Ready to Test

SKILLS & STRATEGIES

D0818127

AMERICAN EDUCATION PUBLISHING™

An imprint of Carson-Dellosa Publishing
Greensboro, NC

American Education Publishing™
An imprint of Carson-Dellosa Publishing LLC
P.O. Box 35665
Greensboro, NC 27425 USA

ISBN 978-1-60996-538-9

01-363117784

Table of Contents

Language Arts
Reading

Chapter 1: Vocabulary

Chapter 2: Reading Comprehension

Language Arts
Language

Chapter 3: Mechanics

Chapter 4: Usage

Chapter 5: Writing

Math

Chapter 6: Concepts

Chapter 7: Computation

Chapter 8: Geometry

Chapter 9: Measurement

Chapter 10: Applications

Letter to Parents

Dear Parents and Guardians:

The *Ready to Test* series will prepare your child for standardized tests by providing him or her with test-taking tips and strategies for success. The sample questions and tests in this book will allow your child to gain familiarity with standardized tests, making him or her more comfortable on test day and, therefore, more likely to do well.

You can help your child with this important part of learning. Allow your child to become familiar with the testing strategies presented in this book. If your child gets stuck at any point when completing the book, encourage him or her to think of those tips to help determine what to do.

Time your child to help him or her learn time management when taking tests. On average, a lesson page in this book should take about 10 minutes to complete. A Practice Test should take about 45–60 minutes to complete. Keep in mind, however, that the goal is not how fast your child can complete each page. Instead, the goal is to provide practice and strategies for success on test day.

Below are some additional suggestions that will help your child make the most of *Ready to Test*:

- Provide a quiet place to work.
- Go over the work with your child.
- Tell your child he or she is doing a good job.
- Remind him or her to use the tips that are included throughout the book.

By preparing your child with test-taking tips and strategies, *Ready to Test* can help take the fear out of standardized tests and help your child achieve the best scores possible.

Introduction

About the Common Core State Standards

The Common Core State Standards Initiative is a state-led effort developed in collaboration with teachers, school administrators, and experts to provide a clear and consistent framework to prepare children for college and the workforce. The standards are based on the most effective models from states across the country. They provide teachers and parents with a common understanding of what students are expected to learn. Consistent standards will provide appropriate benchmarks for all students, regardless of where they live.

The Common Core State Standards provide a consistent, clear understanding of what students are expected to learn, so teachers and parents know how to help them. The standards are designed to be relevant to the real world, reflecting the knowledge and skills that children need for success in college and their future careers. With students fully prepared for the future, our communities and our country will be best positioned to compete successfully in the global economy.

These standards define the knowledge and skills students should have within their education so that they will graduate high school able to succeed in college and in workforce training programs. The standards:

- are aligned with college and work expectations.
- are clear, understandable, and consistent.
- include rigorous content and application of knowledge through high-order skills.
- build upon strengths and lessons of current state standards.
- are informed by other top-performing countries, so that all students are prepared to succeed in our global economy and society.
- are evidence-based.

Common Core Standards: Language Arts

The Language Arts standards focus on five key areas. Students who are proficient in these areas are able to demonstrate independence, build strong content knowledge, comprehend as well as critique, respond to the varying demands of the task, value evidence, use technology strategically and effectively, and understand other perspectives and cultures.

Reading

The Common Core Standards establish increasing complexity in what students must be able to read, so that all students are ready for the demands of college- and career-level reading. The standards also require the progressive development of reading comprehension, so that students are able to gain more from what they read.

Writing

The ability to write logical arguments based on substantive claims, sound reasoning, and relevant evidence is a cornerstone of the writing standards. Research is emphasized throughout the standards but most prominently in the writing strand, since a written analysis and presentation of findings is often critical.

Speaking and Listening

The standards require that students gain, evaluate, and present increasingly complex information, ideas, and evidence through listening and speaking, as well as through media.

Language

The standards expect that students will grow their vocabularies through a mix of conversations, direct instruction, and reading. The standards will help students determine word meanings, appreciate the nuances of words, and steadily expand their vocabulary of words and phrases.

Media and Technology

Skills related to media use are integrated throughout the standards, just as media and technology are integrated in school curriculum for life in the 21st century.

Common Core Standards: Math

The mathematically proficient student must be able to:

Make sense of problems and persevere in solving them. Mathematically proficient students start by thinking about the meaning of a problem and deciding upon the best way to find the solution. They think the problem through while solving it, and they continually ask themselves, "Does this make sense?"

Reason abstractly and quantitatively. Mathematically proficient students make sense of quantities and their relationships in problem situations. Quantitative reasoning entails an understanding of the problem at hand; paying attention to the units involved; considering the meaning of quantities, not just how to compute them; and knowing and using different properties of operations and objects.

Construct viable arguments and critique the reasoning of others. Mathematically proficient students understand and use stated assumptions, definitions, and previously established results in constructing arguments. Students at all grades can listen or read the arguments of others, decide whether they make sense, and ask useful questions to clarify or improve the arguments.

Model with mathematics. Mathematically proficient students can apply the math they've learned to solve problems arising in everyday life.

Use appropriate tools strategically. Mathematically proficient students consider the available tools when solving a mathematical problem and make appropriate decisions about when each of these tools might be helpful.

Attend to precision. Mathematically proficient students try to communicate precisely to others and in their own reasoning. They state the meaning of the symbols they choose. They calculate accurately and express answers efficiently.

Look for and make use of structure. Mathematically proficient students look closely to discern a pattern or structure. Students can also step back for an overview and shift perspective.

Look for and express regularity in repeated reasoning. Mathematically proficient students look for patterns and shortcuts. As they work to solve a problem, students continue to keep the big picture in mind while attending to the details. They continually evaluate whether or not their results make logical sense.

To learn more about the Common Core State Standards, visit corestandards.org.

Name _____ Date _____

Synonyms

Directions: Read each item. Choose the answer that means the same, or about the same, as the underlined word. Fill in the circle for the correct answer.

Example

A frank answer is

- (A) short.
- (B) honest.
- (C) long.
- (D) complicated.

Answer: (B)

1. a <u>tiresome</u> job
   - (A) hurried
   - (B) slow
   - (C) tedious
   - (D) dim

2. an <u>arrogant</u> man
   - (F) heavy
   - (G) proud
   - (H) cunning
   - (J) humble

3. a <u>surly</u> individual
   - (A) wild
   - (B) anxious
   - (C) gruff
   - (D) calm

4. an <u>agile</u> body
   - (F) clumsy
   - (G) heavy
   - (H) nimble
   - (J) thin

5. To be in the <u>midst</u> is to be in the
   - (A) center.
   - (B) dark.
   - (C) crowd.
   - (D) outskirts.

6. A person in <u>peril</u> is in
   - (F) clothing.
   - (G) safety.
   - (H) luck.
   - (J) danger.

7. To <u>thrive</u> is to
   - (A) withdraw.
   - (B) wither.
   - (C) prosper.
   - (D) participate.

8. An <u>ally</u> is a(n)
   - (F) metal.
   - (G) friend.
   - (H) neighbor.
   - (J) enemy.

Look carefully at all the answer choices before you choose one!

Synonyms

10

Directions: Read each item. Choose the answer that means the same, or about the same, as the underlined word. Fill in the circle for the correct answer.

1. prolong the agony

- Ⓐ stretch out
- Ⓑ shorten
- Ⓒ stop
- Ⓓ postpone

2. scour the tub

- Ⓕ preserve
- Ⓖ fill
- Ⓗ scrub
- Ⓙ lug

3. unruly behavior

- Ⓐ ridiculous
- Ⓑ obedient
- Ⓒ calm
- Ⓓ willful

4. concealed the evidence

- Ⓕ avoided
- Ⓖ revealed
- Ⓗ hid
- Ⓙ examined

5. Her bias was plain to see.

- Ⓐ point of view
- Ⓑ loss
- Ⓒ wisdom
- Ⓓ slip

6. The boy had a hunch.

- Ⓕ feeling
- Ⓖ bad attitude
- Ⓗ hump
- Ⓙ cramp

7. The professor rambled.

- Ⓐ got lost
- Ⓑ babbled
- Ⓒ argued
- Ⓓ stopped

8. The twins mustered their courage.

- Ⓕ lost
- Ⓖ faked
- Ⓗ proclaimed
- Ⓙ gathered

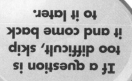

If a question is too difficult, skip it and come back to it later.

Antonyms

Directions: Read each item. Choose the answer that means the opposite of the underlined word. Fill in the circle for the correct answer.

Example

<u>willing</u> to leave

- (A) able
- (B) eager
- (C) reluctant
- (D) allowed

Answer: C

1. <u>dissimilar</u> answers

   - (A) identical
   - (B) strange
   - (C) unusual
   - (D) unlike

2. the play <u>commenced</u>

   - (F) concluded
   - (G) began
   - (H) continued
   - (J) failed

3. a <u>benign</u> host

   - (A) kind
   - (B) spiteful
   - (C) young
   - (D) gracious

4. opened <u>gingerly</u>

   - (F) carefully
   - (G) carelessly
   - (H) swiftly
   - (J) gradually

5. an <u>absurd</u> situation

   - (A) ridiculous
   - (B) horrible
   - (C) funny
   - (D) sensible

6. <u>hoist</u> the sails

   - (F) lift
   - (G) lower
   - (H) display
   - (J) mend

7. a <u>vacant</u> room

   - (A) clean
   - (B) ancient
   - (C) empty
   - (D) inhabited

8. a <u>motivated</u> worker

   - (F) energized
   - (G) uninspired
   - (H) roused
   - (J) new

Since you are looking for antonyms (words that mean the opposite), eliminate answers that mean the same thing as the underlined word.

Antonyms

Directions: Read each item. Choose the answer that means the opposite of the underlined word.

1. During the drought, water was <u>scarce</u>.

(A) foul

(B) limited

(C) abundant

(D) everywhere

2. That knife is too <u>blunt</u> to use.

(F) useless

(G) sharp

(H) dull

(J) old

3. Frankie couldn't <u>conceal</u> the circles under her eyes.

(A) hide

(B) cover-up

(C) remember

(D) reveal

4. Grandmother expects me to be <u>courteous</u>.

(F) rude

(G) polite

(H) generous

(J) friendly

5. The soccer team was excited about their <u>victory</u> on Saturday night.

(A) defeat

(B) achievement

(C) goal

(D) triumph

6. The sky is beautiful at <u>dusk</u>.

(F) evening

(G) dawn

(H) midnight

(J) twilight

7. Does that juice contain <u>artificial</u> flavors?

(A) fake

(B) sweet

(C) healthful

(D) natural

8. What is the <u>singular</u> form of the word *cacti*?

(F) first

(G) common

(H) plural

(J) unusual

Name _____ Date _____

Multiple-Meaning Words

Directions: Read each item. Fill in the circle next to the best answer.

Example

Because of her fever, she felt faint. In which sentence does *faint* mean the same thing as in the sentence above?

- Ⓐ Her dress was a faint pink.
- Ⓑ When he saw the blood, he felt faint.
- Ⓒ The writing on the yellowing paper was very faint.
- Ⓓ Her voice was so faint, I could barely hear it.

Answer: (B)

1. Will you brush my hair? In which sentence does *brush* mean the same thing as in the sentence above?

- Ⓐ She bought a new brush.
- Ⓑ After the storm, the yard was littered with brush.
- Ⓒ I need to brush the dog.
- Ⓓ She felt the kitten brush against her leg.

2. He plans to store the corn in his barn. In which sentence does *store* mean the same thing as in the sentence above?

- Ⓕ She went to the grocery store.
- Ⓖ My dad will store the lawnmower in the shed.
- Ⓗ There is a lot of fun in store when you visit the zoo.
- Ⓙ My favorite store is in the mall.

Use the meaning of the sentences to help you find the correct answer.

Directions: Choose the word that fits in both sentences.

3. The _____ table sits under the window.
The first _____ of the tournament is over.

- Ⓐ square
- Ⓑ part
- Ⓒ round
- Ⓓ circular

4. The second _____ of our encyclopedia set is missing.
Please turn down the _____ on your stereo.

- Ⓕ sound
- Ⓖ volume
- Ⓗ book
- Ⓙ dial

Name _____   Date _____

Homophones

Directions: Fill in the blank with the word that best fits each sentence.

Example

Aunt Theresa has a very sharp _____ (mind, mined).

Answer: mind

1. No one wanted to _____ (by, buy) the book with the wrinkled cover.

2. The cost of the newspaper has increased to 75 _____ (cents, scents).

3. Malik, the social studies report is _____ (do, dew, due) tomorrow!

4. Call me when _____ (it's, its) my turn to use the computer.

5. We can rest when _____ (their, there, they're) is nothing left to put away.

6. The keys were _____ (here, hear) on the table this morning.

7. We'll get tickets when _____ (their, there, they're) in town next year.

8. Nate _____ (red, read) a chapter of the book every day after dinner.

9. Show Braden _____ (where, wear) we keep the extra towels.

10. We can't ride our bikes because the park is _____ (to, too, two) far away.

11. Houston hoped he made the _____ (write, right) decision.

Chapter 1: Vocabulary

Words in Context

Directions: Read the paragraph. Find the word that fits best in each numbered blank.

Example

Ashley was _____ when she won the honor of representing her school in the spelling bee. This annual event gave students the opportunity to represent their schools in a statewide competition.

- Ⓐ disappointed
- Ⓑ indifferent
- Ⓒ bothered
- Ⓓ delighted

Answer: Ⓓ

If you aren't sure which answer is correct, try substituting each answer in the blank.

Which one sounds best?

People who travel or cross the Amazon and Orinoco rivers of South America are careful never to _____ **(1)** a foot or hand from the side of their boat. Just below the surface of these mighty waters _____ **(2)** a small fish feared throughout the _____ **(3)**. That fish is the flesh-eating piranha. It has a nasty _____ **(4)** and an even nastier _____ **(5)**. Although smaller fish make up most of its diet, the piranha will _____ **(6)** both humans and other animals.

1. Ⓐ lift
   Ⓑ dangle
   Ⓒ withdraw
   Ⓓ brush

2. Ⓕ lurks
   Ⓖ nests
   Ⓗ plays
   Ⓙ boasts

3. Ⓐ universe
   Ⓑ town
   Ⓒ continent
   Ⓓ village

4. Ⓕ habit
   Ⓖ friend
   Ⓗ flavor
   Ⓙ disposition

5. Ⓐ smile
   Ⓑ brother
   Ⓒ appetite
   Ⓓ memory

6. Ⓕ befriend
   Ⓖ bully
   Ⓗ attack
   Ⓙ analyze

Words in Context

Directions: Read each item. Choose the correct meaning for each underlined word.

1. The <u>passage</u> appeared in the magazine.

   Ⓐ exit

   Ⓑ crossing

   Ⓒ journey

   Ⓓ quotation

2. I <u>introduced</u> my dad to my teacher.

   Ⓕ proposed

   Ⓖ familiarized

   Ⓗ submitted

   Ⓙ suggested

3. The boat pulled up to the <u>landing</u>.

   Ⓐ touching down

   Ⓑ a dock

   Ⓒ the level part of a staircase

   Ⓓ taking off

4. The horses were <u>sheltered</u> in the barn.

   Ⓕ housed

   Ⓖ shielded

   Ⓗ concealed

   Ⓙ exposed

5. Kayla <u>registered</u> for the computer class.

   Ⓐ listed

   Ⓑ enlisted

   Ⓒ enrolled

   Ⓓ noticed

6. The poet led a <u>colorful</u> life.

   Ⓕ bright

   Ⓖ brilliant

   Ⓗ distinctive or unique

   Ⓙ multicolored

7. The deer was hidden in a <u>stand</u> of trees.

   Ⓐ a small retail business

   Ⓑ a raised platform

   Ⓒ holding a position

   Ⓓ a group of plants

8. Facts about antelopes were found in this <u>obscure</u> book.

   Ⓕ hide

   Ⓖ little-known

   Ⓗ baffling

   Ⓙ mysterious

Having trouble choosing an answer?
Try reading the stem with each option.

Name _____ Date _____

Word Study

Directions: Read each question. Fill in the circle for the correct answer.

Example

Golden retrievers _____ children well. Which of these words would indicate that golden retrievers get along well with children?

- Ⓐ reject
- Ⓑ tolerate
- Ⓒ display
- Ⓓ manipulate

Answer: (B)

---

1. Eggs are to omelet as bread is to _____.

- Ⓐ lunch
- Ⓑ sandwich
- Ⓒ wheat
- Ⓓ cheese

2. Which of these words probably comes from the Greek *gumnastes* meaning *athletic trainer*?

- Ⓕ gumption
- Ⓖ gymnast
- Ⓗ gumshoe
- Ⓙ gusto

3. Carlos did not want to _____. Which word means to *interfere*?

- Ⓐ interval
- Ⓑ insult
- Ⓒ intrude
- Ⓓ surpass

4. The sailors _____ their water supplies. Which word means that the sailors refilled their water supplies?

- Ⓕ detected
- Ⓖ allocated
- Ⓗ participated
- Ⓙ replenished

5. Which of these words probably comes from the Latin *aster* meaning *star*?

- Ⓐ pastor
- Ⓑ asteroid
- Ⓒ mastermind
- Ⓓ plaster

When answering a question, trust your first instinct. It is often right!

Word Study

Directions: Choose the answer that best defines the underlined part of each pair of words.

1. cour<u>ier</u>   **cour<u>ser</u>**

  (A) running

  (B) ruling

  (C) coursing

  (D) turning

2. still<u>ness</u>   **fearful<u>ness</u>**

  (F) quality of

  (G) lacking

  (H) quiet

  (J) in the manner of

3. <u>prim</u>er   **<u>prim</u>eval**

  (A) elementary

  (B) original

  (C) first

  (D) former

4. fold<u>able</u>   **us<u>able</u>**

  (F) quality of

  (G) lacking

  (H) can be

  (J) in the manner of

5. play<u>er</u>   **sing<u>er</u>**

  (A) the study of

  (B) small

  (C) art or skill of

  (D) one who

6. <u>sub</u>zero   **<u>sub</u>marine**

  (F) under

  (G) over

  (H) apart

  (J) backward

7. <u>mis</u>judge   **<u>mis</u>pronounce**

  (A) correctly

  (B) before

  (C) to do after

  (D) wrongly

8. <u>re</u>write   **<u>re</u>arrange**

  (F) many

  (G) to do before

  (H) partly

  (J) to do again

If you are not sure which answer is correct, first eliminate answers you know are wrong.

Chapter 1: Vocabulary

Sample Test 1: Vocabulary

Directions: Choose the word or words that mean the same, or almost the same, as the underlined word.

Example

possessed information

- Ⓐ questioned
- Ⓑ discovered
- Ⓒ had
- Ⓓ lost

Answer: C

1. important data

- Ⓐ computer
- Ⓑ meeting
- Ⓒ information
- Ⓓ announcement

2. promptly returned

- Ⓕ quickly
- Ⓖ quietly
- Ⓗ hesitantly
- Ⓙ gallantly

3. an emphatic reply

- Ⓐ humorous
- Ⓑ forceful
- Ⓒ emotional
- Ⓓ weak

4. a huge commotion

- Ⓕ noise
- Ⓖ concert
- Ⓗ disturbance
- Ⓙ crowd

5. To urge someone is to

- Ⓐ encourage.
- Ⓑ discourage.
- Ⓒ invite.
- Ⓓ conceal.

6. To crouch is to

- Ⓕ crawl.
- Ⓖ jump up.
- Ⓗ stoop.
- Ⓙ shrink.

7. Gnarled means

- Ⓐ grumpy.
- Ⓑ knotted.
- Ⓒ lifelike.
- Ⓓ smooth.

8. If someone is bewildered, he is

- Ⓕ enchanted.
- Ⓖ enlightened.
- Ⓗ confused.
- Ⓙ correct.

GO

Sample Test 1: Vocabulary

Directions: Choose the word that means the opposite of the underlined word.

9. scatter the leaves

(A) move

(B) collect

(C) disperse

(D) rake

10. a ship adrift

(F) sinking

(G) floating

(H) anchored

(J) lost

11. to rouse someone

(A) awaken

(B) anger

(C) soothe

(D) enliven

12. a good chum

(F) quality

(G) deed

(H) friend

(J) stranger

13. acute pain

(A) intense

(B) sharp

(C) intermittent

(D) dull

14. eat with relish

(F) enjoyment

(G) disgust

(H) zest

(J) pleasure

Directions: Choose the word that correctly completes each sentence.

15. The guard had to _____ the suspicious package.

(A) sees

(B) seize

(C) seas

(D) seeze

16. The nurse inserted an IV into the patient's _____.

(F) vein

(G) veign

(H) vane

(J) vain

17. Ivanka _____ the canoe across the lake.

(A) road

(B) raued

(C) rode

(D) rowed

18. The owl _____ on mice and other small creatures.

(F) praise

(G) prays

(H) preys

(J) praze

GO

Name _____ Date _____

Sample Test 1: Vocabulary

Directions: Choose the word that correctly completes both sentences.

19. Please hand me a _____.
She needed a _____ transplant.

- Ⓐ kidney
- Ⓑ hand
- Ⓒ tissue
- Ⓓ hammer

20. That was _____.
There were a(n) _____ number of players.

- Ⓕ strange
- Ⓖ odd
- Ⓗ quick
- Ⓙ outside

21. The stars _____ at night.
You _____ to be ill.

- Ⓐ seem
- Ⓑ pretend
- Ⓒ appear
- Ⓓ shine

22. What's all that _____ ?
He hit the ball with his _____.

- Ⓕ noise
- Ⓖ bat
- Ⓗ commotion
- Ⓙ racket

23. I don't recognize your accent.
In which sentence does *accent* mean the same thing as in the sentence above?

- Ⓐ Place the accent above the second syllable.
- Ⓑ You forgot to include the accent mark.
- Ⓒ She has a southern accent.
- Ⓓ There is an accent on reading programs.

24. The directions were very complex.
In which sentence does *complex* mean the same thing as in the sentence above?

- Ⓕ Alicia had a spider complex.
- Ⓖ This map is too complex for me.
- Ⓗ What is a complex carbohydrate?
- Ⓙ They lived in an apartment complex.

Directions: Choose the answer that best defines the underlined part of each pair of words.

25. manual   manuscript

- Ⓐ hand
- Ⓑ write
- Ⓒ dictate
- Ⓓ instead of

26. mistreat   mispronounce

- Ⓕ almost
- Ⓖ badly
- Ⓗ not
- Ⓙ opposite of

GO

Sample Test 1: Vocabulary

LANGUAGE ARTS
22

Directions: Choose the best answer to each question below.

27. Which of these words probably comes from the Old French word *aaisier*, meaning *to put at ease*?

(A) simple

(B) easy

(C) aisle

(D) alas

28. Which of these words probably comes from the Latin word *ferox*, meaning *fierce*?

(F) ferret

(G) ferment

(H) ferocious

(J) fervor

29. The design was very _____. Which of these words means *elaborate*?

(A) intrepid

(B) serviceable

(C) intricate

(D) exclusive

30. They gave _____ to the officer. Which of these words means *to give honor* to the officer?

(F) homage

(G) flourish

(H) ballast

(J) image

Directions: Read the paragraph. Choose the words that best fit into the numbered blanks.

Laughter is good medicine. Scientists believe that laughter _____ **(31)** the heart and lungs. Laughter burns calories and may help _____ **(32)** blood pressure. It also _____ **(33)** stress and tension. If you are _____ **(34)** about an upcoming test, laughter can help you relax.

31. (A) heals

(B) stresses

(C) weakens

(D) strengthens

32. (F) raise

(G) lower

(H) eliminate

(J) elongate

33. (A) relieves

(B) increases

(C) revives

(D) releases

34. (F) excited

(G) enthusiastic

(H) nervous

(J) knowledgeable

STOP

Main Idea

Directions: Read the passage. Choose the best answer to each question.

Example

The experts are not always right. They advised the big mining companies to pass up the Cripple Creek region. They claimed that no gold could be found there. It was left to local prospectors to uncover the incredible wealth of Cripple Creek. More than $400 million worth of ore was found in this area that experts ignored.

What was the paragraph mainly about?

(A) what experts thought about Cripple Creek

(B) when gold was found at Cripple Creek

(C) how much the ore was worth

(D) how big mining companies operate

Answer: (B)

The practice of wearing rings is an ancient one. Throughout history, people in many lands have decorated their bodies by wearing rings on their fingers, ears, lips, necks, noses, ankles, and wrists. In some cultures, a married woman wore a ring on the big toe of her left foot; a man might have put rings on his second and third toes. Today, the practice of wearing rings in some cases includes multiple facial rings.

1. What is the paragraph mainly about?

(A) why some people wore rings on their toes

(B) what kinds of rings were the most popular

(C) when the practice of wearing rings began

(D) how people throughout history have worn rings

2. Which title best summarizes this passage?

(F) "Rings Worn Today"

(G) "Rings Throughout the Ages"

(H) "Rings in Unusual Places"

(J) "Rings Are Fun"

Name _____ Date _____

Main Idea

Directions: Read the passage. Choose the best answer to each question.

Starfish Regeneration

Starfish and crustaceans can regenerate body parts. This means that if a starfish's arm or a lobster's claw is cut off, it can grow a new one. People do not generate entire body parts, although there have been instances in which young children have grown new fingertips. Starfish and earthworms can regenerate whole new bodies from a part of a body. In the past, this has caused problems for the shellfish industry. Starfish eat oysters, clams, and scallops. They were competition for the fishermen who hoped to catch these mollusks. The fishermen cut the starfish into parts, thinking they were killing them. Instead, parts of the starfish regenerated and created whole new starfish!

Every part of a true sentence must be true.

1. What is the main idea of this passage?

(A) Starfish eat oysters, clams, and scallops.

(B) A lobster is a crustacean.

(C) Some animals, such as starfish, can regenerate body parts.

(D) Some children have grown new fingertips.

2. If the author continued this passage, a logical topic for the next paragraph might be

(F) how starfish regenerate arms.

(G) where starfish live.

(H) the best places to catch lobster.

(J) other problems in the shellfish industry.

3. Which of the following is true?

(A) All animals can regenerate body parts.

(B) Starfish and fishermen were competing for the same mollusks.

(C) Fishermen were hoping to increase the number of starfish in the oceans.

(D) Regeneration refers to animals that are endangered.

4. What is the author's purpose for writing this passage?

(F) to entertain

(G) to persuade

(H) to inform

(J) to convince

Recalling Details

Directions: Read the passage. Choose the best answer to each question.

Example

The frankfurter, named for the city of Frankfurt, Germany, is easily the most popular sausage in the world. Frankfurters, popularly known as *hot dogs*, are sold almost everywhere in the United States. They are consumed in great quantities at sporting events and amusement parks. People from other countries often associate hot dogs with the American way of life.

Where are huge numbers of hot dogs eaten?

(A) in Frankfurt, Germany

(B) in other countries

(C) at sporting events

(D) in stores

Answer: (C)

The Continent of Atlantis

Around the year 370 B.C., the Greek philosopher Plato wrote about a huge continent that once existed in the Atlantic Ocean. Plato called the continent *Atlantis* and estimated it to be approximately the size of Europe. Atlantis was supposedly the home of a mighty nation with powerful armies that had subdued parts of Europe and North Africa.

Plato's account of Atlantis came from his research of the records of an earlier Athenian ruler named *Solon*. Solon was supposed to have visited Egypt several hundred years before, and it was there that he heard about Atlantis.

Atlantis was said to have beautiful cities with advanced technologies. The climate was so ideal that two growing seasons were possible. The land teemed with herbs, fruits, and other plants and was the habitat of many animals. Life was good until, according to Plato, the citizens of Atlantis became greedy and incurred the wrath of the gods. Then, great earthquakes and floods that continued nonstop for a day and night caused the continent to sink into the ocean.

1. Who was Plato?

(A) a citizen of Atlantis

(B) a philosopher

(C) a ruler

(D) a warrior

2. Where did Plato believe the continent of Atlantis was located?

(F) near Egypt

(G) in the Pacific Ocean

(H) in the Atlantic Ocean

(J) in the North Sea

Name _____   Date _____

Recalling Details

Directions: Read the passage. Choose the best answer to each question on the following page.

From Dreams to Reality

People have probably always dreamed of flight. As they watched birds fly, they wished that they could soar into the blue sky. As they watched the night sky, they wished they could explore the distant bright specks called *stars*. These dreams led inventors and scientists to risk their lives to achieve flight.

Orville and Wilbur Wright's first flight at Kitty Hawk in 1903 was only the beginning. Flight continued to improve, and dreams soared further into space. The first manned space flight occurred in 1961 when Russian cosmonaut Yuri A. Gagarin orbited Earth a single time. In 1963, the first woman cosmonaut, Valentina Tereshkova, orbited Earth 48 times.

The Russians led the race for many years. In 1965, another cosmonaut, Aleksei A. Leonov, took the first space walk. In 1968, the Russians launched an unmanned spacecraft that orbited the moon.

The United States became the leader in the space race when *Apollo 11* landed on the moon in 1969. Neil Armstrong was the first man to step on the lunar surface. As he did so, he said these famous words, "That's one small step for a man, one giant leap for mankind." Later, in 1969, Charles Conrad, Jr., and Alan L. Bean returned to the moon. In 1972, the United States completed its last mission to the moon, *Apollo 17.*

Today, people continue their quest for space, gathering data from the Mir Space Station, which was launched in 1986. In addition, unmanned probes have flown deep into space toward the planets, sending back pictures and scientific readings.

Look for key words in the question, and then find the same or similar words in the passage. This will help you locate the correct answer.

Name _____ Date _____

Recalling Details

Directions: Use the passage on the previous page to answer the questions below.

1. What happened first?

(A) The *Mir* Space Station was launched.

(B) Yuri Gagarin orbited Earth a single time.

(C) Neil Armstrong walked on the moon.

(D) The first woman orbited Earth.

2. What is this passage mainly about?

(F) famous cosmonauts

(G) a brief history of human flight

(H) the first flight

(J) the space race

3. The first manned space flight was led by _____.

(A) the United States

(B) China

(C) the Wright Brothers

(D) Russia

4. Who said, "That's one small step for a man, one giant leap for mankind"?

(F) Valentina Tereshkova

(G) Charles Conrad, Jr.

(H) Neil Armstrong

(J) Yuri A. Gagarin

5. Which statement is false?

(A) The first woman in space was Valentina Tereshkova.

(B) The first landing on the moon was in 1969.

(C) Russia achieved the first manned space flight.

(D) The last landing on the moon in 1972 ended the space race.

6. Why do you suppose the race to achieve firsts in space travel was so important?

(F) It prompted the United States to excel.

(G) It encouraged cooperation between the two countries.

(H) It discouraged people from being interested in space travel.

(J) It developed a fierce rivalry that led to many mistakes.

Name _____ Date _____

Making Inferences

Directions: Read the passage. Choose the best answer to each question. Fill in the circle for the answer of your choice.

Example

English women once thought they looked best with wigs that rose two or even three feet above their heads. It certainly made them look taller! Wool, cotton, and goat hair were used to give the hairpieces the desired height. The finest high-piled wigs were often decorated with imitation fruit, model ships, horses, and figurines.

From the paragraph you cannot tell

Ⓐ the color of the wigs.

Ⓑ the height of the wigs.

Ⓒ what the wigs were made of.

Ⓓ how wigs were decorated.

Answer: Ⓐ

Skim the passage so you have an understanding of what it is about. Then, skim the questions. Answer the easiest questions first, and then refer to the passage to find the answers.

Trouble

I'll admit the list is long. I broke Mom's favorite blue vase playing baseball in the house. It was a home run, but that didn't count much with Mom. I also broke the back window. I didn't think I could break a window by shoving my hip against a door. It must have been bad glass. I ruined the living room carpet by leaving a red spot the size of a basketball. I know the rule—no drinking in the living room—but I wasn't really drinking. I didn't even get a sip of my cranberry juice before I dropped the glass.

I guess "Trouble" is my middle name. At least that's what Mom says. You probably won't be surprised when I tell you I'm in trouble once again.

1. What is the main problem in the story?

Ⓐ The narrator drinks cranberry juice in the living room.

Ⓑ The narrator accidentally breaks and destroys things.

Ⓒ The narrator disobeys the rules.

Ⓓ The narrator is in trouble again.

2. What do you think happens next in the story?

Ⓕ The narrator gets a paper route to pay for all the damages.

Ⓖ The narrator apologizes for ruining the carpet.

Ⓗ The narrator tells about the latest trouble he caused.

Ⓙ The narrator asks for a new middle name.

Chapter 2: Reading Comprehension

Making Inference

Directions: Read the passage. Choose the best answer to each question.

Example

By actually fishing for and catching other fish, the anglerfish grows to be almost four feet long. It lies quietly in mud at the bottom of the water. Three wormlike fingers on the top of its head attract other fish. When the fish come close, the anglerfish gets its meal. If fishing is slow, the anglerfish may rise to the surface and swallow ducks, loons, or even geese.

From this passage, what can you conclude about anglerfish?

Ⓐ Anglerfish prefer fish to other animals.

Ⓑ They have worms growing out of their heads.

Ⓒ Birds often eat anglerfish.

Ⓓ They always remain at the bottom of the water.

Answer: (A).

Wishing for a Win

Mason crossed only one set of fingers when he made a wish. He avoided black cats and never stepped on cracks in the sidewalk. He thought he was a perfect candidate to win something, anything.

Mason knew that winning took more than avoiding cracks and black cats. That's why he tried out for the track team. Mason wanted to hear the words, "You are the winner!" He imagined hearing his name announced over the loud speaker. However, Mason didn't work very hard at practice and didn't make the team.

Mason spent his free time kicking stones down the street. He pretended he was an NFL kicker in a championship game. The score was always 0–0, and his kick would cinch the title. In his imagination, he always scored.

Mason believed he would be a football star when he grew up. He would play football when he got to high school. He was such a great kicker, he would easily make the team. He really wanted to be a winner.

1. Which sentence best summarizes this story?

Ⓐ Mason was very superstitious.

Ⓑ Mason really wanted to be a winner.

Ⓒ Mason had a vivid imagination.

Ⓓ Track was not the right sport for Mason.

2. Which sentence best describes what Mason will need to do to be a winner?

Ⓕ Mason will need to stop being so superstitious.

Ⓖ Mason will need to work hard to succeed.

Ⓗ Mason will need to find someone to coach him.

Ⓙ Mason will need to stop kicking stones.

Fact and Opinion

Directions: Read the passage. Choose the best answer to each question.

Case of the Missing Journal

Jessica and Michi were friends and neighbors. Both girls planned to work as criminal investigators someday. In the meantime, they loved to solve mysteries so much that they began their own club, the Super Sleuths.

One Saturday afternoon, the day of their weekly meeting, Michi went to her room at 2:00 to get her journal. She was distressed to discover that it was missing. The journal contained all the information and notes from each of the club's meetings and cases. Michi ran to the meeting place in Jessica's backyard. "My journal is missing!" she exclaimed, trying to catch her breath. "You have to help me find it."

The club members were concerned. They needed the club notes to solve a mystery from the week before. "Tell us all you know," said Jessica.

Michi replied, "I keep the journal in the drawer of my bedside table. Last night, I was writing in it while I ate a sandwich. I don't remember much else except that I was exhausted. I didn't think about my journal again until just now. It wasn't in my drawer where I keep it."

1. Which sentence below is not a fact?

Ⓐ The club met on Saturday.

Ⓑ Jessica and Michi were friends.

Ⓒ Michi went to her room at 2:00 to get the journal.

Ⓓ Someone took Michi's journal.

2. Because Michi has lost her journal, what will the club members probably do next?

Ⓕ The club will buy a new journal.

Ⓖ They will search for the missing journal.

Ⓗ They will move on to the next mystery.

Ⓙ Michi and Jessica will no longer be friends.

Fact and Opinion

Directions: List one fact and one opinion from each paragraph.

> Ryan wanted to find out if people could tell the difference between the taste of cold tap water and cold bottled water. He filled one glass pitcher with tap water and another with bottled water. Then, he placed the pitchers in the fridge overnight. In the morning, his mom sampled both. "This one tastes great!" She held up the glass Ryan had marked with an A.

Fact: _____

Opinion: _____

> People from each part of the United States have special foods that help make that region unique. For example, in the Great Plains region, lefse is a popular favorite. Lefse is a soft flatbread made from potatoes, milk, and flour. The recipe was brought to America by Scandinavian immigrants. Lefse tastes best when eaten with a little jelly.

Fact: _____

Opinion: _____

> At 5:30, Ruby opened her eyes. The chirping birds had woken her up a few minutes before her alarm rang. The sound of that alarm was so annoying! Ruby made a mental note to see if her dad knew how to change the ring. She stretched and then swung her legs over the side of the bed. She peered out the window into the dark backyard. There was nothing quite as beautiful as those moments just before the sun began to peek over the horizon.

Fact: _____

Opinion: _____

Name _____   Date _____

Story Elements

Directions: Read the passages. Choose the best answer to each question.

Afternoon Fun

"What do you want play?" Will asked, as he shoved a bite of pancake into his mouth.

"Scramble. We are Scramble maniacs in this house," said Javier.

Will poured juice into his glass. "I don't feel like thinking that hard."

"How about a game of football?" Erik suggested.

"It's too cold out," said Javier.

"I know—let's dig out your connector sets. I haven't played with those for years," Will said as he pushed his chair back and stood.

"Yeah!" said Javier and Erik as they jumped from their seats.

1. What is the setting for this story?

(A) Javier's bedroom

(B) Javier's living room

(C) Javier's kitchen

(D) Javier's basement

2. What is the problem in this story?

(F) The boys wish there were more pancakes.

(G) The boys cannot decide what they want to do.

(H) They boys do not want to play Scramble.

(J) It's too cold to play football.

Space Flight

The space taxi's engine hummed. Nathan's teeth chattered. Little wells of moisture beaded up on his forehead and palms. *I can't fly*, he thought. *Mars is just around the corner, but it's still too far to be stuck in this taxi.* Nathan knew that his uncle was waiting for him, waiting for help with his hydroponic farm. At first, that didn't matter. But then he thought of his uncle. Nathan knew that if he did not help his uncle, the crops he had worked so hard to nurture and grow would not be ready for the Mars 3 season. He took a deep breath and settled back for the remainder of the flight.

3. What is the setting of this story?

(A) Earth

(B) a space farm

(C) a space taxi

(D) unknown

4. What is Nathan's motivation to stay in the taxi?

(F) His uncle will pay him well.

(G) The taxi can't stop until it gets to Mars.

(H) His parents will be upset with him if he doesn't go.

(J) He knows his uncle needs his help on the farm.

Name _____ Date _____

Story Elements

Directions: Read the passage. Choose the best answer to each question.

Daedalus

According to a Greek myth, Daedalus was a builder who had a son named *Icarus*. Daedalus designed a labyrinth, a maze of complicated passages that is very hard to escape. Minos, the king of the island Crete, used the labyrinth to hide a monster, called *Minotaur*, who was half man and half bull.

Daedalus did something to anger Minos, and the king made Daedalus and Icarus prisoners in the labyrinth. One day, Daedalus got an idea as he was watching birds fly. He asked Icarus to gather up all the bird feathers he could find. Then, using feathers and some wax, Daedalus created two large pairs of wings. Soon, he and Icarus were on their way over the walls of the labyrinth.

1. **Who is the main character in this passage?**

   (A) Minos

   (B) Icarus

   (C) Daedalus

   (D) Minotaur

2. **Which of the following is not a setting for this story?**

   (F) a labyrinth

   (G) the island of Crete

   (H) King Minos's castle

   (J) the sky

3. **This passage would most likely be found in**

   (A) an encyclopedia.

   (B) an atlas.

   (C) a book of Greek mythology.

   (D) a book on learning to speak Greek.

Skim or read the passage quickly for clues to the setting and problem.

4. **Which of these is the resolution to the problem in the story?**

   (F) Minos hid a monster called *Minotaur*.

   (G) Daedalus designed a labyrinth.

   (H) Daedalus made two pairs of wings so he and Icarus could escape.

   (J) The king imprisoned Daedalus and Icarus.

Identifying Literature Genres

Directions: Read each passage below, and write its genre on the line.

> The following list tells you about four types of stories, called *genres*.
>
> **Science Fiction**—a make-believe story based on scientific possibilities.
> **Myth**—a make-believe story that explains how something came to be.
> **Nonfiction**—true stories that include actual details and facts.
> **Realistic Fiction**—a make-believe story that could actually happen.

1. **Juniper trees grow in Arizona. Tiny fairies live in their trunks. During the full moon, the fairies come out and dance at night. While dancing, they place blue berries on each tree for decoration. That's how the juniper gets its berries.**

   _____

2. **"It's a bird!" Farid shouted. "It's a plane!" Audrey said. But it was a spaceship! It landed next to a juniper tree. Little green men got off the spaceship. They clipped off several branches of the tree. "They're collecting tree samples to study on Mars," Audrey whispered. They watched, amazed, as the spaceship disappeared into the sky.**

   _____

3. **Jason and Patrick went for a hike. Because they were in the high desert, they carried water with them. When they got tired, the two boys sat in the shade of a juniper tree to rest and drink their water. That's when the rattlesnake appeared. "Don't move!" Patrick said to Jason. The boys sat still until the snake moved away. "What an adventure!" Jason said as the two boys returned home.**

   _____

4. **Juniper trees are small, gnarly trees that grow in many parts of the world. Members of the evergreen family, they remain green year round. Juniper trees can be easily identified by their tiny blue or red berries. There are 13 different kinds of juniper trees in the United States. One kind of juniper tree is called the *alligator juniper* because its bark looks similar to the skin of an alligator. It grows in the Southwest.**

   _____

Identifying Literature Genres

Directions: Read each passage below, and identify the most likely genre of each. Fill in the circle next to the best choice.

1. Act IV
Timothy enters his apartment and finds the furniture overturned and things thrown from the drawers. He picks up the telephone and dials 9-1-1.

Timothy: (fearfully) Yes, I need to report a break-in! (pause) No, I haven't searched the entire apartment. (pause) Do you really think they could still be here?!

- Ⓐ biography
- Ⓑ poetry
- Ⓒ play
- Ⓓ novel

2. The children awoke to a happy sight.
While they were sleeping, the world had turned white.
Their mother peered into their room and said,
"No school today. Go back to bed!"

- Ⓕ adventure story
- Ⓖ fable
- Ⓗ nonfiction
- Ⓙ poetry

3. Raccoon sat on the beach eating his potato. Before each bite, he dipped the potato into the water. Monkey watched him from his perch in the tree and wondered about this curious habit.

- Ⓐ folk tale
- Ⓑ novel
- Ⓒ play
- Ⓓ autobiography

4. The Himalayas are sometimes called the tallest mountains on Earth. The truth is that several underwater ranges are even higher. Mount Everest may be the highest mountain rising above sea level, but Mauna Kea—the mountain that forms the island of Hawaii—is much taller, even though most of it sits below the surface of the Pacific Ocean.

- Ⓕ legend
- Ⓖ nonfiction
- Ⓗ biography
- Ⓙ how-to manual

5. The flies, big as eagles, swooped and soared around him, but Wild Will had an idea. He snatched up a small pine tree—yanked it right out of the ground—and began swishing it through the air above the gigantic watermelon. Soon the flies scattered, but then a line of ants as big as bicycles marched past Wild Will and straight for the house-sized melon.

- Ⓐ adventure story
- Ⓑ biography
- Ⓒ tall tale
- Ⓓ play

Name _____ Date _____

Identifying Literature Genres

Directions: Read each title below, and identify what genre it most likely is.

1. *King Arthur and the Blazing Sword*

- (A) novel
- (B) play
- (C) legend
- (D) folktale

2. *Adventure to Venus*

- (F) science fiction
- (G) poetry
- (H) legend
- (J) history

3. "Ode to an Owl, the Wisest of Fowl"

- (A) play
- (B) legend
- (C) novel
- (D) poetry

4. *How Zebra Got His Stripes*

- (F) biography
- (G) folk tale
- (H) textbook
- (J) novel

5. *Abraham Lincoln: His Life Story*

- (A) legend
- (B) poem
- (C) novel
- (D) biography

6. *101 Tips to Growing a Better Garden*

- (F) textbook
- (G) how-to manual
- (H) history
- (J) essay

7. *Canals: How America's Waterways Opened the West*

- (A) science fiction
- (B) novel
- (C) biography
- (D) history

8. "Why 12-Year-Olds Should Be Allowed to Vote"

- (F) history
- (G) novel
- (H) essay
- (J) play

Treat each option as a true-false question, and choose the most true answer.

Fiction

Directions: Read the passage. Choose the best answer to each question on the following page.

Example

Excited, the guinea pig squealed with delight when the girl entered the room. Surely the girl would give her a special treat. Instead, the girl threw herself down on the bed. "It's not fair," the girl said. Disappointed, the guinea pig closed her eyes and went back to sleep.

What title best summarizes this story?

- (A) "Squeals of Delight"
- (B) "A Guinea Pig's Perspective"
- (C) "The Sad Girl"
- (D) "A Special Treat?"

Answer: (B)

Saturday Noon

Saturday noon is one of those special times in our house. When I say special, I don't mean good special. By Saturday noon, my sisters and I need to have our bedrooms pristine.

When Dad inspects our rooms, he is like an army sergeant doing the white-glove test. If anything is out of place, if any clothes are left on the floor, or if your dresser isn't clean and shiny, you don't get to go anywhere that day.

That isn't hard for Margaret. She's a neat freak. But Chelsea and I are normal, which is the problem—two normal sisters sharing a bedroom. On Monday, we start our separate piles: dirty clothes, wrinkled clothes, clothes we decided not to wear but forgot to hang up. By Wednesday, it's hard to find the floor. By Friday, the tops of the dressers are loaded. Plus, Mom won't let us throw everything down the laundry chute. "Sort it," she says.

Usually, we have enough time to get our clothes all folded and hung by noon, but last Saturday, Chelsea got sick. She spent the morning asleep on the couch. I was left to clean the room alone. I had plans to go biking with my friend Henry.

At 10:00, Henry was ready to go. I was desperate, so I shoved everything under Chelsea's bed, dusted the dressers, plumped the pillows, and called Dad for a room check.

Dad started his checklist. Everything was okay until Dad got to my closet. He turned and asked, "Where are all your clothes, Sara?"

"Dirty," I confessed.

Dad looked around until he spied the clothes under Chelsea's bed.

"Dirty?" he asked.

I winced. "I must have missed those."

"Call Henry. I don't think you'll be going biking today," he said.

By Saturday noon, I was sick right alongside Chelsea. Mom said, "It's a good thing you didn't go biking." I figured it was just the opposite. If I had gone biking, I would never have gotten sick.

Name _____   Date _____

Fiction

Directions: Use the story on the previous page to answer the questions that follow.

1. The words in the title "Saturday Noon" are used three times in the story. Why is that time important to Sara?

(A) Chelsea wanted to go biking.

(B) It was the deadline for having her room clean, which determined whether or not she could go out that day.

(C) It was the time Sara had to have her laundry done.

(D) It was when she got sick.

2. How is Margaret different from Sara and Chelsea?

(F) She is older.

(G) She is younger.

(H) She is very neat.

(J) She always goes out on Saturdays.

3. What does the word *pristine* mean in this story?

(A) very clean

(B) organized

(C) packed

(D) untidy

4. Which of the following is not one of Sara's excuses for not getting her room clean?

(F) Sara's mom will not let her throw clothes down the laundry chute.

(G) Chelsea got sick and couldn't help.

(H) Henry was ready to leave at 10:00.

(J) Her mom should clean her room.

5. What is this story's plot?

(A) Sara can't wait to go for a bike ride.

(B) Sara knows she needs to have her room clean by Saturday noon, but blames everyone but herself for her room not being clean.

(C) Sara allows her laundry to pile up.

(D) Sara's dad has unrealistic expectations for Sara.

6. Which title below best fits this story?

(F) "The Blame Game"

(G) "Cleaning Is Not Normal"

(H) "Biking with Henry"

(J) "Laundry Woes"

If you have enough time, review both questions and answers. You might see something you missed!

Fiction

Directions: Read the passage. Choose the best answer to each question on the following page.

The Special Gift

T.J. was poised to take a bite of his birthday cake when his mother said, "Not so fast, Mister. I think you have one more present coming."

"Really? What is it?" T.J. asked.

His father rose from his seat and walked around to T.J.'s chair. "I've been waiting for this day to give you a very special gift. My father gave it to me when I was about your age, and it has been one of my most valued possessions. Now, I want to give it to you." He placed an old, dusty shoebox tied with string in front of T.J.

"This is my stamp collection, T.J.," his father began. "Your grandfather and I worked on it together. Now, I'll teach you about the different stamps and how to <u>preserve</u> them. We can go to the post office tomorrow after school, and you can pick out one of the new stamp sets to add to your collection."

T.J. tried to be excited about his gift, but he didn't understand what was so great about a box of old stamps. "Thanks, Dad," he said with a forced smile.

Then, he noticed that his sister, Felicia, had taken the box and was looking at each of the envelopes inside. "Look at this one!" she exclaimed. "It's from the year I was born. "Hey, T.J., here's one from the year you were born, too!"

"That's right," said T.J.'s grandfather. "There are even stamps from my birthday!"

T.J. began to understand why the box was so important to his father and grandfather. He moved close to Felicia so that he could see the stamps better. Twenty minutes later, he didn't even notice that his ice cream was melted all over his cake.

Name _____   Date _____

Fiction

Directions: Use the passage on the previous page to answer the questions below.

1. What is the main idea of this story?

(A) Good manners are best.

(B) T.J. received a very special gift.

(C) Stamps are valuable.

(D) It's the thought that counts.

2. When Felicia discovers the stamps from the years she and T.J. were born, what does T.J. begin to understand?

(F) He and Felicia are about the same age.

(G) Some of the stamps are older than he is.

(H) The stamps are very meaningful.

(J) He was born after the collection was begun.

3. Why didn't T.J. notice that his ice cream was melting?

(A) He was no longer hungry.

(B) He was interested in the stamps.

(C) He did not like chocolate ice cream.

(D) He had already left the table.

4. Which of the following is an opinion?

(F) The stamp collection was very special to T.J.'s dad.

(G) At first, T.J. did not understand why the gift was so special.

(H) Collecting stamps is boring.

(J) Some of the stamps were very old.

5. Who is the main character in this story?

(A) Grandfather

(B) Father

(C) T.J.

(D) Felicia

6. In the sentence, "I'll teach you about the different stamps and how to preserve them," the word *preserve* probably means

(F) to keep in good condition.

(G) to store.

(H) to sell to make money.

(J) to keep from decay.

If you are not sure which answer is correct, take your best guess.

Chapter 2: Reading Comprehension

Fiction

Directions: Read the passage. Choose the best answer to each question on the following page.

Cyber Help

Alex sat next to the girl of his dreams every day in science, math, and computer applications. Every day, Amira smiled at Alex with her pretty silver smile. Like Alex, she wore braces. She wrote notes to him during class and laughed at all his jokes. Alex thought she liked him, but he was too shy to ask. He worried that the year would pass without ever learning for certain.

When Valentine's Day approached, Alex thought he had a chance. He would send Amira a special valentine. Unfortunately, he had no money. He was desperate—so desperate that he broke down and talked to his dad.

When Alex's dad said "Try cyberspace," Alex was confused. He wondered how the Internet could help him. But when he visited the Free Virtual Valentine Web site, he knew his problem was solved. He chose a musical valentine and e-mailed it to Amira at school.

On Valentine's Day, Alex waited patiently for Amira to open her e-mail. He tried to look busy as he watched her out of the corner of his eye. Amira whispered, "You sent me a message," as she clicked on the link to Alex's valentine. A moment later, she turned to Alex and grinned. "You're great," she said.

I'm great, Alex thought to himself. *She likes me. If only I'd thought about cyberspace a long time ago!*

Cover the answer choices, and read the question. Think about your answer before you look at the choices. Choose the option that is closest to your answer.

Name _____   Date _____

Fiction

Directions: Use the passage on the previous page to answer the questions below.

1. Which sentence best summarizes the main idea of this story?

(A) Alex liked school.

(B) Alex was very shy.

(C) Alex wanted to know if Amira liked him.

(D) Cyberspace is a great way to show someone how you feel about them.

2. Which detail from the story does not show that Amira liked Alex?

(F) She smiled at him.

(G) She laughed at his jokes.

(H) She sent him notes.

(J) She and Alex both wore braces.

3. What can you conclude about Amira from the first paragraph?

(A) She had a good sense of humor.

(B) She was intelligent.

(C) She liked Alex.

(D) She liked Alex's braces.

4. Why didn't Alex ask Amira if she liked him?

(F) He didn't think to ask.

(G) He was too shy.

(H) He was pretty sure she didn't like him.

(J) The year went by too quickly.

5. What is the climax of this story?

(A) Alex waits to see Amira's response to his valentine.

(B) Amira tells Alex that he is great.

(C) Alex talks to his dad.

(D) Amira laughs at his jokes.

6. What is the purpose of this story?

(F) To illustrate how to combat shyness with girls.

(G) To explain how Alex discovered that Amira liked him.

(H) To illustrate how to send a valentine through cyberspace.

(J) To illustrate that it pays to ask parents for advice.

Don't be nervous on test day!
You'll do better if you are relaxed.

Nonfiction

Directions: Read the passage. Choose the best answer to each question.

Example

The Trans-Canada Highway is the first ocean-to-ocean highway in Canada and the longest national road in the world. After 12 years of work, the 4,859-mile highway was completed in September 1962. This highway made it possible for a person to drive from coast to coast and remain within Canada for the entire trip.

This paragraph tells mainly

(A) about highways in Canada.

(B) why the Trans-Canada Highway is helpful.

(C) when the Trans-Canada Highway was built.

(D) the location of the longest road.

Answer: (B)

Ice Biking

Imagine this: You wake up to discover that a fresh layer of glistening snow covers the ground. After breakfast, you pull on your cold-weather gear and hop on your bike. Most people would never think of doing this. For others, ice biking is an enjoyable form of recreation—or even a way to commute to work.

If you think that ice biking sounds like fun, it is easy to get started. Ice bikers suggest that starting is as easy as not putting your bike away when the weather grows cold. They suggest that you begin by riding your bike one day at a time. They also advise that you dress appropriately and watch the wind chill—it can be awfully cold when you are riding and an icy breeze comes by!

1. What is the best way to begin ice biking?

(A) Go out and buy a new bike.

(B) Don't put your bike away when it gets cold.

(C) Ride just a few minutes each day.

(D) Watch the wind chill.

2. Which describes an activity enjoyed by ice bikers?

(F) commuting to work

(G) camping

(H) racing

(J) All of the above

Nonfiction

Directions: Read the passage. Choose the best answer to each question on the following page.

The Ship of the Desert

Nomads who crisscross the Sahara Desert of North Africa rely on a most unique animal for transportation—the dromedary, or one-humped camel. Because it is indispensable to desert travel, the dromedary is sometimes called *the ship of the desert.*

Several factors make the dromedary suitable for long desert trips. It can go for long periods without nourishment. The hump on a camel's back serves as its food reserve. When it has little to eat, it converts the fat from its hump into energy. The camel's hump can weigh up to 80 pounds or more. When the animal has to rely on its reservoir of fat, the hump becomes much smaller. As a result, it is easy to recognize a well-fed camel by the size of its hump.

Many people believe that camels store water in their humps. This is not true. Their ability to go for days without drinking is due to other factors. First, camels are able to drink large quantities of water at one time. Some have been known to gulp 53 gallons in one day. Second, the camel sweats very little and can tolerate greater body temperatures. Consequently, it retains most of the water it drinks and can travel several hundred miles before replenishing its supply.

Other physical characteristics enable the camel to endure harsh desert conditions. It can completely close its nostrils, thus protecting it from the stinging effects of sandstorms. Its eyes are shielded from sand and sun by overhanging lids and long lashes, and its broad, padded feet keep it from sinking into the soft sand. No other animal is better equipped for life in the desert than the camel.

Nonfiction

Directions: Use the passage on the previous page to answer the questions below.

1. What is the main idea expressed in this story?

(A) The dromedary is the ideal animal for desert life.

(B) The camel's hump serves as its food reservoir.

(C) The dromedary is called *the ship of the desert.*

(D) Camels do not store water in their humps.

2. Which characteristic does not help the camel to survive in the desert?

(F) A camel can drink up to 53 gallons of water in one day.

(G) A camel can close its nostrils.

(H) A camel sweats very little.

(J) A camel is indispensable to desert travel.

3. What cannot be concluded from reading this passage?

(A) A camel can survive a long time without eating.

(B) A dromedary camel is easier to ride than a Bactrian camel.

(C) Camels have many features that equip them for cold weather.

(D) Both B and C

4. Which of these statements is a fact?

(F) Nomads prefer camels to all other pack animals.

(G) The Bactrian camel is the best camel for desert travel.

(H) A camel's broad, padded feet protect it from sinking in soft sand.

(J) Camels enjoy hot weather.

5. Which additional detail would support the title of this story?

(A) Nomads use camels' hair to weave cloth to make tents.

(B) Camels are strong animals capable of carrying loads up to one thousand pounds.

(C) The camel's meat and milk are often part of the nomad's diet.

(D) Camels can be stubborn.

6. What is the author's purpose for this passage?

(F) to entertain

(G) to inform

(H) to persuade

(J) to sell a product

Does an answer choice seem totally unfamiliar to you?

It probably isn't the correct choice.

Nonfiction

Directions: Read the passage, and then answer the questions on the following page.

Niagara Falls

Niagara Falls is one of the most spectacular natural wonders of the world. Part of the falls is in Ontario, Canada, and part is in New York.

The falls are supplied by the Niagara River, which connects Lake Ontario and Lake Erie. The Niagara Falls are located midway in the river. They pour 500,000 tons of water a minute into a deep gorge.

Scientists believe that Niagara Falls was formed after the last ice sheet from the Ice Age withdrew from the area. The surface of the land was changed by the ice. This caused waterways and streams to form new paths. The result was an overflow of Lake Erie, which produced Niagara Falls. Scientists believe that the falls are approximately 20,000 years old.

The falls are formed over an outer layer of hard dolomitic limestone. This covers a softer layer of shale. The shale is more easily worn away, which causes the harder limestone to form an overhanging edge. This allows the falls to drop straight down at a sharp angle, which produces a spectacular sight.

Over the years, the outer layer has broken off at times. This is causing the falls to gradually move back up the river. This erosion is happening to the American Falls at the rate of three to seven inches a year. The edge of Horseshoe Falls is being worn back at the rate of approximately three feet a year.

Niagara Falls has been a spectacular attraction for sightseers. Observation towers and a special area behind the falls—the Cave of the Winds—have allowed remarkable views. At night, the falls are flooded with lights. A steamer, called *Maid of the Mist*, takes visitors for a ride around the base of the falls.

Niagara Falls also has irresistibly drawn daredevils who have wanted to test their courage. One such man, Charles Blondin, crossed the falls on a tightrope in 1859. Four days later, he crossed again, only this time with a blindfold. A month later, he crossed for the third time carrying a man on his shoulders. And as if that weren't daring enough, he returned to cross the falls once again—on stilts!

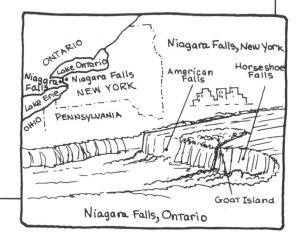

Name _____ Date _____

Nonfiction

Directions: Use the passage on the previous page to answer the questions below.

1. **Scientists believe the falls were formed when**

   (A) an earthquake released water from Lake Erie.

   (B) shale eroded from beneath limestone.

   (C) ice sheets withdrew after the last Ice Age.

   (D) water flowed from a cave.

2. **The Niagara River connects which two Great Lakes?**

   (F) Lake Michigan and Lake Ontario

   (G) Lake Erie and Lake Huron

   (H) Lake Huron and Lake Ontario

   (J) Lake Erie and Lake Ontario

3. **Niagara Falls is a spectacular sight mainly because**

   (A) the water falls straight down.

   (B) the shale is eroding beneath the limestone surface.

   (C) the falls are partly in Canada and partly in the United States.

   (D) the falls are moving slowly upstream.

4. **What is *Maid of the Mist*?**

   (F) a cave behind the falls

   (G) a boat that takes visitors to see the falls

   (H) a legend about how the falls were formed

   (J) a hotel near the falls

5. **What is causing the falls to move gradually back up the river?**

   (A) dams

   (B) overflow from Lake Erie

   (C) ice sheets

   (D) erosion

6. **A tightrope walker crossed the falls several times. According to the passage, which of the following does not describe a way he crossed the falls?**

   (F) blindfolded

   (G) on stilts

   (H) on a bicycle

   (J) with another man on his shoulders

7. **The third paragraph concludes, "Scientists believe that the falls are approximately 20,000 years old." Based on information in the passage, what else can you infer happened approximately 20,000 years ago?**

   (A) The last Ice Age ended.

   (B) Lake Erie and Lake Ontario were formed.

   (C) Horseshoe Falls began eroding at the rate of three feet per year.

   (D) The first humans began coming to visit the falls.

Chapter 2: Reading Comprehension

Ready to Test • Sixth Grade

Nonfiction

Directions: Read the passage. Choose the best answer to each question on the following page.

The Man Behind the Faces

If you have never heard of Gutzon Borglum, you are not alone. Even though Borglum was the sculptor responsible for the carvings on Mount Rushmore, many people do not know him by name.

Gutzon Borglum was born in Idaho in 1867 to Danish parents. He became interested in art early in life. He spent time studying in Paris and then returned home to concentrate on sculpture. At the beginning of his career, Borglum created many large sculptures, some of which are quite famous. He also worked on the early stages of the carving of General Robert E. Lee at Stone Mountain, Virginia.

Borglum was patriotic and outspoken. He lived during a time in American history called *the Colossal Age*, when big things were happening. For this reason, Gutzon Borglum became known as an artist who did things on a grand scale.

Borglum wanted to create a large monument for four American presidents who brought our country into the modern age. He located Mount Rushmore, a 5,725-foot granite mountain in South Dakota and began his sculptures in 1927. Working on one at a time, Borglum and his team carved the faces of George Washington, Thomas Jefferson, Abraham Lincoln, and Theodore Roosevelt into the mountainside.

Gutzon Borglum died in 1941, but his son, Lincoln, continued the work on Mount Rushmore. Today, Mount Rushmore is one of the most-visited national monuments.

If a question sounds confusing, try to restate it in simpler terms. Be sure you understand the question before you choose an answer.

Nonfiction

Directions: Use the passage on the previous page to answer the questions below.

1. **What is this article mainly about?**

   Ⓐ the beginning of the Colossal Age

   Ⓑ Gutzon Borglum's life

   Ⓒ Borglum's great work, Mount Rushmore

   Ⓓ art on a grand scale

2. **According to the passage, Gutzon Borglum did things on a grand scale. What does this mean?**

   Ⓕ creating things with intricate designs

   Ⓖ making things that are very large and impressive

   Ⓗ doing things well and with great care

   Ⓙ doing things that take artistic talent

3. **Based on your answer for question 2, which of the following would you consider to be done on a grand scale?**

   Ⓐ a painting as tall as a house

   Ⓑ a painting of a large royal family

   Ⓒ a drawing of the tallest building in the world

   Ⓓ a life-size sculpture of a man

4. **Which of these statements about Mount Rushmore is true according to the information in the article?**

   Ⓕ Mount Rushmore is located in North Dakota.

   Ⓖ It is located in South Dakota.

   Ⓗ It is more famous than Stone Mountain.

   Ⓙ It is the largest mountain in the country.

5. **Which detail does not support the idea of Borglum as an artist?**

   Ⓐ Borglum went to Paris to study art.

   Ⓑ He became interested in art early in his life.

   Ⓒ Borglum was patriotic and outspoken.

   Ⓓ He created many large sculptures.

6. **How did Borglum decide which presidents to include in his sculpture?**

   Ⓕ He chose presidents who had lived in the West.

   Ⓖ He chose his favorite presidents.

   Ⓗ He chose the first four presidents.

   Ⓙ He chose presidents who brought our country into the modern age.

If any one part of the sentence is false, the whole sentence is false despite many other true statements.

50 # Sample Test 2: Reading Comprehension

Directions: Read the passage. Choose the best answer to each question.

Example

Eliza arrived early at the Sanchez's because it was her first time to babysit for their little girl, Pilar. Pilar's hair was pulled back into two neat ponytails. She had a bright smile and a dimple in one cheek. Right away, Pilar asked Eliza to play with her toy horses.

What do you know about Pilar from reading the paragraph?

(A) She is an intelligent little girl.

(B) She doesn't want to have a baby-sitter.

(C) She likes horses.

(D) Eliza will have no problems baby-sitting Pilar.

Answer: C

Change of Plans

"You said there was a river near here. Why don't we go swimming?" suggested Mara, wiping the sweat off her brow.

"Oh, you wouldn't want to swim in that river!" said Eva.

"Why not?" Mara asked. "I'm a strong swimmer. Even if the river's deep or the current's fast, it won't bother me."

"It's not that the river is deep or fast," said Eva. "If you like swimming with tires, broken bottles, and rusty cans, you can swim there."

"Well," said Mara, "I don't think I want to swim that badly. Unless—isn't there a public pool in town?"

---

1. Why did Mara probably want to go swimming?

(A) It was a warm day.

(B) Mara felt daring.

(C) Mara was practicing for a competition.

(D) It was raining out.

2. What will the girls most likely do next?

(F) visit a friend

(G) go swimming in a pool

(H) swim in the river

(J) go back to Eva's house

Sample Test 2: Reading Comprehension

Directions: Read the passage. Choose the best answer to each question on the following page.

Maternal Fish Father

In the warm and temperate waters of the world live two unusual fish: the sea horse and its relative, the pipefish.

The sea horse, so-called because its head resembles a horse, is a small fish about two to eight inches long. It swims by moving the dorsal fin on its back. It is the only fish with a prehensile tail that it uses, like a monkey, to coil around and cling to seaweed.

The pipefish is named for its long snout, which looks like a thin pipe. When its body is straight, the pipefish resembles a slender snake. Its body forms an S shape and is propelled by its rear fins.

It is not appearance that makes the sea horse and pipefish unique; it is their paternal roles. With both fish, the female's responsibility ends when she lays and deposits her eggs. From that point on, the male takes over, and, in a manner of speaking, gives birth to the babies.

Both the male sea horse and pipefish have pouchlike organs on their undersides in which the female deposits her eggs. Here the young fish stay and are nourished for either a few days or for several weeks, depending on the species. When the baby sea horses are ready to be born, the father sea horse attaches itself to a plant and actually goes through the pangs of childbirth. As the sea horse bends back and forth, the wall of its brood pouch contracts. With each spasm, a baby fish is introduced into the world of the sea. The birth of the baby pipefish is less dramatic. The father's pouch simply opens, and the offspring swim off on their own.

LANGUAGE ARTS

52 Sample Test 2: Reading Comprehension

Directions: Use the passage on the previous page to answer the questions below.

3. What is the main idea of this passage?

(A) The pipefish and the sea horse fathers are unusual because of the way their offspring are born.

(B) Sea horses resemble horses but have tails like monkeys.

(C) Female pipefish and sea horses are lazy.

(D) Sea horses make good pets.

4. Which statement does not describe a sea horse?

(F) The sea horse's head resembles a horse.

(G) The sea horse's body is propelled by a rear fin.

(H) The sea horse uses its snout to cling to seaweed.

(J) The sea horse has a prehensile tail.

5. Which statement seems to say that the role of the male pipefish is less difficult than that of the male sea horse?

(A) The baby pipefish swim off.

(B) The father's pouch simply opens.

(C) The pipefish's body is shaped like an S.

(D) The pipefish has a long, thin snout.

6. Which statement is an opinion?

(F) Male sea horses and pipefish are very good fathers.

(G) Sea horses are from two to eight inches long.

(H) Sea horses move by the use of their dorsal fins.

(J) The wall of the male sea horse's brood pouch contracts.

7. Which statement is a fact?

(A) Pipefish look strange.

(B) Pipefish and sea horses live in warm and temperate waters.

(C) It would be cool to see a sea horse up close.

(D) I bet a pipefish can swim fast.

8. What is the author's purpose?

(F) to compare and contrast two fish

(G) to entertain

(H) to persuade

(J) to confuse

GO ▶

Sample Test 2: Reading Comprehension 53

Directions: Read the passages, and then answer the questions on the following page.

A

Rose, harsh rose,
marred and with stint of petals,
meager flower thin, sparse of leaf,
more precious

than a wet rose
single on a stem—
you are caught in the drift.

B

Born in 1888, Huddie Ledbetter, nicknamed "Leadbelly," was a blues guitarist who inspired generations of musicians. For much of his life, he wandered from place to place, playing anywhere he could. In 1934, he was discovered by John and Alan Lomax, who helped him find a larger audience for his music. Soon, he was playing in colleges, clubs, and music halls. He was featured on radio and television shows. Leadbelly died in 1949, but his music lives on. Musicians in every style credit him with laying the foundation for today's popular music.

C

The grandmother didn't want to go to Florida. She wanted to visit some of her connections in east Tennessee, and she was seizing at every chance to change Bailey's mind. Bailey was the son she lived with, her only boy. He was sitting on the edge of his chair at the table, bent over the orange sports section of the Journal. "Now look here, Bailey," she said, "see here, read this," and she stood with one hand on her thin hip and the other rattling the newspaper at his bald head.

D

What triggers lightning? One theory states that a bigger bit of ice slams into a smaller bit of ice, leaving behind a positive or negative charge. The larger the bit of ice and the faster it is going, the bigger the charge it leaves behind. When enough of these charges collect, lightning occurs.

E

COOK: Short-order cook needed at Flynn's Diner. Shift: 12 midnight to 8 A.M. Must have reliable transportation and references. Good pay and benefits. Two free meals daily. Apply in person at Flynn's Diner, 2000 Wharf Street, near the harbor.

GO

54 Sample Test 2: Reading Comprehension

Directions: Use the passages on the previous page to answer the questions below.

9. Which passage requires you to pay particular attention to figurative language?

(A) passage A

(B) passage B

(C) passage D

(D) passage E

10. Which passage would you most likely find in a local newspaper?

(F) passage A

(G) passage C

(H) passage E

(J) All of the above

11. Which passage could you more easily illustrate on a time line?

(A) passage A

(B) passage B

(C) passage C

(D) passage E

12. Which passage requires you to pay particular attention to a sequence of events?

(F) passage A

(G) passage C

(H) passage D

(J) passage E

13. Which passage would you read for entertainment?

(A) passage B

(B) passage C

(C) passage D

(D) passage E

14. Which passage would you read for information?

(F) passage B

(G) passage D

(H) passage E

(J) All of the above

15. Which passage is biographical?

(A) passage B

(B) passage C

(C) passage D

(D) passage E

16. Which of the following passages are nonfiction?

(F) passage B

(G) passage D

(H) passage E

(J) All of the above

STOP

Practice Test 1: Reading
Part 1: Vocabulary

Directions: Find the word that means the same, or almost the same, as the underlined word.

1. a surprising <u>outcome</u>

- (A) relationship
- (B) appointment
- (C) result
- (D) announcement

2. a <u>hideous</u> mask

- (F) lovely
- (G) funny
- (H) monstrous
- (J) false

3. an <u>audible</u> sigh

- (A) heard
- (B) silent
- (C) austere
- (D) angry

4. a <u>desolate</u> landscape

- (F) forested
- (G) barren
- (H) desirable
- (J) unnatural

5. To <u>subside</u> is to _____.

- (A) continue
- (B) grow louder
- (C) cease
- (D) be intermittent

6. A <u>cunning</u> plan is _____.

- (F) clever
- (G) unoriginal
- (H) original
- (J) detailed

7. A <u>monotone</u> speech is _____.

- (A) exciting
- (B) lively
- (C) dull
- (D) hesitant

8. To <u>assert</u> is to _____.

- (F) declare
- (G) argue
- (H) proceed
- (J) boast

GO ▶

Name _____   Date _____

Practice Test 1: Reading
Part 1: Vocabulary

Directions: Choose the word that means the opposite of the underlined word.

9. an <u>absurd</u> situation

- (A) ridiculous
- (B) sensible
- (C) unbelievable
- (D) embarrassing

10. an <u>arid</u> climate

- (F) dry
- (G) airy
- (H) fertile
- (J) barren

11. an <u>animated</u> conversation

- (A) dull
- (B) lively
- (C) energetic
- (D) one-sided

12. <u>sodden</u> clothing

- (F) soaked
- (G) spongy
- (H) dry
- (J) filthy

13. an <u>essential</u> ingredient

- (A) necessary
- (B) unnecessary
- (C) important
- (D) additional

Directions: Choose the word that correctly completes each sentence.

14. Annabel's change was 75 _____.

- (F) scents
- (G) cents
- (H) sents
- (J) sense

15. The cut should _____ in a couple of days.

- (A) heal
- (B) heil
- (C) he'll
- (D) heel

16. Rico brushed the horse's shiny chestnut _____.

- (F) main
- (G) mayne
- (H) Maine
- (J) mane

GO

Practice Test 1: Reading
Part 1: Vocabulary

Directions: Choose the word that correctly completes both sentences.

17. Connor's arm was in a _____.
Tierra was part of the _____.

- (A) sleeve
- (B) crew
- (C) cast
- (D) mold

18. Akiko had a _____ in her brow.
The farmer made a _____ with his plow.

- (F) furrow
- (G) wrinkle
- (H) trench
- (J) scar

19. Blanca's hair was _____.
The frightened dog _____ at the vet.

- (A) scowled
- (B) wild
- (C) tangled
- (D) snarled

20. He discovered an underground _____.
Rachel read the _____ several times.

- (F) book
- (G) passage
- (H) civilization
- (J) letter

21. Andre bounced the ball.
In which sentence does *bounced* mean the same thing as in the sentence above?

- (A) Kate bounced back after her surgery.
- (B) Mrs. Smith's check bounced.
- (C) The Ping-Pong ball bounced off the table.
- (D) The kangaroo bounced across the field.

22. Will the children spruce up their rooms?
In which sentence does *spruce* mean the same thing as in the sentence above?

- (F) They planted a spruce.
- (G) We used spruce to build our house.
- (H) The volunteers will spruce up the playground.
- (J) Maggie climbed up the spruce.

Directions: Choose the answer that best defines the underlined part of each pair of words.

23. pati<u>ence</u>   obedi<u>ence</u>

- (A) state or condition of being
- (B) full of
- (C) having, tending to
- (D) without

24. <u>pre</u>pare   <u>pre</u>occupy

- (F) after
- (G) before
- (H) because of
- (J) over

Name _____ Date _____

Practice Test 1: Reading
Part 1: Vocabulary

Directions: Choose the best answer to each question below.

25. The man _____ an oak.
Which of these words means *to cut down with an ax*?

(A) hewed

(B) heaved

(C) haunch

(D) sliced

26. Which of these words probably comes from the Latin word *gratia*, meaning *grace*?

(F) grade

(G) grasp

(H) gracious

(J) regret

27. Inhale is to exhale as tense is to _____.

(A) breathe

(B) relax

(C) nervous

(D) gasp

28. Her favorite _____ was "Better safe than sorry."
Which of these words means *saying*?

(F) craving

(G) bias

(H) maxim

(J) gild

Directions: Read the paragraph. Choose the words that best fit in each numbered blank.

In October 1985, a whale caused quite a _____ **(29)** near the _____ **(30)** of California. The whale, a _____ **(31)** so large that its home is the Pacific Ocean, swam under the Golden Gate Bridge and up the Sacramento River. After more than three weeks, the whale finally reversed its _____ **(32)** and headed back toward the ocean.

29. (A) collision

(B) stir

(C) boycott

(D) meddle

30. (F) city

(G) island

(H) coast

(J) coax

31. (A) fish

(B) amphibian

(C) plebeian

(D) creature

32. (F) bow

(G) course

(H) ballasts

(J) opinion

STOP

Practice Test 1: Reading
Part 2: Comprehension

Directions: Read the passage. Choose the best answer to each question on the following page.

One Afternoon in March

One afternoon in March, I found two silver dollars shining in a half-melted snow bank. I instantly thought of buried treasure, so I dug through the snow searching for more. All I ended up with were really cold hands. I slipped the two coins into my pocket and went home colder but richer.

The next morning, Megan and her little sister were searching the snow banks. *Finders keepers* was my first thought. I didn't need to get to the *losers weepers* part since Moira was already crying for real.

"I dropped them right here," she said between tears. Her hands were red from digging in the snow.

"Maybe they got shoved down by the snow plow. Let's try over there," Megan said optimistically.

They'll never know, was my second thought, as I walked past them towards Tyler's house.

"Danny, have you seen two silver dollars?" Megan called. Moira looked up from the snow bank with hope bright in her eyes.

"Coins?" I asked, trying to look innocent.

"Yes, Moira dropped two silver dollars somewhere around here yesterday."

"Yeah," said Moira, "they're big and heavy." She brushed her red hands off on her jacket and wiped the tears from her eyes, which were as red as her hands.

I hesitated. "As a matter of fact, I dug two coins out of that snow bank yesterday. I wondered who might have lost them."

Moira ran to me and gave me a bear hug. "Oh, thank you, thank you!"

I couldn't help but smile.

Practice Test 1: Reading
Part 2: Comprehension

Directions: Use the passage on the previous page to answer the questions below.

1. What is the main idea of this story?

(A) It is okay to lie if you think you can get away with it.

(B) It is always better to be honest than rich.

(C) "Finders keepers, losers weepers" is not a good saying to live by.

(D) Both B and C

2. How did Danny probably feel at the end of the story?

(F) angry with himself for being honest

(G) angry with Megan and Moira

(H) hopeful that he would find another buried treasure

(J) disappointed at having to give up the coins but glad that he had been honest

3. What is the problem in this story?

(A) Moira has lost two silver dollars in the snow.

(B) Danny does not want to give up the coins he found.

(C) Danny does not want to help Moira find her coins.

(D) Megan does not want to help her sister.

4. Which statement below is a fact?

(F) Danny thinks only of his own wants.

(G) Moira cries a lot.

(H) Moira and Danny should be wearing mittens when they are out in the snow.

(J) Moira is crying because she has lost her silver dollars.

5. What is the setting of this story?

(A) outside on a March day

(B) outside on a warm summer day

(C) a cool fall day

(D) the view outside a window

6. What would be another good title for this story?

(F) "Frostbitten Fingers"

(G) "Finders Keepers, Losers Weepers"

(H) "A Fistful of Dollars"

(J) "Honesty Is Best"

Practice Test 1: Reading
Part 2: Comprehension

Directions: Read the passage. Choose the best answer to each question on the following page.

A New Tipi

Fingers of frost tickled Little Deer's feet. It was a chilly fall morning, but there was no time for Little Deer to snuggle beneath her buffalo skins. It was going to be a busy day helping her mother finish the cover for the new tipi.

Little Deer slid her tunic over her head and fastened her moccasins. Wrapping herself up in another skin, she walked outside to survey the work they had done so far. The tipi cover was beautiful and nearly complete. The vast semicircle was spread across the ground, a patchwork in various shades of brown. After her father and brother had killed the buffalo, Little Deer and her mother had carefully cured and prepared the skins, stretching them and scraping them until they were buttery soft. Then, with needles made from bone and thread made from animal sinew, they had sewn the hides together until they formed a huge canvas nearly thirty feet across.

After they finished the cover today, it would be ready to mount on the lodge poles. Little Deer's father had traded with another tribe for fourteen tall, wooden poles. They would stack the poles in a cone shape, lashing them together with more rope made from animal sinew. Then, they would stretch the cover over the poles, forming a snug, watertight home. Little Deer smiled in anticipation. She could imagine the glow of the fire through the tipi walls at night.

Practice Test 1: Reading
Part 2: Comprehension

Directions: Use the passage on the previous page to answer the questions below.

7. What is this story mainly about?

(A) hunting

(B) building a tipi

(C) the uses of buffalo

(D) the life of a Native American girl

8. Which sentence below is not a step in the process of making a tipi?

(F) Stretch the cover over the poles.

(G) Cure and prepare the skins.

(H) Sew the hides together.

(J) Make clothing from the remaining pieces of the hide.

9. How does Little Deer feel about finishing the tipi?

(A) depressed

(B) angry

(C) excited

(D) cold

10. Which of these statements shows personification?

(F) Little Deer smiled in anticipation.

(G) Little Deer slid her tunic over her head and fastened her moccasins.

(H) The tipi cover was beautiful and nearly complete.

(J) Fingers of frost tickled Little Deer's feet.

11. Where would this passage most likely be found?

(A) a historical novel

(B) an encyclopedia

(C) a science fiction story

(D) a diary

12. Which characteristic most accurately describes Little Deer?

(F) lazy

(G) hardworking

(H) clever

(J) intelligent

Practice Test 1: Reading
Part 2: Comprehension

Directions: Read the passage. Choose the best answer to each question on the following page.

Hi-Yo, Silver!

What did people do for entertainment before television? Today, the average child spends more time watching TV than reading. Television is so much a part of daily life that people cannot imagine what life was like before it.

Before television, there was radio. Radio was invented around 1916 from the telegraph. At first, it was used to get information quickly from one part of the country to another. By 1926, radios were common in homes. People listened to music, news, and shows in the same way we watch TV today. Television was not invented until the 1940s, and it did not gain popularity in homes until 1955.

Families gathered around their radios to listen to shows broadcast all over the world. One of the most popular was *The Lone Ranger*. The show was about a Texas Ranger and his faithful friend, Tonto, who tirelessly worked to stop evil. The Lone Ranger rode a white horse named *Silver* and wore a black mask. The Lone Ranger hid his identity because he had been attacked by a violent gang of desperados. His white hat, white horse, black mask, and famous call, "Hi-yo, Silver! Away!" became symbols of the American Wild West hero.

Other famous radio heroes were the Shadow and the Green Hornet. Eventually, radio shows became famous television shows as well. Comedians and vaudeville stars made the transition from the stage to radio to television. Comedians such as Jack Benny, Red Skeleton, and George Burns had radio shows that became television favorites.

Practice Test 1: Reading
Part 2: Comprehension

Directions: Use the passage on the previous page to answer the questions below.

13. What title best captures the main idea of this passage?

(A) "The Lone Ranger Rides Again"

(B) "Before Television Came Radio"

(C) "Radio Stars Hit It Big on TV"

(D) "The History of Radio"

14. What is not true of the passage?

(F) It gives a brief history of radio.

(G) It tells about the transition from radio to television.

(H) It focuses on *The Lone Ranger show.*

(J) It shows how radio was far more popular than television.

15. Which sentence below is an opinion?

(A) *The Lone Ranger* was the best radio show ever.

(B) The Lone Ranger wore a white hat and black mask.

(C) Tonto was the Lone Ranger's faithful companion.

(D) *The Lone Ranger* took place in the American West.

16. Which statement is true?

(F) Tonto rode a white horse named *Silver.*

(G) Radio was invented in 1926.

(H) Several radio shows later became popular TV shows.

(J) Radio stars could not make it as television stars.

17. Why do you suppose *The Lone Ranger* was such a popular radio show?

(A) Families had nothing better to do with their free time.

(B) It had the classic good guy/bad guy theme.

(C) People liked the special effects.

(D) People liked to watch the Lone Ranger and Tonto catch the bad guys.

18. Which sentence below is a fact?

(F) Radio is better than television.

(G) Listening to the radio is boring.

(H) Radios were common in homes in 1926.

(J) *The Lone Ranger* seems like an exciting show.

STOP

Punctuation

Directions: Fill in the circle for the punctuation mark that is needed in the sentence. Fill in the circle for "None" if no more punctuation marks are needed.

Example

Did you remember to brush your teeth

- Ⓐ .
- Ⓑ ?
- Ⓒ !
- Ⓓ None

Answer: B

---

1. The yellow daffodils are very pretty

- Ⓐ ,
- Ⓑ .
- Ⓒ ?
- Ⓓ None

2. The robin, our state bird, lays blue eggs.

- Ⓕ ?
- Ⓖ !
- Ⓗ .
- Ⓙ None

3. "Stop! she called.

- Ⓐ ?
- Ⓑ .
- Ⓒ "
- Ⓓ None

4. We visited Michigan Ohio, and Illinois.

- Ⓕ .
- Ⓖ ,
- Ⓗ :
- Ⓙ None

5. "Hurry! School starts in ten minutes" said Isabel.

- Ⓐ .
- Ⓑ ?
- Ⓒ ,
- Ⓓ None

6. My favorite book A Wrinkle in Time, was already checked out.

- Ⓕ .
- Ⓖ :
- Ⓗ ,
- Ⓙ None

Look carefully at all the answer choices before you choose one.
The missing punctuation mark might be at the end of the sentence or within it. Remember to look in both places!

Punctuation

Directions: Fill in the circle for the choice that has a punctuation error. If there are no mistakes, choose "No mistakes."

1. (A) Our teacher Ms. Su, is

   (B) treating the class to frozen yogurt

   (C) at Dairy Delight, my favorite place.

   (D) No mistakes

2. (F) Do you think you will complete

   (G) your report by Saturday.

   (H) I want to go to the beach on Sunday.

   (J) No mistakes

3. (A) "I miss Grandpa," said Casey,

   (B) "Can we see him again soon?"

   (C) She loved her grandpa very much.

   (D) No mistakes

4. (F) 8789 Rachel Dr.

   (G) Aarontown, MI 49543

   (H) May 22 2012.

   (J) No mistakes

5. (A) Dear Max

   (B) I was so pleased to hear that you won the

   (C) scholarship to computer camp. Good job!

   (D) No mistakes

6. (F) You will have to show me all you learned?

   (G) Love,

   (H) Aunt Margie

   (J) No mistake

Directions: Read each sentence. Choose the word or words that best fits in the blank and shows the correct punctuation.

7. _____ please remember to wash your hands.

   (A) Brewster

   (B) Brewster:

   (C) Brewster,

   (D) "Brewster"

8. The _____ bite was bigger than its bark.

   (F) dogs

   (G) dog's

   (H) dogs's

   (J) dogs'

9. Yoko needed to bring _____ to the picnic.

   (A) plates, napkins, and cups

   (B) plates napkins and cups

   (C) plates, napkins, and cups,

   (D) plates, napkins and, cups

10. This bus is _____ we'll have to catch the next one.

    (F) full

    (G) full,

    (H) full;

    (J) full:

Capitalization and Punctuation

Directions: Fill in the circle for the space that shows the correct capitalization and punctuation.

Example

(A) Yes you can go to the store.

(B) No, you are not going to the mall.

(C) Yes; i will help you.

(D) No: you may not have an iguana.

Answer: (B)

1. (A) I have a new baby sister Nicole.

   (B) When did you see Liam.

   (C) His chinese water dragon eats crickets.

   (D) Chantal, would you like to go to the zoo with me?

2. (F) They have two weeks of school left but we has only one.

   (G) I want to go to Denver colorado to ski.

   (H) Ian and I went to the Detroit Zoo.

   (J) Lets take a trip to Chicago, Illinois.

3. (A) "Where would you like to go?" asked the tour guide.

   (B) Petra's little sister said "She wanted to go home now."

   (C) "can I stay overnight with Maria?" asked Sophie.

   (D) "I would love to visit new york, said Roberto."

4. **Cameron likes the new school but he keeps getting lost.**

   (F) school; but

   (G) school. But

   (H) school, but

   (J) Correct as it is

5. **"Your hamster is cool called Mike.**

   (A) cool, called

   (B) cool," called

   (C) cool?" called

   (D) Correct as it is

6. **Sienna hopes she has Miss Phan's class next year.**

   (F) Miss Phans'

   (G) miss Phans

   (H) Miss Phans

   (J) Correct as it is

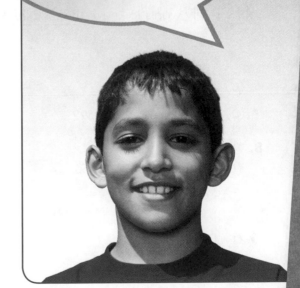

Remember, you are looking for the answer that shows both correct capitalization and punctuation.

Name _____ Date _____

Capitalization and Punctuation

Directions: Fill in the circle for the space that shows the correct capitalization and punctuation. Mark "Correct as it is" if the underlined part is correct.

Have you ever made homemade <u>clay. These</u> **(1)** directions will help you create a small quantity of clay. Take one cup of warm <u>water one</u> **(2)** cup of salt, and two cups of flour. Mix the ingredients together. Squeeze the mixture until it is <u>smooth and</u> **(3)** does not stick to your fingers. <u>Its ready</u> **(4)** for modeling. You may also want to add food coloring.

1. (A) clay, these

   (B) clay? These

   (C) clay; these

   (D) Correct as it is

2. (F) water: one

   (G) water one,

   (H) water, one

   (J) Correct as it is

3. (A) smooth, and

   (B) smooth. And

   (C) smooth; and

   (D) Correct as it is

4. (F) It's ready

   (G) Its' ready

   (H) It's ready,

   (J) Correct as it is

Marble Comix   October 2, 2012
2656 N. Way Blvd.
<u>Characterville, Ca, 12592</u>
<u>Dear mr bulk</u>

   Please tell me how you were able to turn green when you transformed. <u>My friend</u> <u>robin</u> really wants to know. <u>Thanks I think you are cool</u>?

                           Sincerely,

                           Bryce Payne

5. (A) Characterville, Ca 12592

   (B) Characterville, CA 12592

   (C) Characterville CA, 12592

   (D) Correct as it is

6. (F) Dear Mr Bulk

   (G) Dear Mr. Bulk;

   (H) Dear Mr. Bulk,

   (J) Correct as it is

7. (A) My friend, Robin,

   (B) My, Friend Robin,

   (C) My friend Robin

   (D) Correct as it is

8. (F) Thanks; I think you are cool.

   (G) Thanks. I think you are cool.

   (H) Thanks. I think you are cool?

   (J) Correct as it is

Capitalization and Punctuation

Directions: Fill in the circle for the choice that shows the correct capitalization and punctuation.

1. _____ invented a new laborsaving device.

   (A) Prof. Magee

   (B) Prof Magee

   (C) Prof. Magee,

   (D) Prof Magee,

2. **My parents are going to an island in the _____ us.**

   (F) Pacific ocean without

   (G) Pacific, Ocean without

   (H) pacific ocean, without

   (J) Pacific Ocean without

Directions: Fill in the circle for the space that shows the correct capitalization and punctuation. Mark "Correct as it is" if the underlined part is correct.

(1) Some of my buttons are worth money, but most are just valuable to me. (2) I like to look at them because they remind me of people I know or things I have done. (3) My favorite buttons are the ones with jokes or funny pictures. (4) One of these is pink and <u>says Im</u> not just another pretty face, you know!" (5) Others have cartoon characters or animals on them. (6) When I visit a zoo or we go on <u>vacation mom lets</u> me buy a button. (7) She gives me a button every year on my birthday, too. (8) Last year, <u>my cousin miguel</u> sent me a button from <u>Tucson, Arizona?</u>

3. **In sentence 4, <u>says Im</u> is best written _____.**

   (A) says I'm

   (B) says, "I'm

   (C) says "I'm

   (D) Correct as it is

4. **In sentence 6, <u>vacation mom lets</u> is best written _____.**

   (F) vacation mom let's

   (G) vacation, mom lets

   (H) vacation, Mom lets

   (J) Correct as it is

5. **In sentence 8, <u>my cousin miguel</u> is best written _____.**

   (A) my cousin Miguel

   (B) my cousin Miguel,

   (C) my Cousin Miguel,

   (D) Correct as it is

6. **In sentence 8, <u>Tucson, Arizona?</u> is best written _____.**

   (F) Tucson Arizona?

   (G) Tucson, Arizona.

   (H) Tucson, Arizona?

   (J) Correct as it is

Name _____ Date _____

Capitalization and Punctuation

Directions: Fill in the circle for the space that shows the correct capitalization and punctuation. Mark "Correct as it is" if the underlined part is correct.

(1) For many years, people in the United States used streetcars to travel in cities. (2) At first, streetcars were called <u>horse cars because</u> horses pulled them. (3) Later, streetcars were powered by <u>steam in</u> the 1800s, people tried to use electric power, but making electricity was considered to be too expensive. (4) In 1888, a machine was invented that made electricity inexpensively. (5) In that same year, the first electric-powered streetcars were put into <u>use they</u> quickly replaced the steam-powered streetcar. (6) With the invention of the <u>gas engine electric</u> streetcars were soon replaced by buses and cars. (7) By 1930, the streetcar had begun to disappear from the city streets. (8) Interest in streetcars revived in the 1970s.

1. In sentence 2, <u>horse cars because</u> is best written

- (A) horse cars; because
- (B) horse cars, because
- (C) horse cars. Because
- (D) Correct as it is

2. In sentence 3, <u>steam in</u> is best written

- (F) steam; in
- (G) steam, in
- (H) steam. In
- (J) Correct as it is

3. In sentence 5, <u>use they</u> is best written

- (A) use: They
- (B) use. They
- (C) use; they
- (D) Correct as it is

4. In sentence 6, <u>gas engine electric</u> is best written

- (F) gas, engine, electric
- (G) gas, engine electric
- (H) gas engine, electric
- (J) Correct as it is

More than one answer can seem like a good choice. Remember, you are trying to find the best answer.

Spelling

Directions: Find the word that is spelled correctly and fits best in the blank.

Example

The boat _____ toward shore.

- Ⓐ driffed
- Ⓑ drifded
- Ⓒ drifted
- Ⓓ drifteded

Answer: C

---

1. _____ of the dog!

- Ⓐ Beaware
- Ⓑ Beware
- Ⓒ Bewear
- Ⓓ Bewar

2. The _____ hit the moon.

- Ⓕ asteroid
- Ⓖ astroid
- Ⓗ asterood
- Ⓙ asteroyd

3. He spoke with a _____ accent.

- Ⓐ gutteral
- Ⓑ gutterle
- Ⓒ guttural
- Ⓓ gutural

4. My favorite _____ is lemonade.

- Ⓕ beaverage
- Ⓖ beverage
- Ⓗ bevirage
- Ⓙ bevarage

5. Ellen _____ for losing her temper.

- Ⓐ apologised
- Ⓑ apologized
- Ⓒ aplogized
- Ⓓ appologized

6. Do you have any _____ foil?

- Ⓕ alluminum
- Ⓖ aluminum
- Ⓗ alloominem
- Ⓙ aluminem

Read the directions carefully. Be sure you know if you should look for the correctly spelled word or the incorrectly spelled word.

Name _____   Date _____

Spelling

Directions: Read the phrases. Choose the phrase in which the underlined word is not spelled correctly.

1. (A) horizontle line
   (B) install software
   (C) graham cracker
   (D) firm mattress

2. (F) invisible man
   (G) covert operation
   (H) glove compartmant
   (J) contagious disease

3. (A) cast your ballot
   (B) buy a trinkette
   (C) drive the vehicle
   (D) play the lyre

4. (F) our residance
   (G) adhesive tape
   (H) compose a sonnet
   (J) nouns and adjectives

Directions: For each item, choose the underlined word that is not spelled correctly for the way it is used in the phrase.

5. (A) sentence fragment
   (B) Earth's corps
   (C) cancel an appointment
   (D) leaky faucet

6. (F) subtle hint
   (G) sensible plan
   (H) except an offer
   (J) food staples

7. (A) a flare for fashion
   (B) bottle cork
   (C) hunker down
   (D) internal medicine

8. (F) seek help
   (G) mountain peek
   (H) measuring cup
   (J) colorful trend

9. (A) home shopping
   (B) under the bridge
   (C) vivid imagination
   (D) an intense stair

10. (F) a wild bare
    (G) dear friends
    (H) wave the flag
    (J) hold the phone

Spelling

Directions: Fill in the space for the choice that has a spelling error. If there are no mistakes, mark "No mistakes."

1. (A) veer
   (B) request
   (C) surplus
   (D) No mistakes

2. (F) smack
   (G) stitch
   (H) toppel
   (J) No mistakes

3. (A) patter
   (B) schedulle
   (C) mute
   (D) No mistakes

4. (F) aristocrat
   (G) trespass
   (H) gleeming
   (J) No mistakes

5. (A) acsess
   (B) bluff
   (C) valve
   (D) No mistakes

6. (F) ardent
   (G) tripod
   (H) tongue
   (J) No mistakes

Directions: Find the underlined word that is misspelled. If all the words are spelled correctly, fill in the circle for "No mistakes."

7. The <u>abilitie</u> to read is a <u>vital</u> <u>skill</u> for all. <u>No mistakes</u>
   　　(A)　　　　　　　(B)　(C)　　　　　(D)

8. The <u>surly</u> <u>usher</u> <u>sneered</u> at the boy. <u>No mistakes</u>
   　　(F)　　(G)　　(H)　　　　　　　(J)

9. Dr. McCoy played <u>billiards</u> in the <u>lounge</u> with a <u>formidible</u> opponent. <u>No mistakes</u>
   　　　　　　　　　(A)　　　　　(B)　　　　　(C)　　　　　　　　(D)

10. The <u>abbot</u> in the <u>abbie</u> sings <u>alto</u>. <u>No mistakes</u>
    　　(F)　　　　　(G)　　　　(H)　　(J)

11. The twins were dressed in <u>identical</u> <u>khaki</u> pants and <u>calico</u> shirts. <u>No mistakes</u>
    　　　　　　　　　　　　(A)　　　(B)　　　　　　(C)　　　　　　(D)

12. You are <u>indispenseble</u> in your <u>capacity</u> as class <u>secretary</u>. <u>No mistakes</u>
    　　　　(F)　　　　　　　　　(G)　　　　　　(H)　　　　(J)

Sample Test 3: Language Mechanics

Directions: Fill in the circle for the punctuation mark that is needed in the sentence. Fill in the circle for "None" if no more punctuation marks are needed.

1. "That was great" exclaimed Stephen.

- (A) !
- (B) .
- (C) ,
- (D) None

2. We have band on Monday Wednesday, and Friday.

- (F) ;
- (G) ,
- (H) :
- (J) None

3. He said he wanted to go home now.

- (A) ,
- (B) :
- (C) "
- (D) None

4. "When can we leave? Isaac inquired.

- (F) ,
- (G) "
- (H) :
- (J) None

Directions: Fill in the circle for the choice that has a punctuation error. If there are no mistakes, fill in the circle for "No mistakes."

5. (A) Which one is it.
(B) I can't tell
(C) the difference between the two.
(D) No mistakes

6. (F) Whose son is he?
(G) I dont know him.
(H) Does anyone recognize him?
(J) No mistakes

Directions: Read each sentence. Choose the word or words that best fit in the blank and show the correct punctuation.

7. Her list included the _____ clean room, do dishes, feed dog.

- (A) following,
- (B) following:
- (C) following;
- (D) following

8. The _____ we took at the zoo did not turn out.

- (F) pictures
- (G) pictures,
- (H) pictures'
- (J) picture's

GO

Sample Test 3: Language Mechanics

Directions: Read each group of sentences. Fill in the circle next to the sentence that is written correctly and shows the correct capitalization and punctuation.

9. (A) How many days until Memorial Day?

(B) You remind me of my uncle Fester who lives in Bangor Maine.

(C) "Would you like to go swimming, skating or biking." he asked.

(D) "I wont go, Mr Pinsky," Doug insisted.

10. (F) Do you like french bread, with spaghetti?

(G) She should be better in a week, but she needs to rest.

(H) Mrs Patterson the nurse, wont let me go home.

(J) "After breakfast, said Natalie, Let's go swimming."

11. (A) I love to go for walks, and she likes to ride bikes.

(B) We went to the mall and bought jeans, and shirts. and shoes.

(C) "I cant find my homework" said Bill.

(D) "No? she exclaimed!

12. (F) Breakfast is my favorite meal and Lunch is my least favorite.

(G) I like to eat eggs a banana, and toast for Breakfast.

(H) I usually have a boring sandwich for lunch.

(J) We eat dinner and then we go for a walk!

Directions: Read the sentence. Fill in the circle beside the answer choice that fits best in the blank and has correct capitalization and punctuation.

13. Sylvie loves to eat veggie burgers with _____.

(A) sweet potato french fries.

(B) sweet potato French Fries.

(C) sweet potato French fries.

(D) sweet potato French fries;

14. In order to excel at a _____ need to practice.

(F) sport you

(G) sport, you

(H) sport: you

(J) sport. You

15. She lives on _____ just two blocks away.

(A) Fifth street. Its

(B) Fifth Street, its

(C) Fifth Street. It's

(D) fifth street, it's

16. _____ showed us how to care for our teeth.

(F) Dr. Newman and her assistant

(G) Dr. Newman, and her assistant

(H) Dr. Newman and, her assistant,

(J) Dr. Newman and her Assistant

Sample Test 3: Language Mechanics

Directions: Look at the underlined part of each sentence. Fill in the circle of the choice that shows the correct capitalization and punctuation of the underlined words.

17. Toshi <u>exclaimed we</u> need to start practicing now!"

ⓐ exclaimed, we

ⓑ exclaimed. We

ⓒ exclaimed, "We

ⓓ Correct as it is

18. Do you like to travel by <u>bus subway,</u> or car?

ⓕ bus, subway,

ⓖ bus subway

ⓗ bus; subway

ⓙ Correct as it is

19. She lives in the small town of <u>Tykesville, Maine.</u>

ⓐ Tykesville Maine.

ⓑ Tykesville: Maine.

ⓒ Tykesville maine:

ⓓ Correct as it is

20. "Will you visit <u>Grandma she</u> asked.

ⓕ grandma, she

ⓖ Grandma," she

ⓗ Grandma?" she

ⓙ Correct as it is

Directions: Read the passage. Fill in the circle of the choice that shows the correct capitalization and punctuation of the underlined words.

Annie Oakley was a natural. At the age of nine, she shot a walnut off a tree <u>branch the</u> **(21)** very first time she fired her father's old long-barreled rifle. Her skill with the gun proved a blessing for her <u>family because</u> **(22)** her father had died of a fever when she was <u>four Annie</u> **(23)** helped support her <u>mother brother</u> **(24)** and sisters by shooting and selling quail and rabbits.

21. ⓐ branch, the

ⓑ branch. The

ⓒ branch; the

ⓓ Correct as it is

22. ⓕ family. Because

ⓖ family, because

ⓗ family; because

ⓙ Correct as it is

23. ⓐ four Annie,

ⓑ four, Annie

ⓒ four. Annie

ⓓ Correct as it is

24. ⓕ mother, brother,

ⓖ mother brother,

ⓗ mother; brother

ⓙ Correct as it is

Sample Test 3: Language Mechanics

Directions: Find the word that shows the correct spelling and fits best in the sentence.

25. Can I have your _____?

- Ⓐ autograff
- Ⓑ autograph
- Ⓒ ottograff
- Ⓓ autograf

26. Do not cross the _____.

- Ⓕ burrier
- Ⓖ barriere
- Ⓗ barrier
- Ⓙ burier

27. My mother loves to shop for _____.

- Ⓐ antigues
- Ⓑ antikes
- Ⓒ anticues
- Ⓓ antiques

Directions: Choose the phrase in which the underlined word is not spelled correctly.

28. Ⓕ sit on the balcony
- Ⓖ the abominible snowman
- Ⓗ alkaline battery
- Ⓙ the dog yelped

29. Ⓐ apology accepted
- Ⓑ filled with awe
- Ⓒ dispise rainy days
- Ⓓ jostled in the crowd

30. Ⓕ pore the milk
- Ⓖ grammar skills
- Ⓗ vile behavior
- Ⓙ wash with ammonia

31. Ⓐ brief incident
- Ⓑ peal the potatoes
- Ⓒ a bonnie belle
- Ⓓ dance the waltz

32. Ⓕ hold for ransom
- Ⓖ read the text
- Ⓗ serf the waves
- Ⓙ call a truce

STOP

Word Choice

Directions: Correct each underlined verb below.

1. Koalas <u>has</u> an important place in the island continent of Australia. _____

2. They <u>attracts</u> millions of visitors to Australia. _____

3. They <u>is</u> often called *koala bears*, but they are marsupials. _____

4. We <u>has</u> to protect this precious symbol of their country. _____

5. They <u>has</u> sharp, curved claws to protect themselves. _____

6. Koalas <u>climbs</u> trees, often with their babies on their backs. _____

7. They <u>eats</u> only the leaves of eucalyptus trees. _____

8. We <u>is</u> going to get some koalas at our zoo. _____

9. Their habitat <u>are</u> being destroyed to make room for housing developments. _____

10. Killing koalas <u>have</u> been prohibited by law. _____

Remember, pronouns must agree with the verbs to which they refer.

For example:
She **sees** koalas when *she* **visits** Australia.
They **see** koalas when *they* **visit** Australia.
You **see** koalas when *you* **visit** Australia.

Name _____ Date _____

Word Choice

Directions: Write the correct verb form to match each subject in the passage below.

Cormorants _____ (is, are) birds that help people. In some

countries, this type of bird _____ (is, are) used to help catch

fish. Cormorants _____ (fly, flies) around fishing grounds.

Fishermen watching them _____ (know, knows) where the fish

_____ (is, are). Some fishermen _____ (catch, catches)

cormorants. They _____ (tie, ties) long cords to the birds, and

then they _____ (take, takes) them out on their boats. When

the birds _____ (dive, dives) under the water to catch fish, the

fishermen _____ (keep, keeps) them from making off with

the fish. Cormorants _____ (is, are) related to pelicans. Most

cormorants _____ (perch, perches) in trees, on rocks, and on the

edges of cliffs. They _____ (has, have) webbed feet.

> **A singular subject must have a singular verb as a partner. A plural subject must have a plural verb as a partner.**
> For example: *People* **are** living longer in many countries.
>
> **Words such as *everyone, anyone, no one, somebody, someone,* and *something* always require a singular verb.**
> For example: *Everyone* who comes to the party **is** bringing a gift.

Word Choice

Directions: Circle the correct verb in each sentence.

1. Those toys (is, are) loved by most children.

2. There (is, are) two kids who missed the bus.

3. Neither my cat nor my dogs (like, likes) to eat pet food.

4. There (is, are) no reason for you to miss school today.

5. Facts (is, are) facts, and you can't deny them.

6. Many movie monsters (is, are) truly scary.

7. Either you or your sister (has, have) to clean that room.

8. A tomato and a cucumber (sit, sits) on the counter.

9. Every day, someone (take, takes) my favorite seat on the bus.

10. Something in the garbage (smell, smells) really bad!

11. Molly and her friend (wait, waits) outside the store.

12. Neither my pencil nor my books (is, are) in my backpack.

13. Dogs (is, are) my favorite animal.

14. James (kick, kicks) the soccer ball harder than everyone.

15. I can't wait to go home and (read, reads) my favorite book.

Name _____ Date _____

Word Choice

Directions: Choose the word or phrase that best completes the sentence.

1. **He was _____ at math than his twin.**

   (A) best

   (B) better

   (C) more better

   (D) most best

2. **Sally _____ her hair when we arrived.**

   (F) cutting

   (G) were cutting

   (H) was cutting

   (J) are cutting

3. **Pete's Pitas is _____ favorite restaurant.**

   (A) our

   (B) theys

   (C) we

   (D) us

If a question is too difficult, skip it and come back to it later.

Before you mark your answer, say it to yourself. Does it sound right?

Directions: Choose the answer that is a complete and correctly written sentence.

4. (F) Our class buyed souvenirs in the museum's gift shop.

   (G) My dad and uncle builded the house theyselves.

   (H) We enjoyed our tour of the fire station.

   (J) They was shopping at the mall when they saw him.

5. (A) Me and him walked to school together.

   (B) I and Daniel helped Mr. McGinnis paint the walls.

   (C) Marissa and them picked up trash in the playground.

   (D) Angela and I wrote book reports on the same book

Word Choice

Directions: Read each answer choice. Fill in the space for the choice that has a usage error. If there are no mistakes, mark "No mistakes."

1. (A) Lena and I seen
   (B) an accident on the way
   (C) to school this morning.
   (D) No mistakes

2. (F) The driver of a small
   (G) sports car run a stop sign
   (H) and hit a pickup truck.
   (J) No mistakes

3. (A) It's always best
   (B) to obey street signs
   (C) whether you is driving or not.
   (D) No mistakes

4. (F) When Jake grows up,
   (G) he wants to be
   (H) a police officer.
   (J) No mistakes

5. (A) My brother aren't
   (B) feeling well this morning,
   (C) so he isn't going to school.
   (D) No mistakes

6. (F) As she approached,
   (G) we seen that she was
   (H) wearing a new dress.
   (J) No mistakes

7. (A) We visit the zoo
   (B) and saw monkeys
   (C) and two snapping turtles.
   (D) No mistakes

8. (F) Tomorrow will be
   (G) the first day baseball practice
   (H) is held at the new field.
   (J) No mistakes

9. (A) Cody and Trevor is
   (B) excited to play
   (C) in their first game.
   (D) No mistakes

10. (F) Randy and I are
    (G) too busy to go
    (H) outside today.
    (J) No mistakes

82

Word Choice

Directions: Use the passage to answer the questions below. Mark "Correct as it is" if the underlined part is correct.

(1) Abraham Lincoln was a poor farm boy, a lawyer, and a congressman. (2) In 1860, he were elected the sixteenth president of the United States.

(3) Whoever first say that anyone could be president was probably thinking of Abraham Lincoln. (4) As a child, Lincoln was highly motivated to learn. (5) He had little formal education, but he educated hisself by reading books by firelight. (6) He believed anyone who gave him a book was a good friend, since books holds the power of knowledge.

(7) Lincoln was always known for his honesty. (8) Before studying law, he was a shopkeeper. (9) He also worked as a postmaster and a store clerk. (10) As president, he not only freed the slaves, but he also proved to be a master statesman and a wise commander-in-chief.

1. In sentence 2, were elected is best written

A) elected.
B) was elected.
C) will be elected.
D) Correct as it is

2. In sentence 3, say that is best written

F) says that.
G) say that's.
H) said that.
J) Correct as it is

3. In sentence 4, was highly motivated is best written

A) was highly motivates.
B) was highly motivating.
C) were highly motivated.
D) Correct as it is

4. In sentence 5, hisself is best written

F) himself.
G) theyselves.
H) he.
J) Correct as it is

5. In sentence 6, books holds is best written

A) books helds.
B) book holds.
C) books held.
D) Correct as it is

6. In sentence 7, was always known is best written

F) was always knew
G) always knew
H) is always knew
J) Correct as it is

Sentences

Directions: Find the underlined word that is the simple subject of the sentence.

Example

The <u>tiny</u> <u>dog</u> <u>scampered</u> after the <u>horse</u>.
Ⓐ Ⓑ   Ⓒ   Ⓓ

Answer: (B)

1. <u>Their</u> <u>cat</u> <u>meowed</u> at the <u>door</u>.
Ⓐ   Ⓑ   Ⓒ   Ⓓ

2. The <u>large</u> <u>family</u> <u>picnicked</u> in the <u>city</u> park.
      Ⓕ   Ⓖ   Ⓗ   Ⓙ

3. <u>Several</u> <u>other</u> <u>landmarks</u> <u>helped</u> her to remember the way.
   Ⓐ   Ⓑ   Ⓒ   Ⓓ

4. The <u>skilled</u> <u>trumpeter</u> stood and <u>played</u> a <u>solo</u>.
      Ⓕ   Ⓖ   Ⓗ   Ⓙ

Directions: Find the underlined word that is the simple predicate of the sentence.

5. <u>Omar</u> <u>discovered</u> a <u>snapping</u> turtle in his <u>backyard</u>.
   Ⓐ   Ⓑ   Ⓒ   Ⓓ

6. <u>Our</u> <u>dad</u> <u>crawled</u> <u>under</u> the sink to fix the leak.
   Ⓕ   Ⓖ   Ⓗ   Ⓙ

7. Two <u>firemen</u> <u>visited</u> our <u>classroom</u> to <u>talk</u> about their jobs.
      Ⓐ   Ⓑ   Ⓒ   Ⓓ

8. A piece of cut glass <u>hanging</u> in the <u>window</u> <u>created</u> a colorful <u>prism</u> on the floor.
                  Ⓕ   Ⓖ   Ⓗ   Ⓙ

Sentences

Directions: Choose the answer that best combines the underlined sentences.

1. **Mr. Norton called this morning.**
   Mr. Norton said his wife is sick.

   (A) Mr. Norton called this morning and Mr. Norton said his wife is sick.

   (B) Mr. Norton called this morning, and he said his wife is sick.

   (C) This morning, Mr. Norton called and said, his wife is sick.

   (D) Mr. Norton called this morning to say his wife is sick.

2. **George left early.**
   Colette left early.
   They are going to the band festival.

   (F) George and Colette left early because to the band festival they are going.

   (G) George and Colette left early to go to the band festival.

   (H) George left early and Colette because they are going to the band festival.

   (J) Leaving early, George and Colette are going to the band festival.

3. **The birds sing beautifully.**
   The birds are in the tree.

   (A) The birds are in the tree, and they sing beautifully.

   (B) The birds, in the tree, singing beautifully.

   (C) The birds sing beautifully and are in the tree.

   (D) The birds in the tree sing beautifully.

4. **Sadie needed a bath.**
   Sadie had worked in the garden all day.

   (F) Sadie needed a bath, and she had worked in the garden all day.

   (G) Sadie worked in the garden all day, but she needed a bath.

   (H) Sadie needed a bath because she had worked in the garden all day.

   (J) Needing a bath, Sadie had worked in the garden all day.

Directions: Choose the best way of expressing the idea.

5. (A) Because year after year, the salmon struggle upstream to spawn.

   (B) Upstream to spawn, the salmon struggle year after year.

   (C) Year after year, the salmon struggle upstream to spawn.

   (D) The salmon struggle year after year upstream to spawn.

6. (F) The plumber fixed the pipe because it was leaking.

   (G) The plumber fixed the leaking pipe.

   (H) Because the pipe was leaking, the plumber fixed the pipe.

   (J) The pipe was leaking, and the plumber fixed the pipe.

Name _____   Date _____

Sentences

Directions: Use the passage to answer the questions that follow.

(**1**) Years ago, people believed that children could not write until they could spell. (**2**) Children practiced letters or were given spelling words or dictation to copy, but schools did not consider scribbling to be writing. (**3**) Children in early elementary school spent their time painting or playing with blocks or clay. (**4**) Scribbling then was just scribbling.

(**5**) Teachers now <u>believes, that encouraging</u> young children to scribble is an important step in writing. (**6**) Teachers have discovered that it is important for children to write before they even know their alphabet. (**7**) Young children encouraged to write lists and tell stories, leave messages, and make signs. (**8**) They should be asked to read their writing aloud, although unreadable it may be.

1. Which sentence should be added after sentence 5?

(A) Recess was my favorite activity of the day.

(B) This early writing may not be readable, but it is still writing.

(C) Playing dress up and other play activities also are beneficial.

(D) Naptime is a necessary part of the young child's day.

2. How is sentence 8 best written?

(F) Even because it is unreadable, they should be asked to read their writing aloud.

(G) They should be asked to read their writing aloud, even if it is unreadable.

(H) Because they should be asked to read their unreadable writing aloud.

(J) Correct as it is

3. Which group of words is not a complete thought?

(A) sentence 2

(B) sentence 3

(C) sentence 7

(D) sentence 8

4. In sentence 5, <u>believes, that encouraging</u> is best written

(F) believe that encouraging

(G) believes. That encouraging

(H) believe that, encouraging

(J) Correct as it is

Sentences

Directions: Use the passage to answer the questions that follow.

> **(1)** Last May our centennial anniversary for our town was celebrated by us. **(2)** We made a lot of preparations. **(3)** A cleanup committee washed all public buildings. **(4)** They also brushed all public buildings. **(5)** Members of the fire department climbed on high ladders to hang up flags and bunting.
>
> **(6)** At last, the celebration began. **(7)** The high point was when mayor Lopez asked Olga Janssen—at 105, our oldest citizen—what she remembered about the old days. **(8)** Mrs. Janssen recalled how her mother had used a churn to make butter, and her favorite memory was of playing dominoes with her cousins.
>
> **(9)** At the end, we all drank a ginger ale toast to the town's next century. **(10)** We knew most of us would not be here for the next celebration, but we felt happy to be at this one. **(11)** A large bell was struck with a mallet by the mayor to officially close our celebration.

1. How is sentence 1 best written?

(A) Last May our town's centennial anniversary was celebrated by us.

(B) Last May, we celebrated our town's centennial anniversary.

(C) We celebrated last May our town's centennial anniversary.

(D) Correct as it is

2. How are sentences 3 and 4 best combined?

(F) A cleanup committee washed all public buildings and then brushed them.

(G) A cleanup committee washed, and they also brushed, all public buildings.

(H) A cleanup committee washed and brushed all public buildings.

(J) Correct as it is

3. Sentence 11 is best written

(A) The mayor officially closed our celebration with a mallet by striking a bell.

(B) Striking a large bell with a mallet, our celebration officially closed by the mayor.

(C) To officially close our celebration, the mayor struck a large bell with a mallet.

(D) Correct as it is

4. Which sentence should be broken into two sentences?

(F) 2

(G) 5

(H) 8

(J) 10

Sentences

Directions: Write *simple* on the lines after the simple sentences and *compound* on the lines after the compound sentences.

1. It was a beautiful day, and I was ready for adventure.

_____

2. I saw my friend Sofia and invited her to come with me.

_____

3. She strapped on her skates, and she joined me.

_____

4. Sofia and I enjoyed our trip to the park.

_____

5. We reached the park and took a rest.

_____

6. Sofia is new to skating, but I'm not.

_____

7. As I watched, Sofia rolled down a steep part of the path.

_____

8. She skated up to me, and I gave her a high-five.

_____

9. Sofia and I skated around the lake before heading home.

_____

10. We both had a great time, and I can't wait for our next adventure!

_____

Paragraphs

Directions: Read the paragraph. Choose the best topic sentence.

Example

_____ **Some you can pick up and perhaps even take home for pets. But would you believe a lizard exists that can grow up to 10 feet long and weight 300 pounds? Now that's a lizard!**

(A) My favorite pets are dogs.

(B) Some lizards are cute little reptiles no more than a few centimeters in length.

(C) Do you think dinosaurs were the ancestors of reptiles or birds?

(D) Would you like to have a lizard as a pet?

Answer: (B)

---

1. _____ **Ants that live in sandy places, such as dunes and deserts, are plagued by the larvae of two insects. These larvae ambush their prey from concealed sand traps. One of these insects is the tiger beetle. The other is the ant lion.**

(A) People have lots of troubles.

(B) Ants are part of the insect family.

(C) Anteaters are not the only predators ants need to worry about.

(D) Like bees, ants live in a very complex social system.

Directions: Find the answer choice that best develops the topic sentence below.

2. **The sod houses of the Great Plains had their drawbacks.**

(F) They were fireproof, windproof, and, for the most part, bulletproof.

(G) During heavy rains, the roof leaked, and water and mud dripped into whatever happened to be cooking on the stove.

(H) Most were built so strong that they could withstand tornadoes and snowstorms.

(J) The sod house was home to most of those hardy souls who braved life on the Great Plains.

Remember, a paragraph should focus on one idea. The correct answer is the one that fits best with the rest of the paragraph.

Name _____ Date _____

Paragraphs

Directions: Read the paragraph below and answer the question that follows.

> **(1)** Canada is more than a land of great beauty. **(2)** It borders the United States to the south. **(3)** It is also a land of vast forests. **(4)** Lumber and the products that come from lumber make Canada a leader in world paper production. **(5)** The pulp and paper industry continues to grow and is now Canada's leading industry.

1. Which sentence does not belong?

(A) sentence 2

(B) sentence 3

(C) sentence 4

(D) sentence 5

Directions: Read each paragraph. Find the sentence that best fits in the blank.

2. He was greeted by enthusiastic crowds in Paris and London. When he returned to the United States, he was given one of the largest ticker-tape parades in New York history. Overnight, his name became a household word. _____. Aviator Douglas Corrigan, who, following a most unusual feat, was known worldwide as *Wrong-Way Corrigan.*

(F) Whether it was legitimate or not, Douglas Corrigan's flight made him famous.

(G) His ideas were as well-known as the president's.

(H) Who was this new American hero?

(J) Where did this man call his home?

3. In 1937, Douglas Corrigan had requested permission to fly over the Atlantic to Europe. His request was denied after federal aviation officials inspected his plane. _____. One tank was even located directly in front of the pilot's seat and nearly blocked Corrigan's vision.

(A) His plane did not have the capacity to hold enough fuel to cross the ocean.

(B) Corrigan had added so many extra gas tanks to his dilapidated craft that it was considered a deathtrap.

(C) Authorities feared Corrigan would run out of fuel with no land in sight.

(D) His plane had no added room for extra supplies of food and water.

Paragraphs

Directions: Use the paragraphs below to answer the questions that follow.

(1) "This is a pretty good poem," she thought to herself. (2) "it's just that . . ." (3) Grace wondered if she had fed her dog before she left for school. (4) Then her name was called, she stood up, and her knees began to shake. (5) When she turned around and looked at the rest of the class, however, she saw friendly faces.

1. Choose the best first sentence for this paragraph.

(A) Grace waited for her turn to read her poem in front of the class.

(B) Grace could hardly wait to go to lunch.

(C) Grace was looking forward to reading her play.

(D) Grace loved English class.

2. Which sentence should be left out of this paragraph?

(F) sentence 1

(G) sentence 2

(H) sentence 3

(J) sentence 5

3. Choose the last sentence for this paragraph.

(A) "Oh, no," she remembered, "I didn't feed the dog!"

(B) Grace felt like running from the room.

(C) Grace decided that this would be a great time to read all her poems.

(D) "Maybe this won't be so bad after all," Grace thought with relief.

(1) By the late 1800s, many poor people lived in crowded housing in city slums. (2) Progressives worked to change these living conditions. (3) In some cities, they set up settlement houses. (4) There, they provided medical care and worked with slum residents to improve conditions.

4. What would be a logical topic for the next paragraph?

(F) city living conditions today

(G) working conditions for the poor

(H) politics of the late 1800s and early 1900s

(J) the history of the American upper class

5. Which would make the best last sentence for this paragraph?

(A) Factory employees worked long hours for low pay.

(B) As a result of the progressives' work, many states established housing regulations.

(C) Reformers during the Progressive Era were known as *progressives*.

(D) Factory employees often operated unsafe machinery.

Paragraphs

Directions: Use the paragraphs below to answer the questions that follow.

(1) <u>The weather was bad</u> over the mid-Atlantic Ocean. (2) The small plane's engine sputtered. (3) The slim, young woman at the controls knew she was too far out to turn back. (4) Carefully, she coaxed the plane ahead through the storm.

(5) When dawn came, the engine was failing seriously. (6) Just ahead lay the Irish coast. (7) As the engine gasped its last breath, the woman brought her plane down in a cow pasture. (8) An astonished farmer raced over as the young woman climbed out of the airplane. (9) "I'm from America," she said. (10) "My name is Amelia Earhart." (11) The farmer was angry that she had ruined part of his field. (12) She had even set a new speed record: thirteen hours and thirty minutes!

(13) They didn't think a woman was strong enough to keep going through the long night. (14) However, Earhart had strength and courage to spare. (15) She had already made parachute jumps and had explored the ocean floor in a diver's suit. (16) Now, overnight, she had become famous.

1. Which sentence could be added after sentence 10?

(A) The farmer thought she was an alien from outer space.

(B) She had become the first woman to fly over the Atlantic Ocean alone.

(C) She had become the first woman to safely land in a pasture.

(D) She added, "Do you know where I might get something good to eat?"

2. Which sentence could begin the third paragraph?

(F) Many people had told Amelia not to make this flight.

(G) Amelia wanted to give up.

(H) Amelia was a weak woman.

(J) Amelia loved to set world records.

3. Which group of words would be more colorful than the underlined words in sentence 1?

(A) There was lightning

(B) Lightning ripped through the blackness

(C) It was cold and wet

(D) The weather was stormy

4. Which sentence does not belong in the story?

(F) sentence 2

(G) sentence 6

(H) sentence 11

(J) sentence 16

Paragraphs

Directions: Use the paragraphs below to answer the questions that follow.

(1) "We are going to have a good vacation this year, or I'll eat a bug," says Dad, as we pull away from the house. (2) We start laughing because he says that every year. (3) And every year, something goes wrong.

(4) We start out for Lucky Fool Camp the name is enough for my brother and me to know that this is going to be another weird vacation. (5) On the way, Dad takes a couple of wrong turns and gets lost. (6) Fortunately, my brother has a great sense of direction and knows how to get to the camp. (7) We arrive to see a big sign on the gate: *Closed due to mosquito infestation. Sorry! ~ The Mgmt.* (8) The place is swarming with mosquitoes, and one bites me right away. (9) What now?

(10) Dad looks so disappointed, until Mom says, "I knew this would happen, so I've been saving money all year. (11) Here are four plane tickets to Amusement World!" (12) Dad gives each of us a big hug. (13) Next year, we are thinking of going camping or touring Civil War battlefields. (14) We have our first great vacation ever!

1. Which sentence is a run-on sentence?

(A) sentence 4

(B) sentence 6

(C) sentence 8

(D) sentence 13

2. What is the best summary of the second paragraph?

(F) Dad gets lost.

(G) The narrator's brother is good with directions.

(H) The name of the camp is Lucky Fool Camp.

(J) The family arrives at the camp only to find out it is closed.

3. Which sentence does not belong in the last paragraph?

(A) sentence 11

(B) sentence 12

(C) sentence 13

(D) sentence 14

4. If the story continued, what would be a good topic for the next paragraph?

(F) what weather conditions cause mosquito infestations

(G) the narrator's relationship with her brother

(H) Dad's childhood

(J) the family's experiences at Amusement World

Study Skills

Directions: Use the illustration of an encyclopedia set to answer the questions that follow.

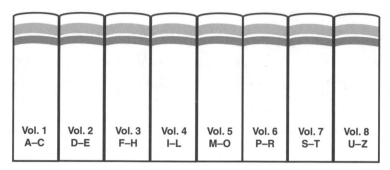

| Vol. 1 A–C | Vol. 2 D–E | Vol. 3 F–H | Vol. 4 I–L | Vol. 5 M–O | Vol. 6 P–R | Vol. 7 S–T | Vol. 8 U–Z |

1. Which volume would include information about amphibians?

- (A) volume 1
- (B) volume 4
- (C) volume 6
- (D) volume 8

2. Which volume would include information on marsupials?

- (F) volume 2
- (G) volume 5
- (H) volume 7
- (J) volume 8

Directions: Use this page from a telephone book to answer the questions below.

Salinsky, Paul   107 Prior Lane 788-8789
Samson, Saul   123 Road Way 798-5434
Simpson, Susan   778 Apple Road 799-2229
Smith, Charles   5555 Oak Avenue 768-8992
Smith, Chuck   111 Prior Lane 788-5456
Soldez, Maria   3579 River Road 779-1133

3. Where does Maria Soldez live?

- (A) 107 Prior Lane
- (B) 778 Apple Road
- (C) 5555 Oak Avenue
- (D) 3579 River Road

4. Paul Salinsky lives very near _____.

- (F) Saul Samson
- (G) Charles Smith
- (H) Chuck Smith
- (J) Susan Simpson

5. Which phone number belongs to Saul Samson?

- (A) 788-8789
- (B) 799-2229
- (C) 779-1133
- (D) 798-5434

Study Skills

Directions: Use this card from an electronic library card catalog to answer the questions that follow.

693.2	GROUCHO MARX
920 Marx	Blue, Alicia One Funny Family / by Alicia Blue. Photographs by Comedians Archives. Cleveland: Dianson Publishing Company, 1974. 244 p.; photos; 24 cm
	1. Marx, Julius "Groucho" 2. Comedians American 3. Movies, Comedies I. Title

2. This listing would be found if you searched by _____.

(F) title

(G) subject

(H) publisher

(J) author

1. From this card, you know that Groucho Marx is

(A) the author.

(B) the publisher.

(C) a comedian.

(D) a photographer.

3. Where did the photographs for this book come from?

(A) Dianson Publishing Company

(B) Alicia Blue

(C) Groucho Marx

(D) Comedians Archives

Directions: Read each question below, and mark the best answer.

4. Which word could be found on the same page as these dictionary guide words?

molehill	monad

(F) molecule

(G) mollusk

(H) monarch

(J) mold

6. Which of these is a main heading that includes the three other words?

(F) mice

(G) hamsters

(H) rodents

(J) gerbils

5. Which word could be found on the same page as these dictionary guide words?

guess	guile

(A) guerilla

(B) guffaw

(C) gulp

(D) guitar

7. Which of these is a main heading that includes the three other words?

(A) tornadoes

(B) hurricanes

(C) earthquakes

(D) natural disasters

Name _____   Date _____

Study Skills

Directions: Choose the best answer.

1. **While doing research for a report, Aaliyah used the book titled *Technology Tomorrow*. Where in the book should Aaliyah look to learn what information is found in each chapter?**

   Ⓐ the index

   Ⓑ the table of contents

   Ⓒ the title page

   Ⓓ the introduction

2. **Where in the book should Aaliyah look to learn when the book was published?**

   Ⓕ the index

   Ⓖ the table of contents

   Ⓗ the copyright page

   Ⓙ the bibliography

3. **Where in the book should Aaliyah look to learn what other sources she might be able to use in her report?**

   Ⓐ the index

   Ⓑ the table of contents

   Ⓒ the title page

   Ⓓ the bibliography

4. **Because Aaliyah has used other sources to write her report, she should**

   Ⓕ explain in her introduction that she has used other sources.

   Ⓖ make photocopies of her sources and attach them to her report.

   Ⓗ acknowledge her sources in citations and a bibliography.

   Ⓙ ignore the sources because she is only writing a report for school.

5. **While doing her research, Aaliyah encounters a word she doesn't know. Where can she look for a definition?**

   Ⓐ the glossary

   Ⓑ the index

   Ⓒ the bibliography

   Ⓓ the title page

6. **When Aaliyah went to the library to borrow *Technology Tomorrow*, she noticed that the library owned two versions. One was published in 1998, and the other was an updated version published in 2011. Which one should she use? Why?**

   _____

   _____

   _____

Study Skills

Directions: The index below appears in a book about trains. Use it to answer the questions that follow.

Index

Engines
  fuel, 32–36
  types of, 30–38

History
  in Africa, 18–22
  in Asia, 20–24
  in Europe, 2–10
  in North America, 8–18
  in South America, 16–18
  legends and stories, 72–78

Tracks
  laying, 26–32
  types, 28–33, 93–95

Workers
  job classifications, 80–85
  unions, 4–8

1. **Which pages would probably tell about a Ghost Train some people say they have seen?**

   (A) 72–78

   (B) 32–36

   (C) 80–85

   (D) 28–33

2. **Which pages would give you information on trains that ran between France and Germany during the 1930s?**

   (F) 4–8

   (G) 18–22

   (H) 2–10

   (J) 16–18

3. **Zara is interested in learning about whether some trains use fuel-efficient engines. What pages should she refer to?**

   (A) 30–38

   (B) 32–36

   (C) 26–32

   (D) 93–95

4. **How many pages are devoted to the discussion of train engines?**

   (F) 6

   (G) 8

   (H) 12

   (J) Not enough information

5. **Which pages would give you information about the first trains in North America?**

   (A) 16–18

   (B) 80–85

   (C) 8–18

   (D) 28–33

Sample Test 4: Usage

Directions: Choose the word or phrase that best completes the sentence.

1. **Last week, my family _____ our relatives in Grand Rapids, Michigan.**

   (A) visit

   (B) will visit

   (C) visited

   (D) visits

Directions: Choose the answer that is a complete and correctly written sentence.

2. (F) I was very pleased with the band's performance.

   (G) We is going to Greenfield Village on Saturday.

   (H) My mom takes me shopping to buy new clothes yesterday.

   (J) Please help she clean your room.

Directions: Fill in the circle for the choice that has a usage error. If there is no mistake, fill in the circle for "No mistakes."

3. (A) I'm wondering if I will ever

   (B) finish this book. I were supposed

   (C) to have it completed today.

   (D) No mistakes

4. (F) Amanda give her report

   (G) on hedgehogs. Ali gave

   (H) his report on chimpanzees.

   (J) No mistakes

5. (A) We don't never get to go

   (B) to the movies. Does your

   (C) family go often?

   (D) No mistakes

Sample Test 4: Usage

Directions: Find the underlined word that is the simple subject of each sentence.

6. <u>Green</u> <u>iguanas</u> <u>are</u> Nico's favorite <u>type</u> of pet.
   - (F) (G) (H)   (J)

7. An <u>editor</u> from a local publishing <u>company</u> <u>spoke</u> to our <u>class</u> on Monday.
   - (A)   (B)   (C)   (D)

Directions: Choose the answer that best combines the underlined sentences.

8. <u>**Gordon is going to the store.**</u>
   <u>**Samantha is going with him.**</u>

   - (F) Gordon is going to the store and so is Samantha.
   - (G) Gordon and Samantha are going to the store.
   - (H) To the store, Gordon and Samantha are going.
   - (J) Gordon and Samantha to the store are going.

9. <u>**Please go to the kitchen.**</u>
   <u>**I would like you to get an orange**</u>
   <u>**for me.**</u>

   - (A) Please go to the kitchen to get me an orange.
   - (B) Please go to the kitchen to get me an orange because I want one.
   - (C) For me, please go to the kitchen to get an orange.
   - (D) I would like for you to please go to the kitchen to get an orange for me.

Directions: Choose the best way of expressing each idea below.

10. (F) In the family room is our television, which we enjoy together as a family.

   - (G) Our television is in the family room, which my family enjoys together.
   - (H) My family enjoys watching television together in the family room.
   - (J) My family enjoys in the family room watching television.

11. (A) Because of the heavy rain, we had to take a detour the police officer said.

   - (B) The police officer said because of the heavy rain, we had to take a detour.
   - (C) The police officer told us to take a detour because of the heavy rain.
   - (D) We had to take a detour, said the police officer, in spite of the heavy rain.

GO

Name _____ Date _____

Sample Test 4: Usage

Directions: Find the best topic sentence for the paragraph below.

12. _____ **When you first begin, all that comes out are high-pitched squeaks. Before long, you can play a simple melody. Eventually, playing your instrument is almost second nature.**

    Ⓕ Learning to ride a bike is a long process.

    Ⓖ Playing a clarinet takes time and practice.

    Ⓗ Playing a clarinet is simple.

    Ⓙ Becoming a concert pianist is difficult.

Directions: Find the answer choice that best develops the topic sentence.

13. **White-water rafting is a thrilling but dangerous sport.**

    Ⓐ Meandering through forests and observing the wildlife is very relaxing.

    Ⓑ Steering the raft together is great teamwork.

    Ⓒ The water can be cold, so dress appropriately.

    Ⓓ If you fall overboard, you can be dashed against the rocks.

Directions: Read the paragraph below. Find the sentence that best fits in the blank.

14. **The Internet can be a great resource for research papers. _____ When doing a research paper, be sure to check facts with several reliable sources. Never rely on one source.**

    Ⓕ When visiting chat rooms, never supply any personal information, such as your name or telephone number.

    Ⓖ Use a filter to screen out objectionable sites.

    Ⓗ Search for sites associated with organizations and institutions.

    Ⓙ Never give out your parents' credit card number.

Sample Test 4: Usage

Directions: Study this table of the wars in which the United States was involved. Use it to answer the questions that follow.

War	Dates	President(s)
War of 1812	1812–1815	Madison
Mexican War	1846–1848	Polk
Civil War	1861–1865	Lincoln
Spanish-American War	1898	McKinley
World War I	1914–1918	Wilson
World War II	1941–1945	F. Roosevelt, Truman
Korean War	1950–1953	Truman, Eisenhower
Vietnam War	1965–1973	Johnson, Nixon
Persian Gulf War	1991	G. Bush
Global War on Terrorism	2001–ongoing	G.W. Bush, Obama

15. Which of these wars was the earliest?

(A) Persian Gulf War

(B) Civil War

(C) War of 1812

(D) Spanish-American War

16. Which president was in office during two wars?

(F) Madison

(G) Nixon

(H) Truman

(J) Wilson

17. Which war is the most recent?

(A) World War II

(B) Persian Gulf War

(C) Global War on Terrorism

(D) Korean War

Directions: Choose the word that would appear first if the words were arranged in alphabetical order.

18. (F) tablet

(G) tableau

(H) tabard

(J) tabulate

19. (A) regret

(B) regress

(C) rekindle

(D) reinforce

20. (F) Roberts, Kevin

(G) Roberts, Cynthia

(H) Roberts, Chiara

(J) Roberts, Clifford

Directions: Choose the best source of information.

21. Which of these would tell you the names of the rivers in Africa?

(A) an atlas

(B) a thesaurus

(C) a dictionary

(D) a book of quotations

22. Which of these would help you to decide which lizard would be the best pet for you?

(F) an encyclopedia

(G) a gardening book

(H) a dictionary

(J) a handbook on lizards

GO

Name _____   Date _____

Sample Test 4: Usage

Directions: Use the table of contents and index from a science book to answer the questions that follow.

Table of Contents

Index

23. In which chapter would you probably find a question about the liver's function?

- (A) Chapter 1
- (B) Chapter 2
- (C) Chapter 4
- (D) Chapter 5

24. From looking at the table of contents and index, which of the topics below would most likely be covered in Chapters 1 and 5?

- (F) mumps and measles
- (G) plants and animals
- (H) earthquakes
- (J) helicopters

25. On which page might you find an answer about why your face turns red when you perspire?

- (A) page 7
- (B) page 38
- (C) page 65
- (D) page 157

26. Who do you think would be most likely to be interested in this book?

- (F) someone who loves to read novels
- (G) someone who enjoys science trivia
- (H) someone who wants to know how to build a tree house
- (J) someone who wants to plant a garden

Pre-Writing

Directions: Saleem is writing a report about orangutans. He began by making the web below. Use it to answer the questions that follow.

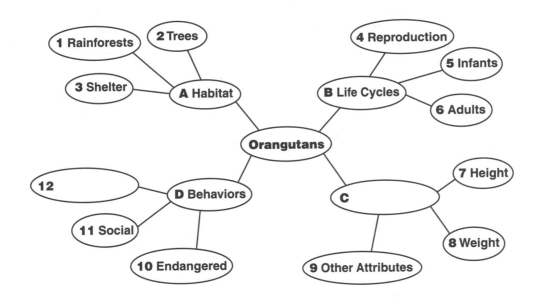

1. **Which of these should go in circle C?**

   (A) Physical Characteristics

   (B) Lifestyles

   (C) Coloration

   (D) Arm Spans

2. **Which idea in Saleem's web does not belong?**

   (F) 2

   (G) 6

   (H) 9

   (J) 10

3. **Which of these belongs in circle 12?**

   (A) Culture

   (B) Communication

   (C) Sports

   (D) Religion

4. **If Saleem wanted to add a circle E to the web, which of these would fit best?**

   (F) Diet

   (G) Education

   (H) Pastimes

   (J) Beliefs

Name _____   Date _____

Point of View

Directions: In each blank, write *1* for first person, *2* for second person, or *3* for third person to identify the point of view of each paragraph below.

1. _____ It's true, you know? You always loved cats more than people. When you first saw what was that cat's name? Oh, yes, Bernard! When your dad brought Bernard home from the shelter, your eyes got teary with happiness.

2. _____ A domestic turkey is not a wise bird. A dog, fox, or weasel that finds its way into a turkey coop merely waits for some lame-brained and curious turkey to waddle over for a visit. The predator has a cooperative victim!

3. _____ I don't think I can stand it any longer. I've got to tell Mom how much I dislike her asparagus custard pie. But how do I do it without hurting her feelings?

4. _____ That stubborn bachelor Patches McCloud had better get out of his termite-infested apartment before the walls come tumbling in on him! No one need warn him again!

5. _____ When you were born, the sun smiled down upon the earth. The moon glowed. The creatures of the night forest whispered that you, a princess, had been born to our people.

6. _____ What? You—become an army sharpshooter? Why, you couldn't hit the broad side of a barn if you were leaning against it!

7. _____ She carried a large basket of laundry on her head. She had done chores like this since she was a tiny child. But this time, things were different. Mikela was working at a real job now. Wouldn't her mother be proud!

8. _____ Oh, it was so dark! We will never know what caused the sudden blackout at the ball game. We hope the game will be rescheduled.

Letter Writing

Directions: Sixth graders wrote the following letters as part of a class project. Read the letter in each box below. Then, answer the questions.

A

Your store is the best grocery store in Orchard Grove. My parents buy all their groceries at your store. Our class is trying to raise money for a class trip. We would like to hold a car wash in your parking lot on Saturday, because we would get lots of business on that day.

B

We have 25 students in our class. Our teacher's name is Mr. Wordsworth. He is a great teacher. He said I should write to ask if we could hold a car wash in your parking lot on Saturday. He thought you would say yes.

C

The students in our class are raising money for our class trip. We would like your permission to hold a car wash in your parking lot on Saturday from 9:00 A.M. to 3:00 P.M. We promise to clean up when we are finished. We appreciate your consideration of this matter.

D

The students in our class think the best place to have a car wash would be in your parking lot. We think we could raise lots of money there. We need money to go on a class trip, since the school will not pay our way. Saturday from 9:00 A.M. to 3:00 P.M. would be a great time for us.

1. What task does the class have?

(A) to raise money for a class trip

(B) to clean their parents' cars

(C) to bring more cars to the parking lot

(D) to have something to do on a Saturday morning

2. To whom are the students writing the letter?

(F) to their teacher

(G) to their parents

(H) to their principal

(J) to the owner of the parking lot

3. Which letter would be the most appropriate in asking permission to use the parking lot for a car wash?

(A) letter A

(B) letter B

(C) letter C

(D) letter D

4. What point of view do the letters use?

(F) first person

(G) second person

(H) third person

(J) first and third person

Writing with Figurative Language

Directions: For each sentence below, write a more colorful way to express the same idea. Use any type of figurative language you want (simile, metaphor, personification, or idiom).

Personification assigns human qualities, feelings, or actions to an animal, an object, or an idea. For example: *The mother bear missed her cub and wondered what time he would be home.*

Similes use *like* or *as* to compare things that may seem unlike each other. For example: *Her smile was as dazzling as the sun.*

Metaphors compare unlike things without using *like* or *as.* For example: *His body was a well-oiled machine.*

Idioms are expressions that mean something different from what they actually say. For example: *She had a chip on her shoulder.*

1. **The weather was bad over the ocean today.**

_____

_____

_____

_____

2. **Jana was very angry with Tomas.**

_____

_____

_____

_____

3. **The knife was sharper than anything Gavin had ever felt.**

_____

_____

_____

_____

4. **These are the best hamburgers I've ever tasted! They're delicious!**

_____

_____

_____

_____

5. **Alex walked slowly as he carried the heavy suitcase back to the attic.**

_____

_____

_____

_____

6. **The loud chirping of the crickets woke Kenya from a deep sleep.**

_____

_____

_____

_____

Writing with Organization

Directions: Write three short paragraphs about ways that you could volunteer in your community. Structure your composition as follows.

Paragraph 1: Choose at least three organizations for which you would be interested in doing volunteer work. Describe them.

Paragraph 2: Give reasons why you would be interested in volunteering for these organizations.

Paragraph 3: Conclude by explaining what contributions you personally could make as a volunteer for these organizations.

_____

_____

_____

_____

_____

_____

_____

_____

_____

_____

_____

_____

_____

_____

_____

Persuasive Writing

Directions: Write three paragraphs about what you think is the biggest problem facing world leaders today. Identify the problem, and explain why you think it is the most serious problem. Then, explain what you think world leaders could do to solve the problem.

_____

_____

_____

_____

_____

_____

_____

_____

_____

_____

_____

_____

_____

_____

_____

_____

_____

_____

_____

_____

Sample Test 5: Writing

Directions: Values are an individual's ideas about what is right and wrong and what is important in life. Who or what has been the most important influence on your values? Give specific examples and details to support your answer.

_____

_____

_____

_____

_____

_____

_____

_____

_____

_____

_____

_____

_____

_____

_____

_____

_____

_____

_____

_____

_____

LANGUAGE ARTS

110

Practice Test 2: Language
Part 1: Language Mechanics

Directions: Fill in the circle for the punctuation that is needed in the sentence. Choose "None" if no further punctuation is needed.

1. I have lived in Flint Detroit, and Philadelphia.

(A) :

(B) .

(C) ,

(D) None

2. Mia you need to decide if you want to play soccer.

(F) .

(G) ;

(H) ,

(J) None

3. "That was the most fun I've ever had!" exclaimed Antoine.

(A) ,

(B) :

(C) "

(D) None

4. "Let's play computer games, said Sammy.

(F) !

(G) "

(H) ,

(J) None

Directions: Read each answer. Fill in the circle next to the choice that has a punctuation error. If there is no mistake, mark "No mistakes."

5. (A) Read the directions carefully

(B) Then, put the set together

(C) one step at a time.

(D) No mistakes

6. (F) I can hardly wait

(G) to see my friend Fiona.

(H) She lives in Alaska.

(J) No mistakes

7. (A) Peter says he wants to be a pilot,

(B) police officer or park ranger

(C) when he grows up.

(D) No mistakes

8. (F) Mr. Wong went to the museum.

(G) At the museum, he bought

(H) a pair of earring's for his wife.

(J) No mistakes

GO

Practice Test 2: Language
Part 1: Language Mechanics

Directions: Read each sentence. Choose the word or words that best fits in the blank and shows the correct punctuation.

9. _____ my dog's fault that my homework is late.

(A) Its

(B) It's

(C) Its'

(D) Its's

10. "How did you do on your _____ asked Mr. Sanchez.

(F) test?"

(G) test?

(H) test?",

(J) test,"

11. Before Miko heads _____ she always finds her little sister first.

(A) home

(B) home,

(C) home;

(D) home:

12. "I love your _____ Lucy said to her mom.

(F) pancakes,

(G) "pancakes,"

(H) pancakes,"

(J) pancakes"

Directions: Rewrite the following sentences using the correct capitalization.

13. The proclamation of 1763 forbade British subjects to settle beyond the appalachian mountains.

_____

_____

_____

14. During the revolutionary war, fighting occurred from quebec in the north to florida in the south.

_____

_____

_____

15. The Americans were angry about paying the taxes required by the stamp act of 1765.

_____

_____

Practice Test 2: Language
Part 1: Language Mechanics

Directions: Read each group of sentences. Find the one that is written correctly and shows the correct capitalization and punctuation.

16. (F) Shaquila and janelle, love to do challenging word puzzles, together.

    (G) In 1970 my mother was born in Saginaw Michigan.

    (H) Would you like to own a skunk. I would but my mom would not.

    (J) We did experiments in Mr. Neuman's class. Dave, our student aide, assisted.

17. (A) In 1964, dad was born to cora and vern in North Carolina.

    (B) Thats Freds' pet frog. Please leave it there.

    (C) Mom and Dad will take us to see our cousins' new home in Columbus.

    (D) We need to go now? Mrs Fairey is waiting.

18. (F) Did you read *wind in the Willows!* Its my favorite book.

    (G) Allie asked, does anyone know where I left jacks coat?"

    (H) "Which way is ivy street?" the man inquired.

    (J) She wants to bring her dog, Hershey, to Ms. Sweet's class.

19. (A) I love french fries, english muffins and german potato salad.

    (B) No, added Abigail, "I will not ride with you"

    (C) "Yes," said Renee. "It's a beautiful day today."

    (D) My teacher Mr Winters is marrying Ms Summers in june.

Directions: Read each sentence. Fill in the circle for the answer choice that fits best in the blank and has correct capitalization and punctuation.

20. **My aunt lives just a few miles from _____.**

    (F) Lake Superior

    (G) lake Superior

    (H) lake, Superior

    (J) lake superior

21. **The bus is _____ we call your mom?**

    (A) late, should

    (B) late? Should

    (C) late should

    (D) late. Should

22. **Maddie found a _____ under her chair.**

    (F) dime, and two nickels,

    (G) Dime and two Nickels,

    (H) dime and two nicke-ls,

    (J) dime and two nickels

Practice Test 2: Language
Part 1: Language Mechanics

Directions: Read the passage below, and use it to answer the questions that follow. Mark "Correct as it is" if the underlined part is correct.

---

(1) For more than a <u>century americans</u> have sung about the mighty deeds of John Henry. (2) You have probably heard the ballad, or folk song, about this giant among railroad workers. (3) The song tells of a "steel-driving man" who competed in a contest with a steam drill.

(4) There really was a person named John Henry. (5) He was an <u>African-American</u> railroad construction worker. (6) But, according to most accounts, he died from an accident in a railroad tunnel. (7) Writers generally contend that the race against the steam drill is invented folklore.

(8) Lovers of legends and <u>folk tales however</u> think otherwise. (9) They believe that the duel with the steam drill actually occurred. (10) Some say it took place in <u>west Virginia, in</u> 1870. (11) Others maintain that it happened in Alabama about the year 1882.

---

23. In sentence 1, <u>century americans</u> is best written _____.

(A) century Americans

(B) Century, Americans

(C) century, Americans

(D) Correct as it is

24. In sentence 5, <u>African-American</u> is best written _____.

(F) African-american

(G) African-American,

(H) african-american

(J) Correct as it is

25. In sentence 8, <u>folk tales however</u> is best written _____.

(A) folk tales, however,

(B) folk tales however,

(C) folktales, however

(D) Correct as it is

26. In sentence 10, <u>west Virginia, in</u> is best written

(F) West Virginia, in

(G) West Virginia in

(H) west Virginia in

(J) Correct as it is

Name _____ Date _____

Practice Test 2: Language
Part 1: Mechanics

Directions: Find the word that is spelled correctly and fits best in the blank.

27. She was in _____.

- (A) anguish
- (B) angish
- (C) enguish
- (D) anguishe

28. Please take out the _____.

- (F) garbage
- (G) gerbage
- (H) garbagge
- (J) gharbage

29. Stop talking _____!

- (A) nonsence
- (B) nonsense
- (C) nonsince
- (D) noncence

30. Don't _____.

- (F) exagerate
- (G) exaggerate
- (H) ecagerate
- (J) excagerate

31. This is an _____ time.

- (A) enconvenient
- (B) incunvient
- (C) inconvenient
- (D) encunvenient

32. Send a _____ greeting.

- (F) courdial
- (G) corgial
- (H) cordial
- (J) courgial

Directions: Read the phrases. Choose the phrase in which the underlined word is not spelled correctly.

33.
- (A) fluorescent light
- (B) garden hose
- (C) one fortnight
- (D) physical characterestics

34.
- (F) northern hemisphere
- (G) sincere congradulations
- (H) impart wisdom
- (J) 2012 census

35.
- (A) condensed version
- (B) the puppy yelped
- (C) quench your thirst
- (D) midnight rade

36.
- (F) razer blade
- (G) gorgeous dress
- (H) blue lagoon
- (J) swift gazelle

GO

Practice Test 2: Language
Part 1: Mechanics

Directions: Read each answer. Fill in the space for the choice that has a spelling error. If there is no mistake, mark "No mistakes."

37. Ⓐ molecule

Ⓑ pavillion

Ⓒ oath

Ⓓ No mistakes

38. Ⓕ nominate

Ⓖ tournament

Ⓗ tradgedy

Ⓙ No mistakes

39. Ⓐ vigerous

Ⓑ revolution

Ⓒ gourd

Ⓓ No mistakes

Directions: Read each phrase. One of the underlined words is not spelled correctly for the way it is used in the phrase. Fill in the circle for the word that is not spelled correctly.

40. Ⓕ fix the <u>leek</u>

Ⓖ change the <u>topic</u>

Ⓗ pay a <u>toll</u>

Ⓙ <u>scant</u> clothing

41. Ⓐ garbage <u>heap</u>

Ⓑ <u>roe</u> the boat

Ⓒ <u>loaf</u> of bread

Ⓓ tie the <u>knot</u>

42. Ⓕ a <u>holy</u> man

Ⓖ run an <u>errand</u>

Ⓗ weather <u>vein</u>

Ⓙ <u>sole</u> survivor

Directions: Find the underlined part that is misspelled. If all the words are spelled correctly, fill in the circle for "No mistakes."

43. It is <u>awful</u> to <u>experience</u> an <u>earthquake</u>. <u>No mistakes</u>
  　　Ⓐ　　　　Ⓑ　　　　　Ⓒ　　　　　Ⓓ

44. <u>Parakeats</u> can <u>mimic</u> many <u>phrases</u>. <u>No mistakes</u>
  　Ⓕ　　　　Ⓖ　　　　Ⓗ　　　　Ⓙ

45. As a <u>neccessary</u> <u>precaution</u>, we <u>recommend</u> that you stay seated. <u>No mistakes</u>
  　　Ⓐ　　　　Ⓑ　　　　　Ⓒ　　　　　　　　　Ⓓ

Name _____   Date _____

Practice Test 2: Language
Part 2: Usage

Directions: Choose the word or phrase that best completes the sentence.

1. It has been snowing _____ for more than two days.

Ⓐ steady

Ⓑ steadier

Ⓒ steadily

Ⓓ steadiest

Directions: Choose the answer that is a complete and correctly written sentence.

2. Ⓕ Taking a vacation at the Outer Banks during the holiday.

Ⓖ They are writing to their.

Ⓗ Because they like roasting marshmallows over campfires.

Ⓙ Janette's family will be renting a cottage for the entire month of July.

3. Ⓐ My brother delivering papers every morning before school.

Ⓑ Has you seen that new TV show yet?

Ⓒ I think their last album was much more better.

Ⓓ Gabe and Addy were upset with themselves for missing the bus.

4. Ⓕ Jumping up and down with excitement.

Ⓖ The choir singing the best they ever had.

Ⓗ He and me will miss you when you're gone.

Ⓙ Li twisted her ankle on the ice yesterday.

5. Ⓐ The best pet I ever had was a parakeet name Maurice.

Ⓑ Lilies and zinnias growed wild in the field.

Ⓒ Whoever put salt in the sugar bowl had better admit to his or her prank.

Ⓓ Holden won't never try to go skating again.

6. Ⓕ When I had trouble changing the tire on my bike.

Ⓖ Next Saturday, the zoo will be letting in kids under 18 for free.

Ⓗ Rain fell in the gutters and drain out into the yard.

Ⓙ The curtains are dusty and needing to be washed.

7. Ⓐ The chipmunk scampered away.

Ⓑ My sister's friend are coming to visit.

Ⓒ Sewing their jeans.

Ⓓ It is hot yesterday.

Practice Test 2: Language
Part 2: Usage

Directions: Find the underlined word that is the simple predicate of each sentence.

8. The <u>amusement</u> <u>park</u> <u>had</u> more than two million <u>visitors</u> each summer.
  Ⓕ   Ⓖ   Ⓗ   Ⓙ

9. Our <u>local</u> <u>restaurant</u> <u>serves</u> the best <u>spaghetti</u>.
  Ⓐ   Ⓑ   Ⓒ   Ⓓ

Directions: Choose the answer that best combines the underlined sentences.

10. <u>Flora walked to the store.</u>
<u>She wanted to buy new shoes.</u>

Ⓕ Flora walked to the store, and she wanted to buy new shoes.

Ⓖ Wanting to buy new shoes, Flora walked to the store.

Ⓗ Although Flora walked to the store, she wanted to buy new shoes.

Ⓙ Flora walked to the store to buy new shoes.

11. <u>Kyle is in line.</u>
<u>Austin is in line, too.</u>
<u>They are waiting in line to ride the roller coaster.</u>

Ⓐ Waiting in line to ride the roller coaster are Kyle and Austin.

Ⓑ Kyle and Austin are waiting in line to ride the roller coaster.

Ⓒ Kyle is in line and Austin is too to ride the roller coaster.

Ⓓ Kyle is in line to ride the roller coaster and so is Austin.

Directions: Choose the best way of expressing the idea.

12. Ⓕ I walked past a pasture to get to school, and there were cows there.

Ⓖ I walked past a cow pasture to get to school.

Ⓗ Cows were in the pasture I walked past to get to school.

Ⓙ I walked to school and passed a pasture with cows in it.

13. Ⓐ I ran in the race, and I came in second, which made my grandfather proud.

Ⓑ I made my grandfather proud when I ran in the race and when I came in second.

Ⓒ When I came in second in the race I ran, my grandfather was proud.

Ⓓ My grandfather was proud when I came in second in the race.

GO

Practice Test 2: Language
Part 2: Usage

Directions: Choose the best way to write the underlined part of each sentence. If the underlined part is correct, fill in the circle next to "No change."

14. The crowd began <u>erupted</u> with cheers as the DJ played the latest hit.

- (F) eruption
- (G) erupting
- (H) erupt
- (J) No change

16. <u>However</u> the bus was crowded, she was able to find a seat near the back.

- (F) Whether
- (G) Although
- (H) Until
- (J) No change

15. As we read the story, we began to better <u>understanding</u> why the problem was so complex.

- (A) understand
- (B) understood
- (C) understands
- (D) No change

17. There were several other children at the museum that day <u>besides</u> just my brother and me.

- (A) otherwise
- (B) additionally
- (C) because
- (D) No change

Directions: Read each answer choice. Fill in the circle for the choice that has a usage error. If there is no mistake, mark "No mistakes."

18. (F) The boys is writing to
(G) their congresswoman
(H) to express their concern.
(J) No mistakes

19. (A) The monkeys at the zoo
(B) enjoy swinging from the branches
(C) and playing with their keepers.
(D) No mistakes

Directions: Find the answer choice that best develops the topic sentence.

20. Making fudge the old-fashioned way is not easy.

- (F) Most recipes allow you to use a microwave oven.
- (G) Just go to the store and pick up a box mix.
- (H) It requires patience and skill, but it can be worth the effort.
- (J) Add butter and vanilla.

GO

Practice Test 2: Language
Part 2: Usage

Directions: Read the paragraph below. Choose the best topic sentence.

21. _____ **I attached the buttons to a t-shirt and hung it on the wall. When friends and family learned of my collection, everyone started to give me buttons. Now, I have so many buttons that I keep them in a large box under my bed.**

(A) Collecting buttons can be expensive.

(B) My grandma had a button collection when she was small.

(C) In the beginning, my collection was very small.

(D) I don't like collecting buttons.

Directions: Read the paragraph below. Find the sentence that does not belong.

> **(1)** Bones are the super-structure of the human body. **(2)** They support muscles and organs and give the body its size and shape. **(3)** Bones grow as a person's body grows. **(4)** Yellow bone marrow contains fat. **(5)** They become thicker and stronger. **(6)** Like other organs, bones require nourishment to remain strong.

22. (F) sentence 2

(G) sentence 3

(H) sentence 4

(J) sentence 5

Directions: Read the paragraph below. Find the sentence that best fits in the blank.

23. Most pictures of Abraham Lincoln that appear in textbooks show him with a beard. _____ It was not until he ran for the presidency in 1860 that he began to grow a beard.

(A) Lincoln was born in a log cabin.

(B) However, for most of his political life, Lincoln was clean-shaven.

(C) His wife, Mary, liked Lincoln with a beard.

(D) Lincoln was too busy with the war to be concerned with his appearance.

Name _____ Date _____

Practice Test 2: Language
Part 2: Usage

Directions: Study the newspaper below. Use it to the answer the questions that follow.

Monday,
June 3

DAILY SENTINEL

Today's Weather—
Sunny, high 82

INDEX

Firefighter Rescues Boy

This morning at 4:00 A.M., a fire erupted in a private residence located at 3345 Palmer Street. The family dog woke the family from their slumber with its insistent barking. All but the youngest son were able to escape from the home. Firefighters were on the scene within minutes after a neighbor alerted them.

(Photo on page A5)

In a daring move, a firefighter was able to rescue the young boy by
(Continued on page A5)

Local Business Volunteers Aid

After the recent earthquake that left thousands homeless, a local business temporarily shut its doors and bused its employees to the scene of the devastation. The employees set up tents to serve hot meals and dispense food and clothing. Ron Wardie, owner of Supply Co., told reporters, "It was my employees' idea. I was reluctant at first. But they were so willing to donate their time, I couldn't help but say yes."

(Continued on page A6)

---

24. How many sections does this paper have?

(F) 1

(G) 2

(H) 3

(J) 4

25. Which of these appears on A5?

(A) Weather

(B) the continuation of the story about the firefighter

(C) World News

(D) the continuation of the story about the local business

26. What was the weather on the day this newspaper was published?

(F) cloudy with a high of 72

(G) The weather is listed on D1.

(H) sunny with a high of 82

(J) It can't be determined.

27. In which section would you be most likely to find job listings?

(A) A

(B) B

(C) C

(D) D

Name _____ Date _____

Practice Test 2: Language
Part 2: Usage

Directions: Matthew is writing a report about baboons in the wild. Keep this purpose in mind as you answer the following questions.

28. Matthew used the book titled *Baboons and Other Primates.* Where in the book should Matthew look to find the definition of the word *bipedal?*

(F) the index

(G) the glossary

(H) the table of contents

(J) the introduction

29. Which of these should Matthew be sure to include in his report?

(A) the habitat and diet of baboons

(B) the location of zoos that feature baboons

(C) baboon as pets

(D) information on chimpanzees

Directions: Study this dictionary entry, and use it to answer the questions that follow.

---

ex•haust (ĭg-zôst) Verb. -hausted, -hausting. 1. To wear out completely. 2. To drain of resources or properties; deplete. 3. To treat completely; cover thoroughly: *exhaust a topic.* —Noun. 4. The escape or release of vaporous waste material, as from an engine. 5. A duct or pipe through which waste material is emitted.

---

30. Which definition of the word *exhaust* is used in this sentence? The car's exhaust gave Hanna a stomachache.

(F) definition 2

(G) definition 3

(H) definition 4

(J) definition 5

31. Which definition of the word *exhaust* means *to cover entirely?*

(A) definition 1

(B) definition 2

(C) definition 3

(D) definition 4

32. Which of these could be guide words on a dictionary page that includes the word *exhaust?*

(F) exert/exit

(G) exhort/exist

(H) exclude/exercise

(J) exhibit/expect

STOP

Practice Test 2: Language
Part 3: Writing

Directions: What do you think are the effects of showing violence on TV, in the movies, and in video games? What are possible solutions to the problem? Clearly state your purpose for writing and develop your topic with supporting details.

Number Sense

Directions: Read and work each problem. Find the answer, and mark your choice.

Example

Which group of numbers is ordered from greatest to least?

Ⓐ 7,834 1,979 7,878 3,876

Ⓑ 1,234 3,456 5,689 7,893

Ⓒ 3,456 4,576 4,579 5,423

Ⓓ 8,778 6,545 2,324 1,645

Answer: Ⓓ

---

1. **Which numeral comes right after XII?**

   Ⓐ XIII

   Ⓑ XIV

   Ⓒ XV

   Ⓓ XX

2. **An employee in a warehouse has 84 games to pack into boxes. Each box can hold 18 games. How many boxes will the employee need for all the games?**

   Ⓕ 6

   Ⓖ 4

   Ⓗ 5

   Ⓙ 8

3. **At her party, Emily wants to serve each of her friends a turkey hot dog and bun. There are 8 hot dogs in a package but only 6 buns in a bag. What is the least amount of hot dogs Emily must buy so that she has an equal number of hot dogs and buns?**

   Ⓐ 48

   Ⓑ 16

   Ⓒ 8

   Ⓓ 24

4. **196 =**

   Ⓕ 14^2

   Ⓖ 8^3

   Ⓗ 16^2

   Ⓙ 63

5. **Which of these numbers is between 5,945,089 and 5,956,108?**

   Ⓐ 5,995,098

   Ⓑ 5,943,787

   Ⓒ 5,947,109

   Ⓓ 5,549,090

Read the problem carefully. Look at all answer choices before you choose one.

Name _____   Date _____

Number Sense

Directions: Read and work each problem. Find the answer, and mark your choice.

1. Which number is 2,000 less than 765,422?

- (A) 565,422
- (B) 763,422
- (C) 745,422
- (D) 765,222

2. The 7 in 68,743 means _____.

- (F) 7,000
- (G) 700
- (H) 70
- (J) 7

3. 7 millions, 8 thousands, 3 tens, and 7 ones =

- (A) 780,037
- (B) 7,080,037
- (C) 7,008,037
- (D) 708,307

4. A number is less than 443 and greater than 397. The sums of the ones digit and the tens digit in the number is 5. The ones digit is 3. What is the number?

- (F) 423
- (G) 432
- (H) 323
- (J) 322

5. Which of these numbers has a 5 in the tens place?

- (A) 4.568
- (B) 5,395
- (C) 8,456
- (D) 7,675

6. thirty thousand, six =

- (F) 36,000
- (G) 30,600
- (H) 306,000
- (J) 30,006

7. 5,078,093 is read

- (A) five hundred seven million, eight thousand, ninety-three
- (B) five million, seventy-eight thousand, ninety-three
- (C) five million seventy-eight, ninety-three
- (D) five hundred seventy-eight million, ninety-three

8. How much would the value of 456,881 be decreased by replacing the 6 with a 5?

- (F) 10,000
- (G) 1,000
- (H) 1
- (J) 100

Number Sense

Directions: Read and work each problem. Find the answer, and mark your choice.

1. Which numeral has a 6 in both the ten thousands and ones places?

   (A) 609,546

   (B) 65,767

   (C) 59,676

   (D) 60,386

2. What is the value of 3 in 9.231?

   (F) 3 tenths

   (G) 3 tens

   (H) 3 hundredths

   (J) 3 thousandths

3. A number has a 7 in the tens place, a 5 in the ones place, and a 3 in the thousands place. Which number is it?

   (A) 753

   (B) 375

   (C) 7,385

   (D) 3,175

Use the number line to answer the following questions.

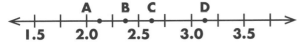

4. What is the range between the first mark and the final mark of this number line?

   (F) 2

   (G) 2.25

   (H) 3.5

   (J) 3.75

5. What is the range between each mark of the number line?

   (A) 0.125

   (B) 0.25

   (C) 0.5

   (D) 0.75

6. What is the value of point B?

   (F) 2.125

   (G) 2.25

   (H) 2.375

   (J) 2.75

7. What is the value of point D?

   (A) 3.0

   (B) 3.5

   (C) 3.625

   (D) 3.125

Name _____ Date _____

Number Sense

Directions: Read and work each problem. Find the answer, and mark your choice.

1. Which of these will have a remainder when it is divided by 12?

(A) 72

(B) 86

(C) 108

(D) 132

2. Which of these numbers cannot be evenly divided into 51?

(F) 1

(G) 3

(H) 9

(J) 17

3. An employee at a pet store had to place 80 fish into 7 aquariums. If the same number of fish were placed into each of the first 6 aquariums, what is the fewest number of fish that would be left over and placed in the seventh aquarium?

(A) 2

(B) 4

(C) 6

(D) 8

Directions: Use the number grid to answer questions 4-5.

1	2	3	4	5	6	7	8	9	10
11	12	13	14	15	16	17	18	19	20
21	22	23	24	25	26	27	28	29	30
31	32	33	34	35	36	37	38	39	40
41	42	43	44	45	46	47	48	49	50
51	52	53	54	55	56	57	58	59	60
61	62	63	64	65	66	67	68	69	70
71	72	73	74	75	76	77	78	79	80
81	82	83	84	85	86	87	88	89	90
91	92	93	94	95	96	97	98	99	100

4. Read the description of each number below. Then, circle the number in the grid above.

- the smallest prime number between 20 and 30
- a multiple of 7 with two digits that, when added together, equal 10
- the greatest prime number between 75 and 85
- a two-digit number whose two digits added together equal 42 and multiplied together equal 82

5. Beginning with the smallest number and working to the greatest number, connect the four circled numbers in the grid above. Which letter have you drawn?

_____

Name _____   Date _____

Number Concepts

Directions: Read each problem. Find the answer, and mark your choice.

Example

How many even numbers are there between 4 and 24?

Ⓐ 6

Ⓑ 8

Ⓒ 12

Ⓓ 9

Answer: D

---

1. $\sqrt{25}$

Ⓐ 7

Ⓑ 5

Ⓒ 4

Ⓓ 6

2. What is the greatest common factor of 16 and 64?

Ⓕ 4

Ⓖ 8

Ⓗ 16

Ⓙ 2

3. Which of these is a multiple of 13?

Ⓐ 169

Ⓑ 196

Ⓒ 133

Ⓓ 159

4. What number is expressed by (8 × 10,000) + (5 × 1,000) + (3 × 100) + (8 × 1)?

Ⓕ 805,308

Ⓖ 85,308

Ⓗ 850,308

Ⓙ 805,380

5. What are all the factors of 16?

Ⓐ 2 and 4

Ⓑ 2, 4, and 8

Ⓒ 32, 48, and 64

Ⓓ 1, 2, 4, 8, and 16

Be on the lookout for key words and numbers that will help you find the answers.

Remember, you might not have to compute to find the correct answer to a problem.

Name _____ Date _____

Number Concepts

Directions: Read each problem. Find the answer, and mark your choice.

1. What is the smallest number that can be divided evenly by 5 and 45?

- (A) 135
- (B) 225
- (C) 90
- (D) 125

2. Which expression shows 50 as a multiple of prime numbers?

- (F) 25×2
- (G) $2 \times 5 \times 5$
- (H) 50×1
- (J) 10×5

3. Which of these is a prime number?

- (A) 6
- (B) 47
- (C) 39
- (D) 8

4. The expanded number for 64,090 is _____.

- (F) $6 + 4 + 0 + 9 + 0$
- (G) $(64 \times 10,000) + (4 \times 1,000) + (9 \times 10)$
- (H) $(64 \times 10,000) + 900$
- (J) $(6 \times 10,000) + (4 \times 1,000) + (9 \times 10)$

5. Which group contains both odd and even numbers?

- (A) 76, 94, 54, 32, 22
- (B) 33, 51, 11, 99, 37
- (C) 72, 44, 68, 94, 26
- (D) 55, 38, 21, 88, 33

6. Which of these is another way to write $7 \times 7 \times 7 \times 7 \times 7$?

- (F) 5^7
- (G) 7^5
- (H) 7×5
- (J) $7 + 5$

7. Which of these is a composite number?

- (A) 27
- (B) 11
- (C) 29
- (D) 51

8. What is the greatest common factor of 42 and 54?

- (F) 6
- (G) 7
- (H) 4
- (J) 9

Number Concepts

Directions: Read and work each problem. Find the answer, and mark your choice.

1. Which number completes the number sentence below?
$7 \times (2 + 5) = \square + 23$

   Ⓐ 11

   Ⓑ 24

   Ⓒ 26

   Ⓓ 13

2. There are 52 weeks in a year. Jenna works 46 weeks each year. During each week, she works 32 hours. Which number sentence below shows how many hours Jenna works in a year?

   Ⓕ $52 \times 32 = \square$

   Ⓖ $46 \times 32 = \square$

   Ⓗ $32 \times 52 = \square$

   Ⓙ $(52 - 46) \times 32 = \square$

3. Which is another name for 55?

   Ⓐ $(5 \times 5) + 10$

   Ⓑ $5 + (5 \times 1)$

   Ⓒ $61 - (2 \times 3)$

   Ⓓ $(3 \times 3) \times 6$

4. You helped your mom plant 40 tulip bulbs in the fall. In the spring, 10 of the tulips did not come up at all, and $\frac{1}{3}$ of the rest had yellow flowers. Which of the number sentences below shows how to find the number of tulips that had yellow flowers?

   Ⓕ $40 - 10 = \frac{1}{3} \times \square$

   Ⓖ $\frac{1}{3} \times (40 - 10) = \square$

   Ⓗ $(\frac{1}{3} \times 40) - 10 = \square$

   Ⓙ $(\frac{1}{3} \times 10) = \square$

5. Which of the tables follows the rule shown below?
Rule: Add 3 to the number in column A, and then multiply by 8 to get the number in column B.

   Ⓐ

A	B
3	49
4	55
5	61
6	67

   Ⓑ

A	B
3	14
4	15
5	16
6	17

   Ⓒ

A	B
3	48
4	56
5	64
6	72

   Ⓓ

A	B
3	46
4	54
5	62
6	70

Name _____ Date _____

Number Concepts

Directions: Complete the table for each function rule given below.

Example

Rule: $m = n + 3$

IN (n)	12	14	16	18	20	22
OUT (m)	15	17	19			

Answer: 21 23 25

1. Rule: $m = 3n$

IN (n)	0	1	2	3	4	5
OUT (m)						

2. Rule: $m = 3n - 3$

IN (n)	2	4	6	8	10	12
OUT (m)						

Directions: Find the function rule for each table below.

3.

IN (x)	6	7	9	11	14	16
OUT (y)	10	11	13	15	18	20

Rule: $y =$ _____

5.

IN (x)	5	8	11	14	17	20
OUT (y)	3	6	9	12	15	18

Rule: $y =$ _____

4.

IN (x)	1	3	6	8	10	13
OUT (y)	4	12	24	32	40	52

Rule: $y =$ _____

6. Graph the ordered pairs for numbers 1, 3, and 5. Label each line using the rule.

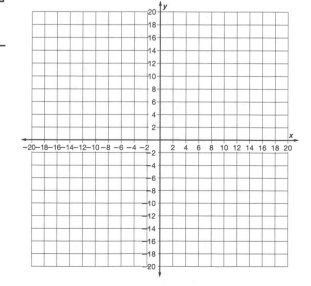

Chapter 6: Concepts

Number Concepts

Directions: Read and work each problem. Find the answer, and mark your choice.

1. **Which number can be expressed as $[(12 \times 6) - (15 \times 2)] \div 7$?**

   (A) 4

   (B) 5

   (C) 6

   (D) 8

2. **Which number can be expressed as $\sqrt{121} \times 3$?**

   (F) 21

   (G) 33

   (H) 36

   (J) 48

3. **Which number can be expressed as $[(5^2 \times 3) \div 15] + 10$?**

   (A) 3

   (B) 11

   (C) 12

   (D) 15

4. **Which number makes this number sentence true?**
   23% of $\Box$ = 126.5

   (F) 5.5

   (G) 550

   (H) 2,909.5

   (J) 5,500

5. **Which number makes this number sentence true?**
   $\frac{3}{5}$ of 900 = $\Box$

   (A) 540

   (B) 1,500

   (C) 3,150

   (D) 5,400

6. **Which number makes this number sentence true?**
   $(3 \times \Box) + 12 = 27$

   (F) 3

   (G) 5

   (H) 7

   (J) 13

7. **Which number makes this number sentence true?**
   $(320 \div 16) - \Box = 13$

   (A) 3

   (B) 5

   (C) 7

   (D) 13

8. **Which number makes this number sentence true?**
   $(\Box^2 \div 2) + 10 = 18$

   (F) 1

   (G) 2

   (H) 3

   (J) 4

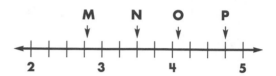

Fractions and Decimals

132

Directions: Read and work each problem. Find the answer, and mark your choice.

Example

How much of the figure below is shaded?

Ⓐ $\frac{1}{3}$

Ⓑ $\frac{1}{8}$

Ⓒ $\frac{1}{2}$

Ⓓ $\frac{1}{4}$

Answer: Ⓓ

---

1. Which of these is six hundredths?

Ⓐ 0.006

Ⓑ 0.060

Ⓒ 0.600

Ⓓ 6.100

2. $\frac{54}{1,000} =$

Ⓕ 5.400

Ⓖ 0.5400

Ⓗ 0.054

Ⓙ 0.54

3. Which of these is greater than $\frac{3}{5}$?

Ⓐ $\frac{1}{4}$

Ⓑ $\frac{1}{2}$

Ⓒ $\frac{7}{8}$

Ⓓ $\frac{1}{3}$

4. On the number line below, which arrow points most closely to 2.8?

M   N   O   P

2   3   4   5

Ⓕ M

Ⓖ N

Ⓗ O

Ⓙ P

5. Which of these is between 0.07 and 0.5 in value?

Ⓐ 0.18

Ⓑ 0.81

Ⓒ 0.007

Ⓓ 0.018

> **Pay close attention to the numbers in the problem and in the answer choices.**
> If you misread even one number, you will probably choose the wrong answer.

Fractions and Decimals

Directions: Read and work each problem. Find the answer, and mark your choice.

1. The length of $\overline{ST}$ is what fraction of $\overline{UV}$?

S | | | | T

U | | | | | | | | | | V

(A) $\frac{1}{6}$

(B) $\frac{1}{3}$

(C) $\frac{2}{3}$

(D) $\frac{1}{5}$

2. What is the least common denominator for $\frac{1}{3}$, $\frac{3}{5}$, and $\frac{1}{2}$?

(F) 15

(G) 30

(H) 45

(J) 60

3. Which decimal is another name for $\frac{5}{1,000}$?

(A) 0.005

(B) 5

(C) 0.050

(D) 0.5000

4. Which group of decimals is ordered from greatest to least?

(F) 3.021, 4.123, 0.788, 1.234

(G) 0.567, 0.870, 0.912, 1.087

(H) 2.067, 1.989, 1.320, 0.879

(J) 0.003, 1.076, 0.873, 0.002

5. Which of these numbers can go in the box to make the number sentence true?

$\frac{1}{\square} > \frac{1}{4}$

(A) 3

(B) 5

(C) 6

(D) 7

6. Which fraction is another name for $3\frac{2}{5}$?

(F) $\frac{6}{5}$

(G) $\frac{11}{5}$

(H) $\frac{37}{5}$

(J) $\frac{17}{5}$

7. Which fraction is in its simplest form?

(A) $\frac{5}{10}$

(B) $\frac{3}{7}$

(C) $\frac{3}{9}$

(D) $\frac{7}{42}$

8. Which of the decimals below is thirty-two and thirteen hundredths?

(F) 3,213

(G) 32.13

(H) 32.013

(J) 3,200.13

Fractions and Decimals

Directions: Write each fraction in decimal form, rounded to the nearest hundredth.

1. $\frac{4}{5}$ _____

2. $\frac{3}{8}$ _____

3. $\frac{5}{3}$ _____

4. $\frac{7}{9}$ _____

5. $\frac{5}{12}$ _____

6. $\frac{14}{5}$ _____

7. $\frac{3}{7}$ _____

Directions: Change each decimal to a fraction.

8. **0.6** _____

9. **0.42** _____

10. **0.025** _____

11. **0.85** _____

12. **1.92** _____

13. **0.56** _____

14. **3.125** _____

> When reducing fractions, be sure to divide the numerator and the denominator by the same number.

Fractions and Decimals

Directions: Read and work each problem. Find the answer, and mark your choice.

1. Which fraction is smallest?

(A) $\frac{1}{4}$

(B) $\frac{1}{5}$

(C) $\frac{3}{8}$

(D) $\frac{3}{16}$

2. Which fraction is greatest?

(F) $\frac{24}{25}$

(G) $\frac{49}{50}$

(H) $\frac{4}{5}$

(J) $\frac{9}{10}$

3. Place these fractions in order from smallest to largest.
$\frac{1}{2}, \frac{3}{16}, \frac{5}{64}, \frac{3}{4}, \frac{5}{8}$

(A) $\frac{1}{2}, \frac{3}{4}, \frac{3}{16}, \frac{5}{8}, \frac{5}{64}$

(B) $\frac{1}{2}, \frac{3}{4}, \frac{5}{8}, \frac{3}{16}, \frac{5}{64}$

(C) $\frac{5}{64}, \frac{3}{16}, \frac{5}{8}, \frac{3}{4}, \frac{1}{2}$

(D) $\frac{5}{64}, \frac{3}{16}, \frac{1}{2}, \frac{5}{8}, \frac{3}{4}$

4. Place these decimals in order from largest to smallest.
0.035, 0.68, 2.056, 1.14, 0.897

(F) 0.897, 0.68, 0.035, 1.14, 2.056

(G) 2.056, 0.897, 0.68, 1.14, 0.035

(H) 2.056, 1.14, 0.897, 0.68, 0.035

(J) 0.035, 0.68, 0.897, 2.056, 1.14

Directions: Look closely at each group of statements. Fill in the circle next to the statement that is not true.

5. (A) $\frac{1}{4} > 0.24$

(B) $\frac{5}{8} < \frac{11}{16}$

(C) $\frac{9}{4} = 2\frac{1}{4}$

(D) $\frac{8}{16} > 0.5$

6. (F) $3.125 = 3\frac{1}{8}$

(G) $\frac{5}{9} < \frac{1}{7}$

(H) $0.06 > \frac{1}{20}$

(J) $\frac{3}{5} < 3.5$

7. (A) $\frac{7}{10} > 0.7$

(B) $\frac{5}{10} = \frac{32}{64}$

(C) $\frac{1}{3} < 0.34$

(D) $2.6 = 2\frac{3}{5}$

8. (F) $0.025 = \frac{25}{1,000}$

(G) $\frac{7}{45} < \frac{2}{15}$

(H) $\frac{16}{17} < \frac{17}{16}$

(J) $\frac{12}{15} = 0.8$

Percentages

Directions: Change each decimal to its percent form.

1. 0.87 _____   3. 0.02 _____

2. 0.45 _____   4. 0.342 _____

Directions: Change each percent to its decimal form.

5. 39% _____   8. 132% _____

6. 7% _____   9. 0.05% _____

7. 1.8% _____

Directions: Find the correct answer to each problem. Mark the space for your choice.

10. **Twenty-five percent of the workers are on third shift. There are 132 workers in all. How many of them are on third shift?**

(A) 25

(B) 12

(C) 33

(D) 3

11. **Forty percent of the class finished their assignment before lunch. There are 25 students in the class. How many students finished before lunch?**

(F) 40

(G) 10

(H) 25

(J) 12

12. **The enrollment at Franklin Middle School has increased 20% from last year. The enrollment last year was 750. By how many students has the enrollment increased?**

(A) 750

(B) 900

(C) 600

(D) 150

Chapter 6: Concepts

Percentages

Directions: Use the pie charts to answer the questions that follow.

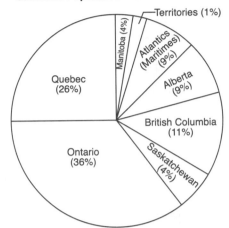

Canadian Population Distribution Chart

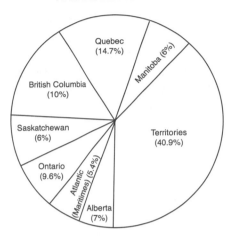

Area Distribution Chart

1. Which province has the greatest population density?

- (A) Quebec
- (B) British Columbia
- (C) Ontario
- (D) Alberta

2. Which province is the largest in area?

- (F) British Columbia
- (G) Manitoba
- (H) Saskatchewan
- (J) Quebec

3. Which two provinces together make up more than 60% of the population?

- (A) Quebec and British Columbia
- (B) Quebec and Ontario
- (C) Ontario and Alberta
- (D) Manitoba and Saskatchewan

4. Quebec is about _____ bigger in area than British Columbia.

- (F) 4%
- (G) 3%
- (H) 5%
- (J) 9%

Directions: Choose the best answer to the question below.

5. Serena had a coupon for 20% off at a local Indian restaurant. Her total before using the coupon was $42.50. How much did she save?

- (A) $8.00
- (B) $8.50
- (C) $6.50
- (D) $7.75

> **Percent** means *per hundred.* It is a ratio that compares a number to 100. It is the number of hundredths.

Name _____ Date _____

Ratios

Directions: Find the correct answer to each problem. Mark the space for your choice.

1. The ratio of the scale drawing of Brittany's bedroom is 1 inch to 5 feet. If the width of Brittany's bedroom is 15 feet, what should be the width of the bedroom on the scale drawing?

   Ⓐ 1 inch

   Ⓑ 3 inches

   Ⓒ 5 inches

   Ⓓ 7 inches

2. The ratio of the scale drawing of Brittany's family room to the actual family room is 1 inch to 5 feet. If the length of Brittany's family room is 20 feet, what should be the length of the family room on the scale drawing?

   Ⓕ 2 inches

   Ⓖ 6 inches

   Ⓗ 4 inches

   Ⓙ 8 inches

3. Fred's Building Company is designing a new volleyball court at Heritage High School. The ratio of the scale drawing to the actual court is 1 inch to 5 feet. If the length of the actual court will be 74 feet, what should be the length of the court on the scale drawing?

   Ⓐ 12.6 inches

   Ⓑ 14.8 inches

   Ⓒ 37.5 inches

   Ⓓ 74 inches

4. The ratio of two days to four weeks is equivalent to _____.

   Ⓕ $\frac{1}{2}$

   Ⓖ $\frac{1}{14}$

   Ⓗ $\frac{1}{7}$

   Ⓙ $\frac{1}{16}$

5. There are 4 apples, 2 bananas, 5 oranges, and 3 pears in a fruit bowl. What is the ratio of apples to oranges?

   Ⓐ 5:4

   Ⓑ $\frac{4}{5}$

   Ⓒ 4 to 14

   Ⓓ $\frac{9}{5}$

6. In the alphabet, the ratio of vowels to consonants is _____.

   Ⓕ $\frac{5}{26}$

   Ⓖ $\frac{1}{5}$

   Ⓗ $\frac{1}{7}$

   Ⓙ $\frac{5}{21}$

If you can't find your answer among the choices, reread the question. You might have misread it the first time.

Name _____   Date _____

Ratios

Directions: Find the correct answer to each problem. Mark the space for your choice.

1. **There are 225 books in a classroom. The ratio of fiction books to nonfiction books is 2:3. How many of each kind of book are in the classroom?**

   (A) 135 fiction books and 90 nonfiction books

   (B) 150 fiction books and 75 nonfiction books

   (C) 75 fiction books and 150 nonfiction books

   (D) 90 fiction books and 135 nonfiction books

2. **There are 165 chickens on a farm. The ratio of roosters to hens is 2:9. How many roosters are there in total?**

   (F) 2

   (G) 9

   (H) 30

   (J) 135

3. **A chess club meets every Tuesday after school. There are 14 students in the club. The ratio of girls to boys in the club is 3:4. If two more girls join the club, which shows the new ratio of girls to boys in the club?**

   (A) 1:1

   (B) 1:2

   (C) 1:3

   (D) 2:3

4. **A large canvas bin contains balls from various sports. There are 12 volleyballs, 15 basketballs, 18 soccer balls, and 6 footballs. The ratio 6:5 expresses**

   (F) the number of volleyballs to soccer balls.

   (G) the number of soccer balls to basketballs.

   (H) the number of footballs to basketballs.

   (J) the number of soccer balls to volleyballs.

5. **There are 56 roses and 96 daffodils growing in a greenhouse. Which of the following is not a proper way to express the ratio of roses to daffodils?**

   (A) 7:12

   (B) $\frac{7}{12}$

   (C) 7 to 12

   (D) 7 out of 12

6. **A group of 19 people are going on a field trip to a museum. The ratio of adults to children is $\frac{3}{16}$. If one more adult joins the group, what is the new ratio of adults to children?**

   (F) $\frac{1}{4}$

   (G) 3 to 17

   (H) 4 to 20

   (J) $\frac{1}{5}$

Properties

MATH
140

Directions: Read and work each problem. Find the answer, and mark your choice.

Example

What is 344 rounded to the nearest hundred?

(A) 350

(B) 340

(C) 300

(D) 400

Answer: C

---

1. The product of 396 × 32.89 is closest to _____.

(A) 900

(B) 9,000

(C) 13,000

(D) 90

2. What number goes in the box to make the number sentence true?
☐ > –7

(F) –15

(G) –1

(H) –8

(J) –9

3. Which of these statements is true?

(A) When a whole number is multiplied by 3, the product will always be an odd number.

(B) When a whole number is multiplied by 4, the product will always be an even number.

(C) All numbers that can be divided by 5 are odd numbers.

(D) The product of an odd and even number is always an odd number.

4. A number rounded to the nearest hundred is 98,400. The same number rounded to the nearest thousand is 98,000. Which of these could be the number?

(F) 98,567

(G) 98,398

(H) 99,123

(J) 98,745

5. In which of the situations below would you probably use an estimate?

(A) You owe your sister some money and need to pay her back.

(B) You are giving a report and want to tell how many ants live in a colony.

(C) You are responsible for counting the votes in a class election.

(D) You are the manager of a baseball team and are calculating the batting averages for the players on your team.

When you use scratch paper, be sure to transfer numbers accurately!

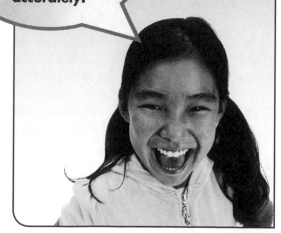

Chapter 6: Concepts

Properties

Directions: Find the number that comes next in the pattern, and mark your choice.

1. 0, 1, 4, 9, 16, 25, _____

- (A) 34
- (B) 36
- (C) 39
- (D) 49

2. 0, 2, 6, 12, 20, 30, _____

- (F) 38
- (G) 40
- (H) 42
- (J) 44

3. 1, 2, 6, 24, 120, _____

- (A) 720
- (B) 216
- (C) 180
- (D) 60

4. 100, 87, 74, 61, 48, _____

- (F) 37
- (G) 39
- (H) 40
- (J) 35

5. 29, 38, 47, 56, 65, _____

- (A) 78
- (B) 76
- (C) 74
- (D) 72

6. 1, 8, 27, 64, 125, 216, _____

- (F) 343
- (G) 307
- (H) 284
- (J) 267

7. Which describes the pattern below?

1, 2, 6, 22, 86, 342, 1,366

- (A) multiply by 4 and subtract 2
- (B) multiply by 3 and add 1
- (C) multiply by 4 and add 2
- (D) multiply by 4 and subtract 4

8. Which describes the pattern below?

0, 6, 18, 42, 90, 186, 378

- (F) multiply by 3
- (G) add 2 times what was added before
- (H) add 6 and multiply by the number of digits
- (J) add 3 and multiply by 2

Algebra

Directions: Read and work each problem. Find the answer, and mark your choice.

Example

What is the value of z in the number sentence $12 \times z = 144$?

(A) 8

(B) 12

(C) 122

(D) 11

Answer: (B)

---

1. Which statement is true if b is a whole number?

(A) If $b - 8 = 16$, then $8 + b = 16$

(B) If $8 \times b = 16$, then $16 \div b = 8$

(C) If $8 \div b = 16$, then $16 \times 8 = b$

(D) If $8 + b = 16$, then $16 + 8 = b$

2. If $y > 98$ and $y < 123$, which of the following is a possible value of y?

(F) 124

(G) 108

(H) 97

(J) 221

3. What is the value of x if $54 \div x = 9$?

(A) 7

(B) 6

(C) 63

(D) 45

4. Evaluate $2a - 3b + 4c$, if $a = 4$, $b = 3$, and $c = 2$.

(F) 25

(G) 38

(H) 7

(J) 12

5. Evaluate $5g + 2h$, if $g = 1$ and $h = 4$.

(A) 13

(B) 28

(C) 22

(D) 7

> Read the question carefully, and think about what you are supposed to do. Then, look for key words, numbers, and figures before you choose an answer.

Algebra

Directions: Read and work each problem. Find the answer, and mark your choice.

1. $a \times (b + c) =$ _____

   Ⓐ $a \times b + a \times c$

   Ⓑ $a \times b + b \times c$

   Ⓒ $a \times b \times c$

   Ⓓ None of the above

2. $a + b =$ _____

   Ⓕ $b + c$

   Ⓖ $c + d$

   Ⓗ $b + a$

   Ⓙ $b - a$

3. $(a + b) + c =$ _____

   Ⓐ $c - (a + b)$

   Ⓑ $a + (b + c)$

   Ⓒ $a \times (b + c)$

   Ⓓ $a + (b \times c)$

4. $(a \times b) \times c =$ _____

   Ⓕ $a \times (b + c)$

   Ⓖ $a + (b \times c)$

   Ⓗ $a \times (b \times c)$

   Ⓙ $(a \times c) - b$

5. If $x > y$ and $y > z$, then _____.

   Ⓐ $x < z$

   Ⓑ $x > z$

   Ⓒ $z > x$

   Ⓓ $x = z$

6. If $z + 8 = 31$, then $z =$

   Ⓕ 39

   Ⓖ 4

   Ⓗ 22

   Ⓙ 23

7. What is the value of a in the equation $a - 9 = 54$?

   Ⓐ 45

   Ⓑ 55

   Ⓒ 63

   Ⓓ 64

8. What is the value of x in the equation $x \div 3 = 16$?

   Ⓕ 84

   Ⓖ 54

   Ⓗ 58

   Ⓙ 48

Algebra

Directions: Read and work each problem. Find the answer, and mark your choice.

1. **A desk normally costs $129. It is on sale for $99. How much would you save if you bought two desks on sale?**

   (A) ($129 + $99) × 2 = s

   (B) ($129 − $99) ÷ 2 = s

   (C) ($129 − $99) × 2 = s

   (D) ($129 + $99) ÷ 2 = s

2. **The highway department uses 6 gallons of paint for every 10 blocks of highway stripe. How many gallons will be needed for 250 blocks of highway stripe?**

   (F) (6 × 10) + 250 = g

   (G) 250 − (10 ÷ 6) = g

   (H) 250 × 10 × 6 = g

   (J) (250 ÷ 10) × 6 = g

3. **A hiker started out with 48 ounces of water. She drank 9 ounces of water after hiking 5 miles and 16 more when she reached mile marker 8. How many ounces of water did she have left?**

   (A) 48 − (9 + 16) = w

   (B) 48 + (9 − 16) = w

   (C) (16 − 9) + 48 = w

   (D) 48 + (9 + 16) = w

4. **A store is open for 12 hours a day. Each hour, an average of 15 customers come into the store. Which equation shows how many customers come into the store in a day?**

   (F) 15 × 24 = c

   (G) 12 + 15 = c

   (H) 12 × 15 = c

   (J) 24 ÷ 12 = c

5. **Matthew spent $\frac{1}{2}$ hour doing his history homework and $\frac{3}{4}$ hour doing his science homework. Which equation shows how much time he spent doing his homework?**

   (A) $\frac{1}{2} \times \frac{3}{4} = t$

   (B) $\frac{3}{4} \div \frac{1}{2} = t$

   (C) $\frac{1}{2} + \frac{3}{4} = t$

   (D) $\frac{1}{2} - \frac{3}{4} = t$

6. **There are 24 people at a meeting. Suppose $\frac{2}{3}$ of the people are women. Which equation shows how many men there are?**

   (F) $6 - (\frac{2}{3} \times 24) = m$

   (G) $24 - (\frac{1}{3} \times 24) = m$

   (H) $24 \times \frac{2}{3} - 4 = m$

   (J) $24 \times \frac{1}{3} = m$

Algebra

Directions: Read and work each problem. Find the answer, and mark your choice.

1. **What is the value of z in the equation 13 × z = 104?**

   (A) 8

   (B) 12

   (C) 122

   (D) 11

2. **What is the value of x if 63 ÷ x = 9?**

   (F) 7

   (G) 6

   (H) 9

   (J) 45

3. **What is the value of r if 17 × r = 68?**

   (A) 51

   (B) 4

   (C) 85

   (D) 6

4. **What is the value of a in the equation a − 22 = 42?**

   (F) 22

   (G) 20

   (H) 63

   (J) 64

5. **If z + 6 = 45, then z =**

   (A) 39

   (B) 4

   (C) 40

   (D) 29

6. **Which expression is equal to 2(3c − 1)?**

   (F) 3c − 2

   (G) 23c − 2

   (H) 6c − 2

   (J) 6c − 1

If two answer choices look a lot alike, one of them is probably correct.

Name _____ Date _____

Sample Test 6: Concepts

Directions: Read each problem. Find the answer, and mark your choice.

Example

What is 7,453 rounded to the nearest hundred?

Ⓐ 7,500
Ⓑ 7,400
Ⓒ 7,000
Ⓓ 7,450

Answer: Ⓐ

1. Which digit means ten thousands in the numeral 5,873,096?

Ⓐ 8
Ⓑ 3
Ⓒ 7
Ⓓ 0

2. Which of these numbers best shows what part of the bar is shaded?

Ⓕ $\frac{1}{4}$
Ⓖ 0.7
Ⓗ $\frac{1}{3}$
Ⓙ 0.5

3. Which letter marks $4\frac{6}{10}$ on this number line?

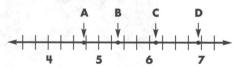

Ⓐ A
Ⓑ B
Ⓒ C
Ⓓ D

4. 7,768 ÷ 17 is between

Ⓕ 300 and 400.
Ⓖ 600 and 700.
Ⓗ 450 and 550.
Ⓙ 250 and 350.

5. Which of these is a composite number?

Ⓐ 13
Ⓑ 31
Ⓒ 57
Ⓓ 14

6. In a book, which chapter comes right after chapter IX?

Ⓕ XI
Ⓖ X
Ⓗ XII
Ⓙ XIV

7. Which of these is another way to write 606,344?

Ⓐ 60 + 63 + 44
Ⓑ 60,000 + 6,000 + 300 + 40 + 4
Ⓒ 600,000 + 6,000 + 300 + 40 + 4
Ⓓ 600,000 + 60,000 + 300 + 40 + 4

Sample Test 6: Concepts

Directions: Read and work each problem. Find the correct answer. Fill in the circle.

8. What number is missing from the pattern below?

$\frac{4}{10}$, 0.5, $\frac{6}{10}$, 0.7, _____, 0.9

(F) $\frac{8}{10}$

(G) $\frac{7}{10}$

(H) 0.8

(J) 0.08

9. Pia had 45 packages of mixed nuts and wanted to put them in bags that could hold 10 packages each. How many bags could she fill completely?

(A) 5

(B) 4

(C) 6

(D) 2

10. Which of these symbols goes in the box to make this number sentence true?

$\frac{8}{10} + \frac{2}{4}$ □ 2

(F) =

(G) >

(H) <

(J) ≥

11. What is 0.465 rounded to the nearest tenth?

(A) 0.5

(B) 0.7

(C) 0.6

(D) 0.05

12. $\sqrt{36}$

(F) 12

(G) 3

(H) 6

(J) 360

13. Which number is three hundred nine thousand, five hundred fifty-eight?

(A) 3,090,558

(B) 309,508

(C) 309,558

(D) 3,009,558

14. What number completes this number sentence?

4 × 35 = 4 × (□ + 5)

(F) 35

(G) 30

(H) 3

(J) 38

15. Using the digits 8, 4, 7, and 6, which of the following are the smallest and the largest decimal numbers you can write?

(A) 0.8476 and 0.6748

(B) 0.8746 and 0.4678

(C) 0.4678 and 0.8764

(D) 0.6748 and 0.8674

Sample Test 6: Concepts

MATH
148

Directions: Read each problem. Find the answer, and mark your choice.

16. What is the value of r if 16 × r = 96?

- (F) 51
- (G) 10
- (H) 70
- (J) 6

17. Sergio spent $3.80 on heavy-duty string for his project. He bought 20 feet of string. Which equation could you use to find out the price per foot of the string?

- (A) $3.80 + 20 = s
- (B) $3.80 − 20 = s
- (C) $3.80 × 20 = s
- (D) $3.80 ÷ 20 = s

18. If z + 20 = 38, then z = ☐

- (F) 18
- (G) 11
- (H) 20
- (J) 4

19. If 27 students each brought in 6 photos, which equation shows how many photos they brought in all?

- (A) 27 + 6 = c
- (B) 27 × 6 = c
- (C) 27 − 6 = c
- (D) 27 ÷ 6 = c

Directions: Use the information below to answer the question that follows.

The base of Sandy Mountain is 5,400 feet above sea level. The top of the mountain is 10,700 feet above sea level. A trail runs from the base of the mountain to the top. The trail is 8 miles long, and it takes about 5 hours to hike from the base of the mountain to the top.

20. Which of the following equations could be used to determine the vertical distance from the base of the mountain to the top?

- (F) t − b = 5,300
- (G) t + b = 16,100
- (H) t × b = 57,780,000
- (J) t ÷ b = 1.98

GO

Sample Test 6: Concepts

Directions: Read each problem. Find the answer, and mark your choice.

21. Daniel is using a scale drawing to design his dream house. The ratio for the scale drawing to the actual house is 1 inch to 3 feet. If the length of the actual living room will be 24 feet, what should the length of the living room be on the scale drawing?

(A) 5 inches

(B) 8 inches

(C) 12 inches

(D) 2.4 inches

22. **Which statement is not true?**

(F) $\frac{5}{25} < \frac{1}{5}$

(G) $12\frac{3}{4} > \frac{48}{4}$

(H) $3\frac{1}{2} = \frac{14}{4}$

(J) $\frac{3}{19} < \frac{19}{38}$

23. $\frac{3}{\square} = \frac{18}{36}$

(A) 5

(B) 8

(C) 6

(D) 4

24. **Which decimal is another name for $\frac{3}{1,000}$?**

(F) 0.003

(G) 3

(H) 0.030

(J) 0.3000

25. **Which is a multiple of 15?**

(A) 55

(B) 45

(C) 70

(D) 5

26. **There are 6 red mittens, 9 navy mittens, 5 green mittens, and 2 purple mittens in the lost-and-found bin. What is the ratio of green mittens to navy mittens?**

(F) 9:5

(G) 5:9

(H) $\frac{9}{5}$

(J) 5 to 14

27. **What number is missing from the pattern shown below?**

2, 6, 14, _____, 62, 126

(A) 18

(B) 22

(C) 30

(D) 28

STOP

Computing Whole Numbers

Directions: Read and work each problem. Be sure you are performing the correct operation. Find the answer, and mark your choice.

Example

4,988
+ 8,765

(A) 12,753

(B) 13,853

(C) 13,753

(D) None of these

Answer: C

1.   678
1,234
+ 679

(A) 2,491

(B) 1,591

(C) 2,591

(D) None of these

2. 6,789 ÷ 13 =

(F) 522 R3

(G) 521 R7

(H) 52 R3

(J) None of these

3. 756 × 432 =

(A) 236,592

(B) 326,592

(C) 336,592

(D) None of these

4.   123,489
– 79,654

(F) 42,835

(G) 93,143

(H) 43,834

(J) None of these

5.   45,676
+ 78,543

(A) 124,219

(B) 115,219

(C) 134,129

(D) None of these

6. 24)6,998

(F) 292 R11

(G) 291 R14

(H) 392 R7

(J) None of these

7. 812 × 789 =

(A) 1,640,668

(B) 560,668

(C) 640,668

(D) None of these

8.   45,678
123,602
+ 345,999

(F) 525,279

(G) 815,279

(H) 515,278

(J) None of these

If the answer you find is not one of the choices given, rework the problem on scratch paper before you mark "None of these."

Computing Whole Numbers

Directions: Read and work each problem. Be sure you are performing the correct operation. Find the answer, and mark your choice.

1. 215 × 328 =

- (A) 70,520
- (B) 69,520
- (C) 68,420
- (D) None of these

2. 34)$\overline{2,658}$

- (F) 78 R1
- (G) 78 R6
- (H) 78
- (J) None of these

3. 25,698 − 4,588 =

- (A) 21,910
- (B) 20,910
- (C) 21,110
- (D) None of these

4. 9,524 + 10,997 =

- (F) 20,511
- (G) 20,421
- (H) 20,521
- (J) None of these

5. 563 ÷ 110 =

- (A) 5 R13
- (B) 5 R3
- (C) 5 R1
- (D) None of these

6.   258,603
         25,544
    + 104,620

- (F) 387,767
- (G) 388,766
- (H) 377,767
- (J) None of these

7.   2,534
    ×   24

- (A) 59,716
- (B) 60,816
- (C) 60,716
- (D) None of these

8. 21)$\overline{25,432}$

- (F) 1,211
- (G) 1,211 R1
- (H) 1,211 R2
- (J) None of these

You can check your answers in a division problem by multiplying your answer by the divisor.

Order of Operations

Directions: Read and work each problem. Be sure you are performing the operations in the correct order. Find the answer, and mark your choice.

1. $\dfrac{56 \div 7) \times (4 \times 3)}{3}$ = _____

   Ⓐ $3\frac{1}{2}$

   Ⓑ 32

   Ⓒ 9.42

   Ⓓ 96

2. $3 + [6 \div (6 \times 3)] \times \frac{1}{2}$ = _____

   Ⓕ $3\frac{1}{6}$

   Ⓖ $3\frac{1}{2}$

   Ⓗ 6

   Ⓙ $\frac{1}{4}$

3. $(5 \times 4 \times 100 - 1{,}000) \div \sqrt{625}$ = _____

   Ⓐ 1.6

   Ⓑ 375

   Ⓒ −720

   Ⓓ 40

4. $3(\sqrt{16} - 4) + (54 \div 12)$ = _____

   Ⓕ 16.5

   Ⓖ 7.5

   Ⓗ 4.5

   Ⓙ 48.5

5. $\dfrac{[830 - (9 \times 35 \times 2)] + 50}{1{,}000 \div 20}$ = _____

   Ⓐ 5

   Ⓑ 0.01

   Ⓒ 2.7

   Ⓓ 1

6. $(4 \times 12 - 99 \div 3) \times (7 \times 2)$ = _____

   Ⓕ 210

   Ⓖ −238

   Ⓗ −414

   Ⓙ −1,176

7. $\sqrt{49} - \sqrt{36} + 20 - (63 \div 9)$ =

   Ⓐ 26

   Ⓑ $-4\frac{2}{3}$

   Ⓒ 14

   Ⓓ −9

8. $\frac{7}{8}(112 \div 2) + [45 \div (36 - (7 \times 3))]$ = _____

   Ⓕ $29\frac{1}{4}$

   Ⓖ 54

   Ⓗ 118

   Ⓙ 59

> **This phrase can help you remember the standard order of operations:**
>
> **P**lease **E**xcuse **M**y **D**ear **A**unt **S**ally
>
> (Parentheses) (Exponents) (Multiplication) (Division) (Addition) (Subtraction)

Order of Operations

Directions: Read and work each problem. Show your work.

1. $35 + 50 + 5 \times 5 - (8 + 11)$

5. $\frac{1}{2} (-16 - 4)$

2. $(-16 + 20) \times 6 \div (6 + 2) + 31$

6. $50 \div (4 \times 5 - 36 \div 2) + -9$

3. $3 + 2(4 + 9 \div 3)$

7. $4 [-4(3 - 12) - 17]$

4. $5 - [48 \div (12 + 4)] - 16$

8. $15 - 8 \times 2 + 11 - 5 \times 2$

Name _____ Date _____

Inverse Relationships

Directions: Find the correct answer to each problem. Mark the space for your choice.

1. If 28,153 − 17,745 = 10,408
   then 10,408 + 17,745 = _____

   Ⓐ 7,337

   Ⓑ 27,153

   Ⓒ 28,153

   Ⓓ 38,561

2. If 872 − 593 = 279
   then 279 + 593 = _____

   Ⓕ 872

   Ⓖ 314

   Ⓗ 593

   Ⓙ 558

3. If x − 356 = y
   then y + 356 = _____

   Ⓐ z

   Ⓑ y

   Ⓒ x

   Ⓓ None of these

4. If 362 × 16 = 5,792
   then 5,792 ÷ 16 = _____

   Ⓕ 462

   Ⓖ 362

   Ⓗ 1,362

   Ⓙ 92,192

5. If a × b = c, then c ÷ b = _____

   Ⓐ a

   Ⓑ b

   Ⓒ c

   Ⓓ x

6. If x ÷ y = z, then z × y = _____

   Ⓕ x^2

   Ⓖ y^2

   Ⓗ z^2

   Ⓙ None of these

No need to solve these problems.
Just use the inverse relationships of addition/ subtraction and multiplication/division to find the answers!

Inverse Relationships

Directions: Find the correct answer to each problem. Mark the space for your choice.

1. If $414 \div 18 = 23$
   then $18 \times 23 =$ _____

   (A) 48

   (B) 18

   (C) 23

   (D) None of these

2. If $r - 2,981 = s$
   then $s + 2,981 =$ _____

   (F) r

   (G) s

   (H) t

   (J) None of these

3. If $42 \times 9 = 378$
   then $378 \div 42 =$ _____

   (A) 378

   (B) 42

   (C) 9

   (D) None of these

4. If $656 - 201 = 455$
   then $455 + 201 =$ _____

   (F) 201

   (G) 601

   (H) 455

   (J) None of these

5. If $m + n = o$, then $o - n =$ _____

   (A) m

   (B) n

   (C) o

   (D) None of these

6. If $14,325 - 762 = 13,563$
   then $13,563 + 762 =$ _____

   (F) 4,325

   (G) 762

   (H) 13,563

   (J) None of these

7. **Write your own pair of inverse relationship equations using addition and subtraction.**

   _____

   _____

8. **Write your own pair of inverse relationship equations using multiplication and division.**

   _____

   _____

MATH
156

Prime Factorization

Directions: Find the factorization of each composite number. Write the prime factors in numerical order on the leaves of the factor tree. Check your answers by completing the factor tree.

1. Prime Factorization = _____ 100

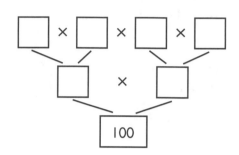

2. Prime Factorization = _____ 210

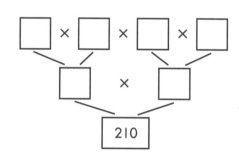

3. Prime Factorization = _____ 44

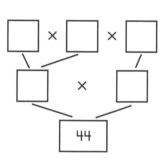

4. Prime Factorization = _____ 1,050

Prime Factorization

Directions: Read and work each problem. Find the answer, and mark your choice.

1. **What are the prime factors of 64?**
   A. 2^6
   B. $2^4 \times 8$
   C. $2^3 \times 16$
   D. $2^4 \times 32$

2. **What are the prime factors of 42?**
   F. $2 \times 3 \times 8$
   G. $1 \times 3 \times 14$
   H. 21×2
   J. $2 \times 3 \times 7$

3. **What are the prime factors of 81?**
   A. $1 \times 3 \times 9$
   B. $2 \times 3^2 \times 9$
   C. 3^4
   D. 3^3

4. **What are the prime factors of 108?**
   F. $2^2 \times 3^3$
   G. 2×27
   H. $2 \times 3 \times 9$
   J. $2^2 \times 9 \times 3$

5. **What are the prime factors of 1,000?**
   A. 10^3
   B. $2^3 \times 5^3$
   C. 100^2
   D. $2^2 \times 25^2$

6. **What are the prime factors of 315?**
   F. $5 \times 7 \times 9$
   G. $5^2 \times 9$
   H. 5×63
   J. $3^2 \times 5 \times 7$

7. **What are the prime factors of 325?**
   A. $5^2 \times 13$
   B. 13×25
   C. 5×13
   D. $2 \times 3 \times 5^3$

8. **What are the prime factors of 625?**
   F. 5×25
   G. 5^4
   H. $5^3 \times 15$
   J. $3 \times 5^2 \times 7$

> When writing out the prime factors for a number, use exponents. For example:
> $24 = 2 \times 2 \times 2 \times 3 = 2^3 \times 3$

MATH
158

Adding and Subtracting Fractions

Directions: Read and work each problem. Find the answer, and mark your choice.

Example

$\frac{7}{10} + \frac{8}{10} =$

- (A) $1\frac{7}{10}$
- (B) $\frac{10}{18}$
- (C) $1\frac{4}{5}$
- (D) None of these

Answer: D

1. $\frac{5}{6} + \frac{1}{12} + \frac{1}{3} =$

- (A) $\frac{7}{3}$
- (B) $1\frac{1}{4}$
- (C) $\frac{11}{12}$
- (D) None of these

2. $20\frac{2}{5} + 5\frac{5}{6} =$

- (F) $26\frac{7}{30}$
- (G) $25\frac{7}{12}$
- (H) $36\frac{3}{10}$
- (J) None of these

3. $4\frac{2}{10}$
$-3\frac{4}{5}$

- (A) $1\frac{4}{10}$
- (B) $\frac{2}{5}$
- (C) $\frac{2}{8}$
- (D) None of these

4. $12\frac{2}{3} - 9\frac{5}{6} =$

- (F) $2\frac{2}{3}$
- (G) $22\frac{1}{2}$
- (H) $2\frac{5}{6}$
- (J) None of these

5. $18\frac{3}{4}$
$+13\frac{5}{8}$

- (A) $33\frac{5}{8}$
- (B) $5\frac{1}{8}$
- (C) $32\frac{3}{8}$
- (D) None of these

6. $8\frac{1}{3} - 6\frac{5}{6} =$

- (F) $1\frac{1}{3}$
- (G) $2\frac{1}{6}$
- (H) $15\frac{1}{6}$
- (J) None of these

7. $1\frac{4}{5} + 6\frac{2}{3} =$

- (A) $7\frac{1}{3}$
- (B) $8\frac{2}{15}$
- (C) $5\frac{7}{15}$
- (D) None of these

After you add the fractions, reduce the answer to its lowest term.

Adding and Subtracting Fractions

Directions: Read and work each problem. Find the answer, and mark your choice.

1. $\frac{3}{5} + 2\frac{3}{4} =$
   - (A) $5\frac{3}{20}$
   - (B) $3\frac{7}{20}$
   - (C) $3\frac{1}{4}$
   - (D) None of these

2. $8\frac{4}{9} - 4\frac{1}{27} =$
   - (F) $4\frac{11}{27}$
   - (G) $4\frac{3}{29}$
   - (H) $4\frac{1}{3}$
   - (J) None of these

3. $22\frac{1}{2} - 22\frac{4}{15} =$
   - (A) $\frac{7}{30}$
   - (B) $\frac{7}{15}$
   - (C) $\frac{11}{30}$
   - (D) None of these

4. $5\frac{3}{8} + 12\frac{5}{6} =$
   - (F) $17\frac{5}{24}$
   - (G) $17\frac{5}{16}$
   - (H) $18\frac{4}{7}$
   - (J) None of these

5. $\frac{23}{24} - \frac{1}{16} =$
   - (A) $1\frac{1}{48}$
   - (B) $\frac{11}{12}$
   - (C) $\frac{43}{48}$
   - (D) None of these

6. $1\frac{1}{3} + 4\frac{12}{21} =$
   - (F) $5\frac{19}{21}$
   - (G) $5\frac{3}{4}$
   - (H) $6\frac{19}{21}$
   - (J) None of these

7. $8\frac{6}{17} - 2\frac{6}{51} =$
   - (A) $6\frac{4}{51}$
   - (B) $6\frac{4}{17}$
   - (C) $7\frac{4}{17}$
   - (D) None of these

8. $2\frac{12}{15} - \frac{4}{9} =$
   - (F) $2\frac{16}{45}$
   - (G) $2\frac{11}{45}$
   - (H) $3\frac{11}{45}$
   - (J) None of these

9. $3\frac{5}{8} + \frac{5}{7} =$
   - (A) $3\frac{19}{56}$
   - (B) $4\frac{19}{56}$
   - (C) $4\frac{3}{7}$
   - (D) None of these

10. $\frac{1}{7} + \frac{1}{2} + \frac{2}{3} =$
   - (F) $5\frac{5}{42}$
   - (G) $1\frac{1}{4}$
   - (H) $1\frac{13}{42}$
   - (J) None of these

MATH
160

Multiplying and Dividing Fractions

Directions: Read and work each problem. Find the answer, and mark your choice.

Example

$7 \times \frac{1}{9} =$

- (A) 63
- (B) $\frac{7}{9}$
- (C) $7\frac{1}{9}$
- (D) None of these

(B)

---

1. $\frac{3}{5} \div \frac{1}{15} =$

- (A) $\frac{1}{5}$
- (B) $\frac{8}{15}$
- (C) 9
- (D) None of these

2. $2\frac{1}{2} \div 5 =$

- (F) 1
- (G) 2
- (H) 5
- (J) None of these

3. $\frac{7}{12} \times \frac{3}{12} =$

- (A) $\frac{3}{24}$
- (B) $\frac{3}{48}$
- (C) $\frac{21}{44}$
- (D) None of these

4. $12 \times \frac{4}{5} =$

- (F) $9\frac{2}{8}$
- (G) $8\frac{2}{5}$
- (H) $9\frac{4}{5}$
- (J) None of these

5. $\frac{2}{3} \div \frac{7}{8} =$

- (A) $\frac{7}{12}$
- (B) $\frac{16}{21}$
- (C) $\frac{1}{3}$
- (D) None of these

6. $\frac{4}{5} \times 11 =$

- (F) $7\frac{3}{5}$
- (G) $8\frac{4}{5}$
- (H) $12\frac{3}{8}$
- (J) None of these

7. $\frac{7}{3} \times \frac{6}{9} =$

- (A) $\frac{2}{27}$
- (B) $\frac{1}{9}$
- (C) $1\frac{5}{9}$
- (D) None of these

8. $\frac{3}{10} \div \frac{9}{20} =$

- (F) $\frac{9}{10}$
- (G) $\frac{2}{3}$
- (H) $\frac{4}{10}$
- (J) None of these

Multiplying and Dividing Fractions

Directions: Read and work each problem. Find the answer, and mark your choice.

1. $\frac{3}{15} \times \frac{7}{8} =$

   (A) $\frac{7}{40}$

   (B) $\frac{21}{32}$

   (C) $\frac{10}{23}$

   (D) None of these

2. $2\frac{5}{9} \times 2\frac{1}{3} =$

   (F) $4\frac{6}{27}$

   (G) $5\frac{26}{27}$

   (H) $5\frac{1}{27}$

   (J) None of these

3. $5 \div \frac{7}{9} =$

   (A) $7\frac{3}{7}$

   (B) $3\frac{6}{7}$

   (C) 8

   (D) None of these

4. $\frac{3}{20} \div \frac{9}{10} =$

   (F) $\frac{1}{6}$

   (G) $\frac{2}{9}$

   (H) $1\frac{2}{7}$

   (J) None of these

5. $\frac{1}{6} \times 36 =$

   (A) $\frac{1}{12}$

   (B) 1

   (C) 6

   (D) None of these

6. $7\frac{1}{2} \div 5\frac{5}{8} =$

   (F) $1\frac{1}{3}$

   (G) $2\frac{2}{5}$

   (H) $1\frac{3}{8}$

   (J) None of these

7. $\frac{5}{12} \times 2\frac{1}{6} =$

   (A) $\frac{11}{72}$

   (B) $\frac{65}{72}$

   (C) $2\frac{5}{72}$

   (D) None of these

8. $9 \times \frac{1}{81} =$

   (F) $\frac{1}{9}$

   (G) 1

   (H) 9

   (J) None of these

9. $\frac{4}{7} \div \frac{12}{13} =$

   (A) $\frac{13}{21}$

   (B) $\frac{48}{91}$

   (C) $\frac{4}{5}$

   (D) None of these

10. $\frac{7}{15} \times \frac{2}{3} =$

   (F) $\frac{1}{2}$

   (G) $\frac{14}{45}$

   (H) $1\frac{2}{15}$

   (J) None of these

Multiplying and Dividing Fractions

Directions: Read and work each problem. Find the answer, and mark your choice.

Example

$\frac{1}{7} \div 6 =$

(A) 42

(B) $\frac{1}{42}$

(C) $\frac{1}{23}$

(D) None of these

Answer: (B)

1. $\frac{7}{12} \div \frac{3}{4} =$

(A) $\frac{21}{48}$

(B) $\frac{1}{3}$

(C) $\frac{7}{9}$

(D) None of these

2. $\frac{5}{6} \div \frac{5}{18} =$

(F) 3

(G) $\frac{1}{3}$

(H) $\frac{5}{9}$

(J) None of these

3. $1\frac{1}{4} \times 3 =$

(A) $3\frac{3}{4}$

(B) $3\frac{1}{4}$

(C) $4\frac{1}{4}$

(D) None of these

4. $\frac{5}{7} \times \frac{2}{3} =$

(F) $\frac{7}{10}$

(G) $\frac{1}{3}$

(H) 1

(J) None of these

5. $2\frac{1}{10} \div 8\frac{2}{5} =$

(A) $\frac{1}{10}$

(B) $\frac{1}{4}$

(C) $\frac{1}{9}$

(D) None of these

6. $\frac{12}{13} \times \frac{13}{12} =$

(F) 1

(G) 12

(H) 156

(J) None of these

7. $\frac{8}{9} \div \frac{1}{4} =$

(A) $5\frac{1}{3}$

(B) $\frac{1}{36}$

(C) $3\frac{5}{9}$

(D) None of these

Pay close attention when dividing fractions. It's easy to make a mistake by forgetting to invert fractions!

Multiplying and Dividing Fractions

Directions: Read and work each problem. Find the answer, and mark your choice.

1. $\frac{5}{8} \times \frac{4}{15} =$

   Ⓐ $\frac{2}{15}$

   Ⓑ $\frac{1}{6}$

   Ⓒ $\frac{1}{3}$

   Ⓓ None of these

2. $1\frac{2}{3}$
   $\times\ 5$

   Ⓕ $2\frac{3}{5}$

   Ⓖ $8\frac{1}{3}$

   Ⓗ $5\frac{2}{3}$

   Ⓙ None of these

3. $\frac{7}{9} \div \frac{1}{9} =$

   Ⓐ $\frac{6}{9}$

   Ⓑ 1

   Ⓒ 7

   Ⓓ None of these

4. $\frac{5}{12} \div \frac{3}{4}$

   Ⓕ $\frac{15}{48}$

   Ⓖ $\frac{5}{9}$

   Ⓗ $\frac{1}{4}$

   Ⓙ None of these

5. $\frac{2}{9}$
   $\times \frac{7}{8}$

   Ⓐ $\frac{7}{36}$

   Ⓑ $\frac{16}{63}$

   Ⓒ $\frac{7}{9}$

   Ⓓ None of these

6. $6\frac{2}{3} \div 4\frac{1}{4} =$

   Ⓕ 4

   Ⓖ $28\frac{1}{3}$

   Ⓗ $1\frac{29}{51}$

   Ⓙ None of these

7. $\frac{5}{9} \div \frac{5}{8} =$

   Ⓐ $\frac{8}{9}$

   Ⓑ $\frac{10}{17}$

   Ⓒ $\frac{25}{72}$

   Ⓓ None of these

8. $1\frac{1}{12} \times \frac{3}{8} =$

   Ⓕ $\frac{31}{32}$

   Ⓖ $\frac{1}{4}$

   Ⓗ $\frac{3}{32}$

   Ⓙ None of these

9. $\frac{2}{5} \times 4 =$

   Ⓐ $\frac{5}{8}$

   Ⓑ $1\frac{3}{8}$

   Ⓒ $1\frac{3}{5}$

   Ⓓ None of these

10. $1\frac{3}{8} \div \frac{8}{11} =$

   Ⓕ 1

   Ⓖ $1\frac{3}{11}$

   Ⓗ $1\frac{57}{64}$

   Ⓙ None of these

Adding and Subtracting Decimals

Directions: Read and work each problem. Find the answer, and mark your choice.

Example

0.4567 + 0.2369 =

- (A) 0.6723
- (B) 0.8693
- (C) 0.6936
- (D) None of these

Answer: C

1. 0.4509 + 0.768 =

- (A) 1.289
- (B) 2.783
- (C) 0.1289
- (D) None of these

2. 1.871
   +0.554

- (F) 1.995
- (G) 0.347
- (H) 2.425
- (J) None of these

3. 3.945 – 1.774 =

- (A) 0.334
- (B) 2.167
- (C) 2.992
- (D) None of these

4. 0.0456
   +1.847

- (F) 2.964
- (G) 5.935
- (H) 1.8926
- (J) None of these

5. 7.302 + 6.0073 =

- (A) 13.9033
- (B) 14.3093
- (C) 1.3309
- (D) None of these

6. 3.338
   –1.774

- (F) 1.564
- (G) 15.64
- (H) 0.1564
- (J) None of these

7. 0.0887 + 0.5534 =

- (A) 0.0642
- (B) 0.6421
- (C) 1.6421
- (D) None of these

> When adding and subtracting decimals, always make sure that the decimal points are lined up correctly before you begin to solve the problem.

Adding and Subtracting Decimals

Directions: Read and work each problem. Find the answer, and mark your choice.

1. 2.873
      −0.620

   Ⓐ 1.253

   Ⓑ 0.654

   Ⓒ 2.253

   Ⓓ None of these

2. 12.854 + 3.055 =

   Ⓕ 9.799

   Ⓖ 13.1595

   Ⓗ 15.909

   Ⓙ None of these

3. 5.24 − 0.032 =

   Ⓐ 5.208

   Ⓑ 5.272

   Ⓒ 4.92

   Ⓓ None of these

4. 0.8423 − 0.458 =

   Ⓕ 0.7965

   Ⓖ 0.3843

   Ⓗ 1.3003

   Ⓙ None of these

5. 3.211
      +0.475

   Ⓐ 2.846

   Ⓑ 2.736

   Ⓒ 3.868

   Ⓓ None of these

6. 1.2066 − 0.5201 =

   Ⓕ 0.7765

   Ⓖ 0.7865

   Ⓗ 0.6865

   Ⓙ None of these

7. 10.251
      − 9.033

   Ⓐ 1.182

   Ⓑ 1.122

   Ⓒ 1.228

   Ⓓ None of these

8. 0.5897 + 1.2232 =

   Ⓕ 1.8129

   Ⓖ 1.8119

   Ⓗ 0.71202

   Ⓙ None of these

9. 0.6687
      +0.9447

   Ⓐ 1.6134

   Ⓑ 1.6024

   Ⓒ 1.5024

   Ⓓ None of these

10. 0.6235 − 0.0451 =

   Ⓕ 0.1725

   Ⓖ 0.5784

   Ⓗ 0.5884

   Ⓙ None of these

MATH 166

Multiplying and Dividing Decimals

Directions: Read and work each problem. Find the answer, and mark your choice.

Example

0.7 × 12 =

(A) 7.8

(B) 8.4

(C) 4.8

(D) None of these

Answer: (B)

---

1. 2.8 × 0.092 =

(A) 2.576

(B) 0.0257

(C) 0.2576

(D) None of these

2. 52 ÷ 3.07 =

(F) 17.2845

(G) 16.93811

(H) 1.693811

(J) None of these

7.   3.90
   ÷   3

(A) 1.26

(B) 13.1

(C) 1.3

(D) None of these

4. 4.877 × 1.567 =

(F) 76.42259

(G) 4.8765

(H) 5.7647

(J) None of these

---

5. 9)389.25

(A) 4.325

(B) 13.12

(C) 43.25

(D) None of these

6. 12 × 0.43

(F) 0.516

(G) 5.16

(H) 6.15

(J) None of these

7. 78.6 ÷ 0.5 =

(A) 157.2

(B) 15.27

(C) 15.72

(D) None of these

To determine the decimal point in a product, count the number of decimal places in the factors.

Multiplying and Dividing Decimals

Directions: Read and work each problem. Find the answer, and mark your choice.

1. 0.44 ÷ 0.22 =

  (A) 0.2

  (B) 2

  (C) 1.2

  (D) None of these

2. 0.3475 × 6.084 =

  (F) 21.1419

  (G) 0.4799

  (H) 2.11419

  (J) None of these

3.   8
   × 7.082

  (A) 5.6656

  (B) 56.656

  (C) 0.5665

  (D) None of these

4. 5)166.65

  (F) 33.33

  (G) 3.333

  (H) 8.923

  (J) None of these

5. 3.192 ÷ 0.42 =

  (A) 6.7

  (B) 0.76

  (C) 7.6

  (D) None of these

6. 0.5)1.38

  (F) 2.96

  (G) 0.276

  (H) 27.6

  (J) None of these

7.   6.35
   × 0.841

  (A) 5.34035

  (B) 7.8055

  (C) 0.534035

  (D) None of these

8. 174.5 ÷ 3.2 =

  (F) 34.8776

  (G) 54.53125

  (H) 5.45312

  (J) None of these

9.   67.04
   × 0.206

  (A) 13.81024

  (B) 14.665

  (C) 16.9912

  (D) None of these

MATH 168

Sample Test 7: Computation

Directions: Read and work each problem. Find the answer, and mark your choice.

Example

789 × 768 =

(A) 65,952

(B) 705,952

(C) 605,952

(D) None of these

Answer: C

1. 6.44 ÷ 46 =

(A) 40.44

(B) 0.14

(C) 7.14

(D) None of these

2. $540.56 + $467.48 =

(F) $1,008.04

(G) $987.65

(H) $1,109.08

(J) None of these

3. 35)‾4,565

(A) 160 R5

(B) 130 R15

(C) 171

(D) None of these

4. $\frac{4}{9} + \frac{5}{6} =$

(F) $1\frac{1}{3}$

(G) $1\frac{5}{18}$

(H) $1\frac{4}{9}$

(J) None of these

5. 12 ÷ 0.75 =

(A) 15

(B) 12.6

(C) 16

(D) None of these

6. $1\frac{5}{8}$
     $\times\ 2\frac{3}{4}$

(F) $4\frac{15}{32}$

(G) $4\frac{3}{8}$

(H) $5\frac{1}{4}$

(J) None of these

7. 567 × 492 =

(A) 378,964

(B) 216,877

(C) 458,443

(D) None of these

8. 6.54 ÷ 3 =

(F) 1.9

(G) 2.18

(H) 2.9

(J) None of these

GO

Sample Test 7: Computation

Directions: Read and work each problem. Find the answer, and mark your choice.

9. 0.3 × 61.7 =

(A) 1.851

(B) 18.51

(C) 0.1851

(D) None of these

10. 78.45
**   − 0.63**

(F) 77.82

(G) 67.92

(H) 78.26

(J) None of these

11. $9\frac{5}{6} + 4\frac{3}{8}$

(A) $13\frac{7}{8}$

(B) $14\frac{5}{24}$

(C) $11\frac{7}{24}$

(D) None of these

12. 31.65 − 22.32

(F) 7.34

(G) 9.32

(H) 9.33

(J) None of these

13. 34$\overline{)569}$

(A) 14 R21

(B) 16 R25

(C) 17 R3

(D) None of these

14. 56.432 ÷ 32 =

(F) 17.635

(G) 1.7635

(H) 1.543

(J) None of these

15.   1,235
**   × 4,897**

(A) 6,047,795

(B) 604,779

(C) 5,886,554

(D) None of these

16. $5\frac{1}{9} \div 2\frac{3}{4}$

(F) $1\frac{53}{62}$

(G) $1\frac{55}{61}$

(H) $1\frac{85}{99}$

(J) None of these

17. 574.436 + 239.08 =

(A) 8,135.16

(B) 813.516

(C) 814.658

(D) None of these

18. 0.769 × 0.56 =

(F) 0.42065

(G) 4.3064

(H) 0.37587

(J) None of these

Name _____ Date _____

Sample Test 7: Computation

Directions: Read and work each problem. Find the answer, and mark your choice.

19. Which of the following correctly lists the order of mathematical operations?

- (A) parentheses, exponents, division, multiplication, addition, subtraction
- (B) multiplication, division, addition, subtraction, parentheses, exponents
- (C) parentheses, exponents, multiplication, division, addition, subtraction
- (D) exponents, parentheses, multiplication, division, addition, subtraction

20. What are all the prime factors of 12?

- (F) 2, 3, 4
- (G) 24, 36, 4
- (H) 2×6
- (J) 2, 3

21. If $144 \times 25 = 3,600$ then $3,600 \div 144 =$ _____

- (A) 144
- (B) 12
- (C) 25
- (D) 5

22. $2\frac{4}{7} + 2\frac{3}{7} =$

- (F) 6
- (G) $4\frac{6}{7}$
- (H) 5
- (J) None of these

23. What are the prime factors of 76?

- (A) 4×19
- (B) 2×19
- (C) $2^2 \times 19$
- (D) $2^2 \times 52$

24. $818 \div 20 =$

- (F) 40 R18
- (G) 40
- (H) 40 R8
- (J) 36

25. $81 - 6 \times 4 + 12 - 8 \times 2 =$ _____

- (A) 24
- (B) 79
- (C) 85
- (D) 53

26. $9 + 15(6 + 12 \div 2)$

- (F) 189
- (G) 180
- (H) 150
- (J) 156

27. $(27 + 13) \div 4 + (16 \times 2) =$ _____

- (A) 38
- (B) 10
- (C) 42
- (D) 72

GO

Sample Test 7: Computation

Directions: Read and work each problem. Find the answer, and mark your choice.

28. 312 × 49 =

(F) 361

(G) 15,288

(H) 15,268

(J) 263

29. What are the prime factors of 273?

(A) 21 × 13

(B) 3 × 7 × 13

(C) 7 × 39

(D) $7^2 \times 3$

30. (6 × 12 − 18 ÷ 3) × (36 × 2) = _____

(F) 1,296

(G) 4,257

(H) 4,752

(J) None of these

31. If $j \times k = l$**, then** $l \div k =$ _____

(A) j

(B) k

(C) l

(D) None of these

**32. If 1,420 − 816 = 604
then 604 + 816 =** _____

(F) 406

(G) 816

(H) 604

(J) 1,420

**33. If 12,889 − 4,242 = 8,647
then 8,647 + 4,242 =** _____

(A) 12,889

(B) 4,242

(C) 8,647

(D) 6,487

34. $145.67 + $63.25 =

(F) $108.82

(G) $208.92

(H) $298.92

(J) None of these

35. 2.03
     ×0.02
     _____

(A) 0.406

(B) 0.0402

(C) 2.006

(D) None of these

STOP

Lines and Angles

Directions: Read each problem. Find the answer, and mark your choice.

Example

A right angle measures _____.

- (A) 180°
- (B) 90°
- (C) 360°
- (D) 60°

Answer: (B)

1. Which of the following lines are parallel?

- (A)
- (B)
- (C)
- (D)

2. Two lines in the same plane that intersect at a right angle are

- (F) curved.
- (G) perpendicular.
- (H) parallel.
- (J) similar.

3. Which line segment is 12 units long?

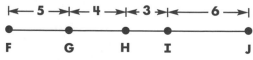

|← 5 →|← 4 →|← 3 →|← 6 →|

F   G   H   I   J

- (A) $\overline{FH}$
- (B) $\overline{GI}$
- (C) $\overline{FJ}$
- (D) $\overline{FI}$

4. The intersection of two sides of an angle is called

- (F) the vertex.
- (G) the circumference.
- (H) an acute angle.
- (J) a ray.

5. Which of the angles below is acute?

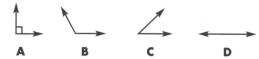

A   B   C   D

- (A)
- (B)
- (C)
- (D)

6. What is not shown in the diagram?

- (F) parallel lines
- (G) intersecting lines
- (H) line segment
- (J) perpendicular lines

Lines and Angles

Directions: Look at each triangle. Write the type of triangle (*right*, *acute*, or *obtuse*) on the line. Then, write the measurement of the missing angle.

1.

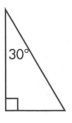

_____

2.

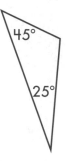

_____

3.

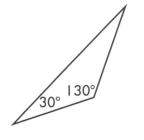

_____

4.

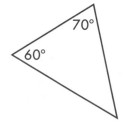

_____

5.

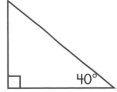

_____

6.

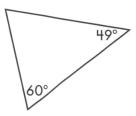

_____

The angle measures in a triangle always add up to 180°.

Lines and Angles

Directions: Look at each quadrilateral. Write the measurement of the missing angle.

1.

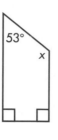

53°
x

_____

The angle measures in any quadrilateral always add up to 360°.

2.

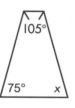

105°
75°   x

_____

3.

x   60°
125°   120°

_____

5.

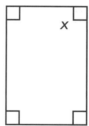

x

_____

4.

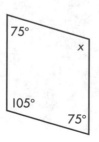

75°
x
105°
75°

_____

6.

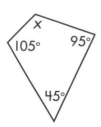

x
105°   95°
45°

_____

Symmetry and Transformations

Directions: Choose the best answer.

1. Parallelogram **QRST** slid to a new position on the grid as shown. Which moves describe the slide?

Ⓐ 1 right, 4 down

Ⓑ 1 right, 5 down

Ⓒ 2 right, 4 down

Ⓓ 1 right, 3 down

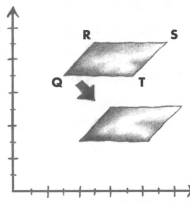

Directions: Compare the following images to their transformed images. Describe each transformation. Be as specific as possible.

2.

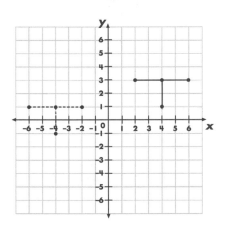

_____

4.

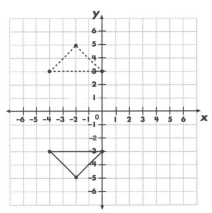

_____

3.

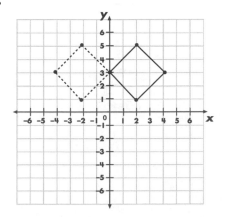

_____

MATH
176

Symmetry and Transformations

Directions: Write *yes* beneath each object that has rotational symmetry and *no* beneath objects that do not have rotational symmetry.

To check if an object has rotational symmetry, follow these steps:
- Trace the object using a small square of tracing paper.
- Place the traced image on top of the original image. Hold the traced image by a pencil-point in the center of the image.
- Rotate your tracing paper around the center point. If the traced image matches exactly with the original image before you have rotated the paper in one full circle, then the shape has rotational symmetry.

1.

_____

4.

_____

2.

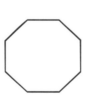

_____

5.

_____

3.

_____

6.

_____

Symmetry and Transformations

Directions: Draw dotted lines to represent the lines of symmetry on polygons that have reflection symmetry. A polygon may have more than one line of symmetry. If there are no lines of symmetry, write *none* below the shape.

1.

4.

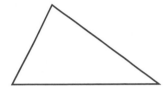

2.

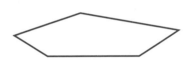

5.

3.

6.

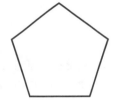

Shapes and Figures

Directions: Read each problem. Find the answer, and mark your choice.

1 Which of the figures below are congruent?

A   **B**   **C**   **D**

(A) B and C

(B) A and C

(C) B and D

(D) A and D

2. Which of these would you use to draw a circle?

(F) compass

(G) protractor

(H) ruler

(J) graph

3. A plane figure with 6 sides is called

(A) an apex.

(B) an octagon.

(C) a hexagon.

(D) a pentagon.

4. Which pair of shapes is congruent?

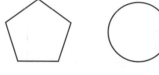

(F)

(G)

(H)

(J)

Directions: Name and draw the described polygon.

5. polygon with opposite sides equal and four right angles

shape: _____

6. polygon with three sides of different lengths

shape: _____

Shapes and Figures

Directions: Give the name for each quadrilateral. Then, find each missing angle measurement.

Name	Description	Example
trapezoid	one pair of opposite sides is parallel	
parallelogram	opposite sides are parallel opposite sides and opposite angles are congruent	
rhombus	parallelogram with all sides congruent	
rectangle	parallelogram with four right angles	
square	rectangle with four congruent sides	

1.

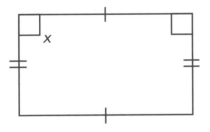

_____

2.

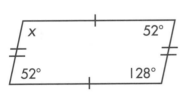

_____

3.

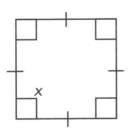

_____

4.

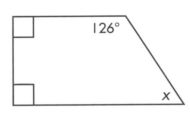

_____

5.

_____

6.

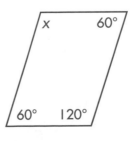

_____

MATH
180

3-D Shapes

Directions: Under each shape below, write *prism*, *pyramid*, or *neither* to show which type of 3-dimensional object it is.

Prisms are 3-dimensional shapes with the following characteristics:
- two opposite, identical bases shaped like polygons
- rectangular faces

Pyramids are 3-dimensional shapes with the following characteristics:
- one base shaped like a polygon
- triangular faces
- a point on one end

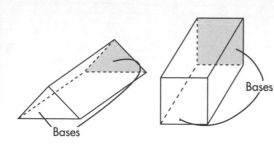
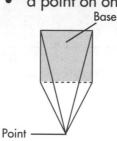

1.

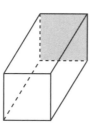

_____

2.

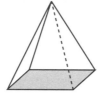

_____

3.

_____

4.

_____

5.

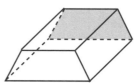

_____

6.

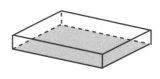

_____

Name _____ Date _____

3-D Shapes

Directions: This chart lists the number of faces, edges, and vertices each shape has. Fill in the missing information.

	cone	cube	rectangular prism	pyramid	sphere	cylinder
Faces	_____	_____	_____	5	_____	2
Edges	_____	_____	12	_____	0	_____
Vertices	0	8	_____	_____	_____	_____

Directions: For each 2-D shape listed below, write the 3-D shape(s) that has at least one face with that shape.

1. triangle _____

2. circle _____

3. square _____

4. rectangle _____

Drawing pictures can help you find the answers to many problems.

Circumference and Area of Circles

MATH
182

Directions: Find the circumference and area of each circle below. Include the appropriate units in your answer.

The **circumference** of a circle is the distance around the outside of the circle.
$C = \pi d$, where d = diameter

The **area** of a circle is the space inside the circle.
$A = \pi r^2$, where r = radius

$\pi = 3.14$

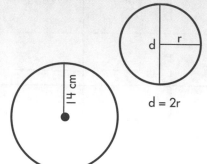

$d = 2r = 2 \times 14 = 28$ cm
$C = \pi d = 3.14 \times 28 = 87.92$ cm
$A = \pi r^2 = 3.14 \times 14^2 = 3.14 \times 196 = 615.44$ cm²

1.

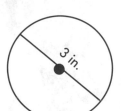

8 in.

C = _____

A = _____

2.

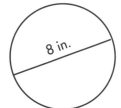

100 mm

C = _____

A = _____

3.

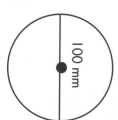

3 in.

C = _____

A = _____

4.

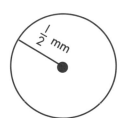

20 ft.

C = _____

A = _____

5.

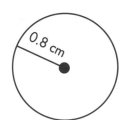

0.8 cm

C = _____

A = _____

6.

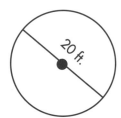

$\frac{1}{2}$ mm

C = _____

A = _____

Circumference and Area of Circles

Directions: Read and work each problem. Find the answer, and mark your choice.

1. Sienna just got a new circular rug for her bedroom. The radius of the rug is 1.5 feet. What is its circumference?

(A) 6 feet

(B) 3 feet

(C) 4.71 feet

(D) 9.42 feet

2. The circumference of a CD is 28.26 centimeters. How would you find the diameter?

(F) $28.26 \times 3.14 = d$

(G) $28.26 \div 3.14 = d$

(H) $28.26 + 3.14 = d$

(J) $(28.26 \div 2)3.14 = d$

3. What is the radius of the CD in question 2?

(A) 9 cm

(B) 4.5 cm

(C) 6 cm

(D) 7.5 cm

4. What is the circumference of a nickel if its diameter is 2 centimeters?

(F) 6.28 cm

(G) 3.14 cm

(H) 0.637 cm

(J) 6.32 cm

5. What is the area of the nickel in question 4?

(A) 12.56 cm²

(B) 3.14 cm²

(C) 6.28 cm²

(D) 4 cm²

6. The circumference of a bicycle wheel is 47.1 inches. What is the diameter?

(F) 13

(G) 15

(H) 17

(J) 14

7. How would you find the area of the bicycle wheel in question 6?

(A) $A = \pi \times \frac{17^2}{2}$

(B) $A = \pi \times 15^2$

(C) $A = \pi \times \frac{15}{2}$

(D) $A = \pi \times \frac{15^2}{2}$

Use hints from questions you know how to answer to help you with problems you are having trouble with.

Chapter 8: Geometry

Name_____   Date_____

Perimeter, Area, and Volume

Directions: Read and work each problem. Find the answer, and mark your choice.

1. The plans for a park call for a rectangular pond measuring 300 feet wide by 100 feet long, with an area of 30,000 square feet. What would the area of the pond be if the length were increased to 300 feet?

   Ⓐ 40,000 ft.^{2}

   Ⓑ 60,000 ft.^{2}

   Ⓒ 90,000 ft.^{2}

   Ⓓ 24,000 ft.^{2}

2. For the pond described in question 1, what are the perimeters for both of the possible sizes?

   Ⓕ 100 ft.; 300 ft.

   Ⓖ 200 ft.; 600 ft.

   Ⓗ 800 ft.; 1,200 ft.

   Ⓙ 2,000 ft.; 2,400 ft.

3. If the circumference of a plate with a diameter of 8 inches is 25.1 inches, what is the circumference of a plate that is 2 inches larger in diameter?

   Ⓐ 23.4 in.

   Ⓑ 35.1 in.

   Ⓒ 27.1 in.

   Ⓓ 31.4 in.

4. A box of laundry detergent measures 12 inches high by 10 inches wide and 2 inches deep, and has a volume of 240 inches cubed. If the manufacturer wants to make a smaller box by decreasing each dimension by 1 inch, what would be the volume of the new box?

   Ⓕ 99 in.^{3}

   Ⓖ 120 in.^{3}

   Ⓗ 21 in.^{3}

   Ⓙ 84 in.^{3}

5. Look at the nested rectangles below. Use a table to determine the dimensions of the next larger rectangle.

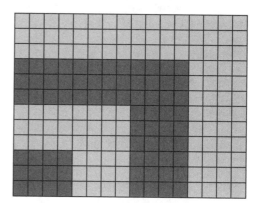

   Ⓐ 20 × 15

   Ⓑ 4 × 3

   Ⓒ 16 × 12

   Ⓓ 8 × 6

Perimeter, Area, and Volume

Directions: Read and work each problem. Find the answer, and mark your choice.

1. What is the perimeter of the figure on the right?

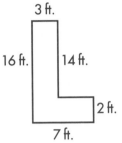

3 ft.

16 ft.   14 ft.

2 ft.

7 ft.

Ⓐ 34 ft.

Ⓑ 42 ft.

Ⓒ 224 ft.

Ⓓ 37 ft.

2. What is the area of the shaded shape?

 = 1 square unit

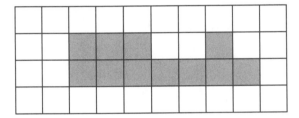

Ⓕ 9 square units

Ⓖ 8 square units

Ⓗ 11 square units

Ⓙ 22 square units

3. What is the area of a classroom that is 17 meters long and 8 meters wide?

Ⓐ 50 square meters

Ⓑ 136 square meters

Ⓒ 25 square meters

Ⓓ 9 square meters

4. What is the volume of a rectangular prism with a length of 8 feet, a height of 6 feet, and a width of 2 feet?

Ⓕ 16 cubic feet

Ⓖ 18 cubic feet

Ⓗ 96 cubic feet

Ⓙ 32 cubic feet

5. The measure of the amount of liquid a glass can hold is called its

Ⓐ volume.

Ⓑ capacity.

Ⓒ circumference.

Ⓓ inside surface area.

Do you know how much time you have? Knowing how much time you have can help you decide what strategies to use.

Name _____   Date _____

Perimeter, Area, and Volume

Directions: Choose the best answer. Find the volume of each space figure by counting the cubes.

A

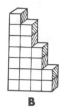
B

C

D

1. What is the volume of shape A?

- (A) 38
- (B) 14
- (C) 42
- (D) 50

2. What is the volume of shape B?

- (F) 38
- (G) 19
- (H) 10
- (J) 26

3. What is the volume of shape C?

- (A) 26
- (B) 16
- (C) 32
- (D) 28

4. What is the volume of shape D?

- (F) 48
- (G) 46
- (H) 40
- (J) 38

Always read the directions carefully!

Perimeter, Area, and Volume

Directions: Find the volume of the following rectangular prisms. Include the appropriate units in your answer.

1.

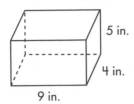

5 in.

4 in.

9 in.

Volume: _____

5.

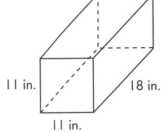

6 cm

11 cm

8 cm

Volume: _____

2.

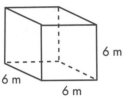

6 m

6 m

6 m

Volume: _____

6.

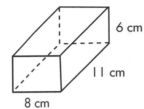

11 in.   18 in.

11 in.

Volume: _____

3.

3 mm   22 mm

3 mm

Volume: _____

7.

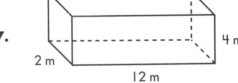

4 m

2 m

12 m

Volume: _____

4.

5 in.

20 in.

0.2 in.

Volume: _____

8.

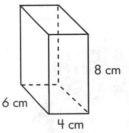

8 cm

6 cm

4 cm

Volume: _____

Using Coordinates

MATH 188

Directions: Write the coordinate pairs for each figure plotted.

> ### Example
>
> Look at the example point graphed on the grid below. This point is 5 units to the left of zero and 4 units above zero. Therefore, it would be labeled (–5, 4). The point (–5, 4) is called a *coordinate pair* or an *ordered pair*.

1. FLAG

F = (,)

L = (,)

A = (,)

G = (,)

2. BOXD

B = (,)

O = (,)

X = (,)

D = (,)

3. SHAPE

S = (,)

H = (,)

A = (,)

P = (,)

E = (,)

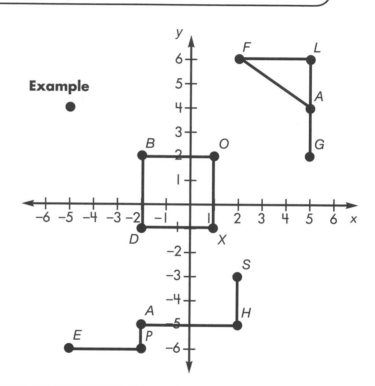

> **The first number in an ordered pair shows the horizontal distance from zero.**
>
> A positive number means to move right. A negative number means to move left. The second number shows the vertical distance from zero. A positive number means to move up. A negative number means to move down.

Using Coordinates

Directions: Use the map to answer the questions below.

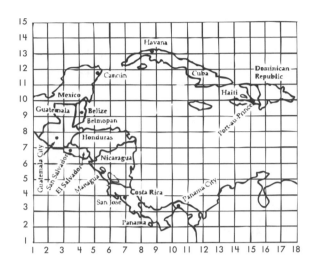

1. What are the coordinates for San Jose, Costa Rica?

- Ⓐ (7, 3)
- Ⓑ (3, 7)
- Ⓒ (7, 4)
- Ⓓ (8, 3)

2. What city is located at (15, 10)?

- Ⓕ Havana, Cuba
- Ⓖ Port-au-Prince, Haiti
- Ⓗ Cancun, Mexico
- Ⓙ Panama City, Panama

3. What are the coordinates for Havana, Cuba?

- Ⓐ (12, 9)
- Ⓑ (12, 8)
- Ⓒ (9, 13)
- Ⓓ (8, 13)

4. What city is located approximately at (5, 12)?

- Ⓕ Havana, Cuba
- Ⓖ Port-au-Prince, Haiti
- Ⓗ Cancun, Mexico
- Ⓙ Panama City, Panama

5. Which set of coordinates is north of (7, 4)?

- Ⓐ (7, 2)
- Ⓑ (9, 4)
- Ⓒ (8, 4)
- Ⓓ (7, 9)

6. Which set of coordinates is east of (4, 9)?

- Ⓕ (6, 9)
- Ⓖ (2, 8)
- Ⓗ (1, 11)
- Ⓙ (4, 6)

Sample Test 8: Geometry

190

Directions: Read each problem. Find the answer, and mark your choice.

1. What is the perimeter of this rectangle?

18 cm ⌐—————————⌐
                    24 cm

(A) 42 cm

(B) 84 cm

(C) 432 cm

(D) 82 cm

2. Which of these shows a radius?

(F)

(G) [parallelogram]

(H) D●————————●E→

(J) [circle with radius]

3. The area of Mr. White's classroom is 981.75 square feet. The gym is 4.50 times as large. What is the area of the gym?

(A) 4,500.12 square feet

(B) 4,417.875 square feet

(C) 986.25 square feet

(D) 4,411.78 square feet

4. A shoe box is 6 inches wide, 11 inches long, and 5 inches high. What is the volume of the box?

(F) 330 cubic inches

(G) 22 cubic inches

(H) 230 cubic inches

(J) Not given

5. Which pair of shapes below forms mirror images?

(A)

(B)

(C)

(D)

6. What is the area of the shape below?

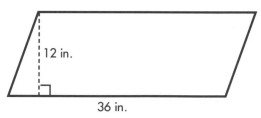

12 in.

36 in.

(F) 532 in.²

(G) 432 in.²

(H) 48 in.²

(J) 96 in.²

GO

Sample Test 8: Geometry

Directions: Read each problem. Find the answer, and mark your choice.

7. Which of these is not a cone?

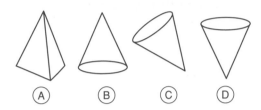

Ⓐ   Ⓑ   Ⓒ   Ⓓ

8. Micah is shipping a gift to his grandpa. The box he needs to ship the gift must have a volume of at least 130 cubic inches but not more than 160 cubic inches. Which of these boxes could he use?

Ⓕ a 5 in. × 3 in. × 5 in. box

Ⓖ a 4 in. × 6 in. × 5 in. box

Ⓗ a 6 in. × 4 in. × 6 in. box

Ⓙ a 5 in. × 5 in. × 5 in. box

9. What is the volume of a rectangular prism with a length of 6 feet, a height of 4 feet, and a width of 3 feet?

Ⓐ 36 cubic feet

Ⓑ 288 cubic feet

Ⓒ 72 cubic feet

Ⓓ 216 cubic feet

10. Which point is at (6, 2)?

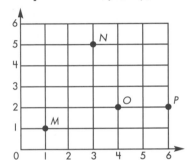

Ⓕ M

Ⓖ N

Ⓗ O

Ⓙ P

Directions: Under each shape below, write *prism*, *pyramid*, or *neither* to show which type of 3-dimensional object it is.

11.

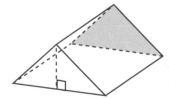

_____

12.

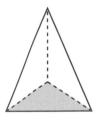

_____

Sample Test 8: Geometry

Directions: Find the circumference and area of each circle below. Include the appropriate units in your answer.

13.

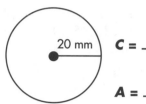

C = _____

A = _____

14.

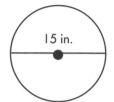

C = _____

A = _____

15.

C = _____

A = _____

16. Compare the following image to its transformation image. What type of transformation was performed? Be as specific as possible.

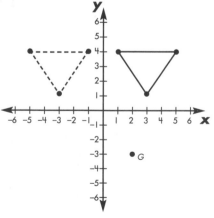

17. In the graph for question 16, what are the coordinates for point G?

Ⓐ (2, 3)

Ⓑ (2, –3)

Ⓒ (3, 2)

Ⓓ (–3, 2)

18. Which figure is a pyramid?

Ⓕ figure 1

Ⓖ figure 2

Ⓗ figure 3

Ⓙ None of these

19. What is the missing measure in this triangle?

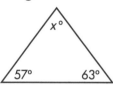

Ⓐ 30°

Ⓑ 50°

Ⓒ 60°

Ⓓ 90°

_____

GO

Sample Test 8: Geometry

Directions: Read each problem. Find the answer, and mark your choice.

20. What is the missing measure in this triangle?

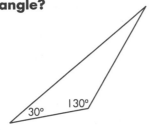

(F) 20°

(G) 100°

(H) 200°

(J) 160°

21. What is the area of a circle with a radius of 2?

(A) 50.24

(B) 6.28

(C) 12.56

(D) 25.12

22. What is the circumference of a circle with a diameter of 4?

(F) 50.24

(G) 6.28

(H) 12.56

(J) 25.12

23. What is the missing measure in this quadrilateral?

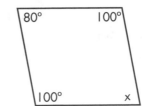

(A) 80°

(B) 120°

(C) 200°

(D) 30°

24. What is the missing measure in this quadrilateral?

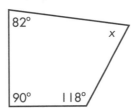

(F) 60°

(G) 70°

(H) 140°

(J) 20°

25. Which of the following statements is not true?

(A) Prisms have two opposite, identical bases shaped like polygons.

(B) A polygon may have more than one line of symmetry.

(C) A figure with 5 sides is a pentagon.

(D) A right angle measures 180°.

STOP

Name _____   Date _____

Measuring

Directions: Find the correct answer to each measurement problem. Fill in the circle for your answer choice.

Example

About how many centimeters long is the pencil pictured to the right?

(A) 5 centimeters

(B) 7 centimeters

(C) 6 centimeters

(D) 4 centimeters

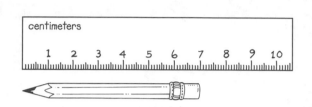

Answer: (B).

---

1. A hot dog weighs

(A) a few pounds.

(B) a few ounces.

(C) a few grams.

(D) a few milligrams.

2. What fraction of a pound is 4 ounces?

(F) $\frac{1}{8}$

(G) $\frac{1}{4}$

(H) $\frac{1}{2}$

(J) $\frac{1}{5}$

3. A map scale shows that 1 inch equals 8 miles. About how long would a section of highway be that is 4.5 inches on the map?

(A) 36 miles

(B) 32.5 miles

(C) 30 miles

(D) 18 miles

4. Which unit of measure would be best to use when weighing a ship?

(F) pounds

(G) grams

(H) kilograms

(J) tons

5. Antonio's trampoline is about 3 yards across. About how many inches across is his trampoline?

(A) 108 inches

(B) 36 inches

(C) 54 inches

(D) 30 inches

Look carefully at where objects begin and end on the rulers.

Measuring

Directions: Find the correct answer to each measurement problem. Fill in the circle for your answer choice.

1. About how many centimeters long is this ticket stub?

 Ⓐ 7 cm

 Ⓑ 5 cm

 Ⓒ 4 cm

 Ⓓ 6 cm

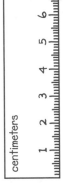 

2. One inch is equal to about 2.5 centimeters. About how many inches long is a meter?

 Ⓕ 250 inches

 Ⓖ 100 inches

 Ⓗ 25 inches

 Ⓙ 40 inches

3. Julio is 54 inches tall. His older brother is one foot taller. How tall is Julio's brother?

 Ⓐ 5 feet 6 inches

 Ⓑ 5 feet 8 inches

 Ⓒ 4 feet 10 inches

 Ⓓ 4 feet 8 inches

4. Randall wants to run a mile. If each city block is 400 feet long, at least how many blocks will he need to run to reach a mile?

 Ⓕ 12

 Ⓖ 13

 Ⓗ 14

 Ⓙ 15

5. A truck needs to cross a bridge with a weight limit of 5 tons. If the truck weighs 3.5 tons when it's empty, what is the maximum load in pounds that it can carry across the bridge?

 Ⓐ 1,500 lb.

 Ⓑ 3,000 lb.

 Ⓒ 3,500 lb.

 Ⓓ 5,000 lb.

6. A CD jewel case is $\frac{3}{8}$ inch thick. How tall is a stack of 32 CD jewel cases?

 Ⓕ 8 inches

 Ⓖ 32 inches

 Ⓗ 1 foot

 Ⓙ 12 feet

7. A field is 60 feet long by 88 feet wide. What is the area of the field?

 Ⓐ 1 square mile

 Ⓑ 1 square kilometer

 Ⓒ 1 acre

 Ⓓ 296 square feet

8. Mr. Washington bought a bag of coffee beans that weighs 18 ounces. The weight of the coffee can also be described as

 Ⓕ a little more than a gram.

 Ⓖ a little more than a pound.

 Ⓗ a little less than a pound.

 Ⓙ about one kilogram.

MATH
196

Measuring

Directions: Find the correct answer to each measurement problem. Fill in the circle for your answer choice.

1. **If you want to measure the amount of water in a fish tank, which unit would you most likely use?**

   Ⓐ kilogram

   Ⓑ milliliter

   Ⓒ decimeter

   Ⓓ liter

2. **What fraction of a pound is 8 ounces?**

   Ⓕ $\frac{1}{8}$

   Ⓖ $\frac{1}{4}$

   Ⓗ $\frac{1}{3}$

   Ⓙ $\frac{1}{2}$

3. **Which of the following shows the correct order from largest to smallest?**

   Ⓐ gram, kilogram, milligram, metric ton

   Ⓑ metric ton, kilogram, milligram, gram

   Ⓒ metric ton, kilogram, gram, milligram

   Ⓓ kilogram, metric ton, gram, milligram

4. **What fraction of a kilometer is one meter?**

   Ⓕ $\frac{1}{10}$

   Ⓖ $\frac{1}{100}$

   Ⓗ $\frac{1}{1,000}$

   Ⓙ $\frac{1}{10,000}$

5. **A map's scale shows that 1 inch equals 250 miles. If it is 3,750 miles between two cities, how many inches would that be on the map?**

   Ⓐ 15 inches

   Ⓑ 14.5 inches

   Ⓒ 13.5 inches

   Ⓓ 12 inches

6. **A paper clip weighs about**

   Ⓕ 15 milligrams

   Ⓖ 1 gram

   Ⓗ 15 grams

   Ⓙ 0.05 kilograms

7. **Which is a realistic measurement for the width of a house?**

   Ⓐ 300 feet

   Ⓑ 10 yards

   Ⓒ 0.1 mile

   Ⓓ None of these

8. **Which is a realistic measurement for the amount of water in a drinking glass?**

   Ⓕ 0.75 pint

   Ⓖ 65 ounces

   Ⓗ $\frac{1}{2}$ gallon

   Ⓙ None of these

Comparing Units of Measurement

Directions: Read each problem. Find the answer, and mark it.

1. A recipe calls for 6 quarts of water. How many gallons is that?

- (A) 1 gallon
- (B) $1\frac{1}{2}$ gallons
- (C) 2 gallons
- (D) $2\frac{1}{2}$ gallons

2. Kenny's book is 30 mm thick. How many centimeters thick is the book?

- (F) 0.3 cm
- (G) 3 cm
- (H) 33 cm
- (J) 300 cm

3. 1 kilogram = _____

- (A) 100 milligrams
- (B) 10 grams
- (C) 100 grams
- (D) 1,000 grams

4. A hair comb weighs about 35 grams. How many milligrams does that equal?

- (F) 3.5 milligrams
- (G) 35,000 milligrams
- (H) 350 milligrams
- (J) 3,500 milligrams

5. 30 ft. = _____

- (A) 5 yd.
- (B) 10 yd.
- (C) 15 yd.
- (D) 20 yd.

6. A football field is 100 yards long. About how many inches is that?

- (F) 800 inches
- (G) 3,600 inches
- (H) 33 inches
- (J) 400 inches

7. 4 gallons = _____

- (A) 40 cups
- (B) 8 quarts
- (C) 16 pints
- (D) 64 cups

8. 16 cups is equivalent to all of the following except _____.

- (F) 8 pints
- (G) 1 gallon
- (H) 4 quarts
- (J) 100 fluid ounces

Comparing Units of Measurement

Metric Units of Length
1 centimeter (cm) = 10 millimeters (mm)
1 meter (m) = 100 centimeters (cm)
1 kilometer (km) = 1,000 meters (m)

Metric Units of Capacity
1 liter (L) = 1,000 milliliters (mL)
1 decaliter (daL) = 10 liters (L)
1 hectoliter (hL) = 100 liters (L)
1 kiloliter (kL) = 1,000 liters (L)

Metric Units of Mass
1 gram (g) = 1,000 milligrams (mg)
1 decagram (dag) = 10 grams (g)
1 hectogram (hg) = 100 grams (g)
1 kilogram (kg) = 1,000 grams (g)
1 metric ton (t) = 1,000 kilograms (kg)

Directions: Read and work each problem. Find the answer, and mark it.

1. 75 mm =
- (A) 75 m
- (B) 0.75 m
- (C) 0.075 m
- (D) 7.5 m

2. 6 km =
- (F) 6,000 m
- (G) 600 m
- (H) 60 m
- (J) 6 m

3. 30 g =
- (A) 3 mg
- (B) 300 mg
- (C) 3,000 mg
- (D) 30,000 mg

4. 22 L =
- (F) 2.2 kL
- (G) 0.22 kL
- (H) 0.022 kL
- (J) 220 kL

5. 11.5 t =
- (A) 1,500 kg
- (B) 11,500 kg
- (C) 1.5 kg
- (D) 115,000 kg

6. 36,000 mL =
- (F) 3.6 L
- (G) 3,600 L
- (H) 360 L
- (J) 36 L

Comparing Units of Measurement

Directions: Read and work each problem. Find the answer, and mark it.

1. **32.75 feet =** _____
   - (A) 3,275 inches
   - (B) 393 inches
   - (C) 384.75 inches
   - (D) None of these

2. **4,578 inches =** _____
   - (F) 1,526 yards
   - (G) 0.75 mile
   - (H) 381.5 feet
   - (J) None of these

3. **456 feet =** _____
   - (A) 152 yards
   - (B) 38 yards
   - (C) 5,472 yards
   - (D) None of these

4. **Estella buys a cantaloupe that weighs 3.25 pounds. How many ounces does it weigh?**
   - (F) 48.5 ounces
   - (G) 52 ounces
   - (H) 15 ounces
   - (J) None of these

5. **Boxes are stacked inside a storage shed. Each box is 20 inches tall, and the storage shed is tall enough for each stack to be 7 boxes high at most. How high is the shed's ceiling?**
   - (A) 10 feet
   - (B) 12 feet
   - (C) 14 feet
   - (D) None of these

6. **An elevator can carry a maximum load of 1.5 tons. At an average weight of 180 pounds per person, how many people at most can ride the elevator at one time?**
   - (F) 14
   - (G) 15
   - (H) 16
   - (J) None of these

7. **Chelsea travels 2.5 feet with each step she takes. How many steps would she take if she walked a mile?**
   - (A) 2,112 steps
   - (B) 5,280 steps
   - (C) 13,200 steps
   - (D) None of these

8. **348 ounces =** _____
   - (F) 34.8 pounds
   - (G) 29 pounds
   - (H) 21.75 pounds
   - (J) None of these

9. **624 inches =** _____
   - (A) 52 feet
   - (B) 18 meters
   - (C) 15 yards
   - (D) None of these

Time and Temperature

Directions: Read and work each problem. Find the answer, and mark it.

1. You go to bed at 10 P.M. You are excited because in 11 hours you are leaving for a vacation. Which clock shows what time you will be leaving for your vacation?

(A)

(B)

(C)

(D)

2. What is the ratio of four days to four weeks?

(F) $\frac{1}{14}$

(G) $\frac{1}{7}$

(H) $\frac{1}{2}$

(J) $\frac{1}{15}$

3. A soccer game started at 11:15 A.M. and lasted 2 hours and 10 minutes. What time did the game end?

(A) 1:25 A.M.

(B) 2:25 P.M.

(C) 1:25 P.M.

(D) 1:35 P.M.

Directions: Use the information below to answer the questions that follow.

7:00 A.M. was –7°C. By noon, the temperature increased to 13°C, but it fell 3° by 6:00 P.M.

4. How much did the temperature increase between 7:00 A.M. and noon?

(F) 6°C

(G) 20°C

(H) –6°C

(J) –20°C

5. What is the average hourly temperature gain between 7:00 A.M. and noon?

(A) –4°C

(B) 20°C

(C) 4°C

(D) –20°C

6. Which equation shows the average hourly temperature gain between 7:00 A.M. and 6:00 P.M.?

(F) $(13 - 7) \div 11 = t$

(G) $(7 + 13 - 3) \div (5 + 6) = t$

(H) $(13 - 3 - 7) \times (5 + 6) = t$

(J) $(12 - 7 + 6) \times 11 = t$

Name _____   Date _____

Time and Temperature

Directions: Read and work each problem. Find the answer, and mark it.

1. Venus sometimes rises above the horizon before the sunrise, when it is often the brightest object in the sky. Predict the day that Venus will rise at 6:00 A.M.

Day	Time Venus Rises
Sunday	6:24 A.M.
Monday	6:20 A.M.
Tuesday	6:16 A.M.
Wednesday	6:12 A.M.
Thursday	6:08 A.M.

(A) Thursday

(B) Friday

(C) Saturday

(D) Sunday

2. Venus rose _____ of an hour earlier on Wednesday than on Sunday.

(F) $\frac{1}{5}$

(G) $\frac{1}{4}$

(H) $\frac{1}{3}$

(J) $\frac{1}{2}$

Directions: Use the chart below to answer the questions that follow.

Date	Moon Phase
December 29	Full moon
January 5	Last quarter
January 11	New moon
January 19	First quarter
January 27	Full moon
February 3	Last quarter
February 10	New moon
February 18	First quarter
February 26	Full moon

3. How many days were there between the first and second full moon on the chart?

(A) 29 days

(B) 33 days

(C) 26 days

(D) Not enough information

4. Approximately how long is there in between full moons?

(F) 2 weeks

(G) 3 weeks

(H) 1 month

(J) 2 months

5. What will the moon phase probably be on March 27?

(A) new moon

(B) last quarter

(C) first quarter

(D) full moon

Time and Temperature

Directions: Read and work each problem. Find the answer, and mark it.

1. The temperature is 80°F. What is it in degrees Celsius? Round to the nearest hundredth.

Ⓐ 24.06°C

Ⓑ 27.66°C

Ⓒ 26.67°C

Ⓓ 29.76°C

2. The temperature is 19°C. What is it in degrees Fahrenheit?

Ⓕ 64.1°F

Ⓖ 66.2°F

Ⓗ 62.6°F

Ⓙ 61°F

3. The temperature is 104°F. What is it in degrees Celsius?

Ⓐ 40°C

Ⓑ 42°C

Ⓒ 36°C

Ⓓ 30°C

4. The temperature is 4°C. What is it in degrees Fahrenheit?

Ⓕ 41.4°F

Ⓖ 39°F

Ⓗ 36.2°F

Ⓙ 39.2°F

5. DeShawn and his dad are going to visit his grandma in Wilmington, North Carolina. They told her they would arrive at 4:00. The drive takes 3 hours and 20 minutes. A detour along the way will add another 17 minutes to their trip. What time do they need to leave?

Ⓐ 1:23

Ⓑ 12:11

Ⓒ 12:23

Ⓓ 1:32

6. What time will this clock show in 2 hours and 45 minutes?

Ⓕ 12:55

Ⓖ 11:55

Ⓗ 10:45

Ⓙ 11:50

Convert **Celsius to Fahrenheit** by taking the temperature in Celsius and multiplying it by 1.8. Then, add 32 degrees.

To convert **Fahrenheit to Celsius**, take the temperature in Fahrenheit and subtract 32. Then, divide by 1.8.

Money

Directions: Read and work each problem. Find the answer, and mark it.

1. Keiko has been hired by the supermarket as a part-time worker. She will earn $7.50 an hour, and she will work 12 hours each week. How much will she earn in a week?

(A) $90.00

(B) $96.50

(C) $29.50

(D) $72.00

2. Bess has 7 quarters, 8 nickels, 9 dimes, 67 pennies, and 3 half-dollars. How much money does she have altogether?

(F) $8.43

(G) $5.22

(H) $7.32

(J) $6.22

3. Last summer, Aaron earned $378 doing odd jobs for his neighbors. This year, he had a regular job baby-sitting his cousin. He earned 2.5 times as much. How much did Aaron earn this summer?

(A) $756

(B) $945

(C) $940

(D) $685

4. Foster ordered some school supplies online. His total at checkout was $68.50. He entered a code to receive 15% off. Shipping and handling cost an additional $6.95. What was Foster's final total?

(F) $58.22

(G) $60.08

(H) $65.17

(J) $67.17

5. How much did Foster save by using the coupon code in question 4?

(A) $10.28

(B) $8.28

(C) $6.18

(D) $11.75

6. Amelia is saving for a trip to Washington, D.C. Her parents have offered to pay for half the trip, but Amelia needs to earn the other $250 herself. If she saves $18 a week, how many weeks will it take her to save enough?

(F) 13 weeks

(G) 14 weeks

(H) 11 weeks

(J) 19 weeks

If you are confused by a problem, read it again. If you are still confused, skip the problem and come back to it later.

Money

Directions: Read and work each problem. Find the answer, and mark your choice.

Example

Simple interest is calculated using the following formula:

$I = P \times r \times t$

I = interest owed P = principal, or the amount invested or borrowed
r = interest rate t = the amount of time that has passed

Anna borrowed $400. The interest rate is 1% each month. How much will Anna owe after 6 months?

$P = \$400$ $r = 0.01$ $t = 6$ months
$I = 400 \times 0.01 \times 6 = \$24$

Anna will owe $24 in interest. If she makes no payments during the six months, then she will owe the principal plus interest, or $424.

---

1. **Tomas borrowed $1,500 at an interest rate of 13% per year. How much interest will he owe after 3 years?**

   (A) $58,500

   (B) $5,850

   (C) $585

   (D) $58.50

2. **The Daffodil Dreams Flower Shop took out a loan for $12,000 to replace old coolers. The owners borrowed the amount at an annual rate of 9.5%. If they make no payments for 2 years, how much will they owe in total? Round your answer to the nearest whole dollar.**

   (F) $14,280

   (G) $13,140

   (H) $22,800

   (J) $228,000

3. **Mr. Wingston invested $6,500 into a savings account. He earns 1.5% interest each month. How much will his investment be worth in 9 months?**

   (A) $8,775

   (B) $87,750

   (C) $6,597.50

   (D) $7,377.50

4. **If $2,000 is put into a savings account that earns 4% interest every six months, how much interest will be earned in 3 years?**

   (F) $240

   (G) $480

   (H) $2,880

   (J) $2,400

Money

Directions: Read and work each problem. Find the answer, and mark your choice.

Example

Compound interest is different than simple interest. When interest is calculated for a certain period of time, any previously accumulated interest is first added to the principle. Use the following formula to calculate compound interest:

$M = P(1 + r)^t$

M = the total amount owed P = principal, or the amount invested or borrowed
r = interest rate t = the amount of time that has passed

William borrowed $1,000 at an annual interest rate of 12%, compounded once each year. How much will he owe total after 6 years, rounded to the nearest whole dollar?

$P = \$1,000$ $r = 0.12$ $t = 6$ months
$M = 1,000(1 + 0.12)^6 = 1,000 \times 1.12 \times 1.12 \times 1.12 \times 1.12 \times 1.12 \times 1.12 = \$1,974$

---

1. A family borrowed $80,000 to buy a house. The annual interest rate is 3%. How much will they owe total after 2 years?

- (A) $83,200
- (B) $84,800
- (C) $84,872
- (D) $82,400

2. Celia invested $4,500. She earns a monthly interest rate of 2.5%, compounded each month. How much will she have total after 4 months, rounded to the nearest whole dollar?

- (F) $4,967
- (G) $10,986
- (H) $9,467
- (J) $45,000

3. If you invested $500 at a monthly interest rate of 1.25%, compounded each month, how much would you have after 6 months?

- (A) $539
- (B) $1,907
- (C) $3,750
- (D) $901

4. If you took out a loan for $1,200 at an annual interest rate of 11.5%, compounded annually, how much would you owe after 3 years?

- (F) $4,140
- (G) $1,338
- (H) $1,825
- (J) $1,663

MATH
206

Estimating Measurement

Directions: Draw a line from the description on the left to the unit of measurement you would most likely use to measure it on the right.

1. weight of a catalog	feet
2. amount of liquid in an eyedropper	meters
3. height of a wall	milliliters
4. length of a bus	millimeters
5. weight of a sack of potatoes	grams
6. amount of water in a pool	tons
7. weight of a train engine	miles
8. amount of water in a fish tank	gallons
9. width of an electrical cord	pounds
10. distance to the bottom of the ocean	liters

Estimating Measurement

Directions: Find the answer for each question, and mark your choice.

1. **The height of a door is about**

    (A) 2 yards.

    (B) 84 inches.

    (C) 3 meters.

    (D) 100 centimeters.

2. **Lincoln wants to race his friends around the outside of his house. About how far will they run?**

    (F) $\frac{1}{2}$ a mile

    (G) 400 yards

    (H) 75 meters

    (J) 120 feet

3. **A large watermelon weighs about**

    (A) 15 pounds.

    (B) 15 ounces.

    (C) 15 grams.

    (D) 15 milligrams.

4. **A truck weighs 3 metric tons. This amount is about the same as**

    (F) 30,000 kilograms.

    (G) 3,000 pounds.

    (H) 30 standard tons.

    (J) 3,000,000 grams.

5. **2 liters is about the same as**

    (A) 2 quarts.

    (B) 2 gallons.

    (C) 2 pints.

    (D) 2 cups.

6. **A yard stick is about how many centimeters long?**

    (F) 36

    (G) 90

    (H) 360

    (J) 1,000

7. **A mile is about how many kilometers long?**

    (A) 0.5

    (B) 1

    (C) 1.5

    (D) 2

8. **Which is a realistic measurement for the height of a skyscraper?**

    (F) 2 miles

    (G) 2,500 feet

    (H) 2 kilometers

    (J) 300 meters

Name _____   Date _____

Sample Test 9: Measurement

Directions: Read and work each problem. Find the answer, and mark it.

1. **Phil's van is 1.7 meters tall. About how many millimeters tall is it?**

   (A) 170

   (B) 1,700

   (C) 17,000

   (D) None of these

2. **A DVD player normally costs $119. It is on sale for $99. Which equation shows how much you would save if you bought 2 DVD players on sale?**

   (F) ($119 + $99) × 2 = ☐

   (G) ($119 − $99) ÷ 2 = ☐

   (H) ($119 − $99) × 2 = ☐

   (J) ($119 + $99) ÷ 2 = ☐

3. **Sven went to the grocery store with his mother. The groceries totaled $36.37. Sven's mom paid for the food with two $20 bills. Which of these is the correct amount of change she should receive?**

   (A) 2 one-dollar bills, two quarters, two dimes, and three pennies

   (B) 3 one-dollar bills, two quarters, one dime, and three pennies

   (C) 3 one-dollar bills, three quarters, one nickel, and three pennies

   (D) None of these

4. **One box of nails weighs 3.6 pounds, and another box weighs 5.4 pounds. How much more does the heavier box weigh?**

   (F) 1.8 pounds

   (G) 1.6 pounds

   (H) 18 pounds

   (J) 1.2 pounds

5. **Chris put 72 kilograms of jam into jars. He put 0.4 kilogram into each jar. How many jars did he use?**

   (A) 90 jars

   (B) 180 jars

   (C) 80 jars

   (D) None of these

6. **Charlotte kept track of the rainfall for one week. She recorded 0.8 inch on Monday, 0.5 inch on Tuesday, and 0.5 inch on Friday. How much rain fell during the week?**

   (F) 1.5 inches

   (G) 2 inches

   (H) 3 inches

   (J) 1.8 inches

GO ▷

Sample Test 9: Measurement

Directions: Read and work each problem. Find the answer, and mark it.

7. About how long is the paper clip below?

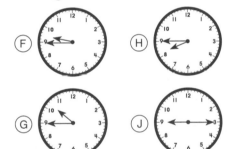

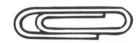

centimeters

1 2 3 4 5 6 7

(A) 3.5 cm

(B) 4 cm

(C) 4.5 cm

(D) None of these

8. Which clock shows the time 3 hours and 15 minutes before midnight?

(F)   (H)

(G)   (J)

9. Jeremy opened a savings account. He deposited $23.45 into his account. The monthly rate of interest on his account is 5%. How much interest would Jeremy receive on that amount at the end of the month?

(A) $1.17

(B) $117.25

(C) $17.25

(D) $0.17

10. What temperature will the thermometer show if the temperature rises 12°?

10°
9°
8°
7°
6°
5°
4°
3°
2°
1°
0°
-1°
-2°
-3°
-4°
-5°
-6°
-7°
-8°
-9°
-10°

(F) −15°

(G) −9°

(H) 9°

(J) 15°

11. 75,000 g = _____

(A) 7.5 kg

(B) 75 kg

(C) 750 kg

(D) 7,500 kg

12. On Tuesday, a truck dropped off 3 metric tons of cans at the recycling center. On Wednesday, it dropped off 2.5 tons, and on Thursday, it dropped off 1 ton. How many kilograms of recycling did the truck drop off at the center?

(F) 6,500 kg

(G) 6.5 kg

(H) 650 kg

(J) 650,000 kg

13. Ms. Ling left her house at 2:35. She arrived at the bank 13 minutes later. It took her 6 minutes to drive to the grocery store, and 28 minutes to do her shopping. Next, she drove to her son's school to pick him up. What time did she pick him up?

(A) 3:22

(B) 2:54

(C) 3:17

(D) Not enough information

GO

Sample Test 9: Measurement

Directions: Read and work each problem. Find the answer, and mark it.

14. The temperature is 22°C. What is it in degrees Fahrenheit?

(F) 66.7°F

(G) 72°F

(H) 71.6°F

(J) 54°F

15. The temperature is 32°F. What is it in degrees Celsius?

(A) 0°C

(B) 32°C

(C) 30°C

(D) 16°C

16. Emma has 7 quarters, 3 dimes, and 16 nickels. Carlos has 2 quarters, 12 dimes, 10 nickels, and 9 pennies. Kris has 1 half dollar and 6 quarters. Which of the following statements is not true?

(F) Emma has $2.85.

(G) Carlos has the least money.

(H) Kris has less money than Emma.

(J) If Carlos had 3 more quarters, he'd have the most money.

17. 42 feet =

(A) 21 yards

(B) 16 yards

(C) 504 yards

(D) 14 yards

18. About how much water does it take to fill a bathtub?

(F) 25 gallons

(G) 100 gallons

(H) 25 ounces

(J) 10 liters

19. At her check-up, Meena's baby sister weighed 16 pounds. How many ounces is this?

(A) 192 ounces

(B) 164 ounces

(C) 256 ounces

(D) 128 ounces

20. About how much does it cost to buy a box of cereal, a gallon of milk, and a bunch of bananas?

(F) $2.50

(G) $8.00

(H) $22.00

(J) $27.00

Probability

Directions: Draw a tree diagram or make a list to show all possible outcomes.

Example

A **tree diagram** shows all possible outcomes. For example, if a car can be ordered in black, red, or tan, and the seats can be leather or fabric, the possible outcomes can be shown as follows:

black < leather
        fabric

red < leather
      fabric

tan < leather
      fabric

1. Phones come in two styles: wall and desk. They come in four colors: red, white, black, and beige. Show the outcomes.

2. The lunch room serves 3 types of fruit, 4 types of vegetables, and 2 types of meat. How many different combinations can be made from these choices? Draw the tree diagram to show all the outcomes.

3. Gabrielle sees an ad in the newspaper for a sale at a local clothing store. Sundresses are selling for $35.88 each. Earrings have dropped to the price of 2 pairs for $5.99, and sandals have slipped to $23.48 a pair. If Gabrielle buys 2 sundresses, 6 pairs of earrings, and 3 pairs of sandals, draw a tree diagram that shows how many outfits she can make with her purchases.

Probability

Directions: Read and work each problem. Find the answer, and mark it.

1. **What is the theoretical probability of randomly picking a face card from a standard 52-card deck? (Hint: There are four suits in standard deck, and each suit has three face cards.)**

   Ⓐ $\frac{1}{52}$

   Ⓑ $\frac{12}{52}$

   Ⓒ $\frac{2}{5}$

   Ⓓ $\frac{1}{2}$

2. **Jose randomly picks a card from a standard 52-card deck and selects the 9 of hearts. He puts the card back into the deck and picks again. This time, he selects the queen of clubs. From this experiment, he can predict that the empirical probability of randomly picking a face card from a standard 52-card deck is _____.**

   Ⓕ $\frac{1}{52}$

   Ⓖ $\frac{12}{52}$

   Ⓗ $\frac{2}{5}$

   Ⓙ $\frac{1}{2}$

3. **Suppose instead of picking cards from the deck just twice, as described in question 2, Jose picks cards 100 times. What do you think the effect will be on his prediction of the empirical probability of randomly picking a face card from the deck?**

   _____

   _____

   _____

   _____

   _____

   _____

   _____

   _____

   _____

   _____

   _____

   _____

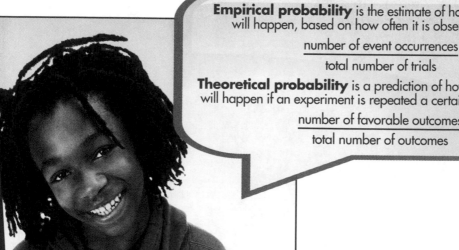

Empirical probability is the estimate of how often an event will happen, based on how often it is observed to occur.

$$\frac{\text{number of event occurrences}}{\text{total number of trials}}$$

Theoretical probability is a prediction of how often an outcome will happen if an experiment is repeated a certain number of times.

$$\frac{\text{number of favorable outcomes}}{\text{total number of outcomes}}$$

Probability

Directions: Read each problem. Find the answer, and mark your choice.

1. **One letter is randomly chosen from the word *correction*. Which statement is true?**

   (A) The letter *c* is most likely to be chosen.

   (B) The letter *c* and the letter *t* are equally likely to be chosen.

   (C) The letter *c* and the letter *r* are equally likely to be chosen.

   (D) The letter *r* is more likely to be chosen than the letter *o*.

2. **A bag contains 12 red marbles, 8 blue marbles, and 5 green marbles. Pilar reaches into the bag without looking and draws out a green marble. She does not put the green marble back into the bag. If she reaches into the bag a second time, what is the probability that she will draw another green marble?**

   (F) $\frac{1}{6}$

   (G) $\frac{1}{4}$

   (H) $\frac{1}{5}$

   (J) $\frac{1}{3}$

3. **A fish tank holds 35 fish of several different types. If you use a net to randomly scoop out one fish, the chance of catching a goldfish is 1 in 7. How many goldfish are in the tank?**

   (A) 5

   (B) 7

   (C) 17

   (D) Not enough information

A bookshelf contains 5 science fiction books, 3 nonfiction books, 4 adventures, 2 fairy tale collections, and 7 mysteries.

4. **You pull a book randomly from the shelf. What is the probability that it will be a mystery?**

   (F) $\frac{1}{21}$

   (G) $\frac{7}{14}$

   (H) $\frac{1}{2}$

   (J) $\frac{1}{3}$

5. **You pull a mystery book from the shelf and set it on a table. Now, you pull a second book from the shelf randomly. What is the chance that it will be an adventure story?**

   (A) $\frac{1}{5}$

   (B) $\frac{1}{7}$

   (C) $\frac{4}{21}$

   (D) $\frac{2}{21}$

6. **You pull an adventure book from the shelf, and then set it on the table with the mystery book. You randomly pull a third book from the shelf. What is the chance it will be another adventure story?**

   (F) $\frac{1}{3}$

   (G) $\frac{1}{7}$

   (H) $\frac{4}{20}$

   (J) $\frac{3}{19}$

Solving Word Problems

Directions: Read and work each problem. Find the answer, and mark it.

Example

Sabrina and Sophie together have more money in their piggy banks than Toby has in his. If Toby has $45 and Sabrina has $23, then Sophie must have

(A) less than $23.

(B) more than $22.

(C) exactly $22.

(D) between $21 and $23.

Answer: (B)

---

1. Computer headphones cost $13.95 a pair. Ms. Jackson wants to buy 24 pairs of headphones for the school computer lab. How much will it cost altogether to buy the headphones?

(A) $335.90

(B) $334.80

(C) $324.80

(D) None of these

2. A train has 160 seats. Passengers are in 97 of them. Which equation would you use to find out how many seats are empty?

(F) $160 \div 97 = \square$

(G) $160 - 97 = \square$

(H) $160 + 97 = \square$

(J) $160 \times 97 = \square$

3. There are 2,464 monkeys in a nature preserve. They live in groups of 16. How many groups of monkeys are there?

(A) 154 groups

(B) 164 groups

(C) 153 groups

(D) None of these

4. Mason, Clare, and Clark bought fruit at the store so they could make a fruit salad. The three types of fruit they bought weighed $2\frac{3}{4}$ pounds, $4\frac{5}{6}$ pounds, and $3\frac{7}{8}$ pounds. How many pounds of fruit did they buy in all?

(F) $12\frac{11}{2}$

(G) $11\frac{1}{24}$

(H) $10\frac{11}{24}$

(J) None of these

Choose "None of these" only if you are sure the right answer is not one of the choices. If you have time, rework the problem.

Solving Word Problems

Directions: Read and work each problem. Find the answer, and mark your choice.

1. There are 10 white socks and 10 black socks in a drawer. Bruce reaches into his drawer without looking. What is the probability that he will pick a white sock?

   (A) $\frac{1}{2}$

   (B) $\frac{1}{3}$

   (C) $\frac{1}{4}$

   (D) None of these

2. Olivia is helping her dad build a deck. The surface of the deck will be 12 feet wide and 14 feet long. The boards they are using can cover an area of 4 square feet each. Which of these shows how many boards they will need to cover the surface of the deck?

   (F) $(12 \times 14) \div 4 = \square$

   (G) $(12 \times 14) \times 4 = \square$

   (H) $12 + 14 + 4 = \square$

   (J) $(12 \div 14) \times 4 = \square$

3. Darnell's speech took $12\frac{3}{4}$ minutes. Tara's speech lasted $\frac{8}{12}$ as long. How long was Tara's speech?

   (A) 9 minutes

   (B) $8\frac{1}{2}$ minutes

   (C) 11 minutes

   (D) $9\frac{1}{2}$ minutes

4. Aleesha saved $2.45 out of her allowance for several weeks so that she could buy a new poster for her bedroom for $14.00. How many weeks did she need to save?

   (F) 6 weeks

   (G) 4 weeks

   (H) 3 weeks

   (J) 5 weeks

5. Last summer, 6 friends ran their own lawn care business. The friends made a total of $498.54. They agreed to share the profits equally. How much did each friend make?

   (A) $73.09

   (B) $83.09

   (C) $84.09

   (D) $79.09

6. Mike received 65% of the votes cast for class treasurer. What fraction of the votes did Mike receive?

   (F) $\frac{13}{20}$

   (G) $\frac{12}{19}$

   (H) $\frac{11}{20}$

   (J) None of these

7. Cole made a base hit on 25% of his official times at bat. What is his batting average?

   (A) .450

   (B) .250

   (C) .025

   (D) .275

Solving Word Problems

Directions: Read and work each problem. Find the answer, and mark your choice.

1. **Lena wants to frame an 8-inch by 10-inch picture with a 3-inch mat. What size frame does she need?**

   (A) 8″ × 10″

   (B) 9″ × 11″

   (C) 14″ × 16″

   (D) 30″ × 32″

2. **Mrs. Mulligan looked at the chart below to determine how many ounces of strawberry sauce she needs to prepare for the yogurt parfaits she'll serve her guests at brunch.**

Servings	1	2	3	4	5
Ounces of Sauce Needed	2	4	6	8	10

   Mrs. Mulligan has invited 6 guests who will each get one serving of her famous parfaits. She also plans to make 12 extra ounces of strawberry sauce to give to one of the guests to take home. Which expression can be used to determine how many ounces of sauce Mrs. Mulligan needs to make?

   (F) 12 + (2 × 6)

   (G) (12 + 2) × 6

   (H) (2 × 12) + (8 × 6)

   (J) 6 × (2 + 8) + 12

3. **A group of teachers are ordering sandwiches from the deli. They can choose ham, beef, turkey, or bologna on white bread, wheat bread, or rye bread. How many different meat and bread combinations are possible?**

   (A) 12

   (B) 16

   (C) 7

   (D) None of these

4. **It takes 5 workers about 50 hours to build a house. How long would it take if there were 10 workers?**

   (F) 25 hours

   (G) $12\frac{1}{2}$ hours

   (H) 100 hours

   (J) None of these

5. **13 people ride to school in 2 cars. One car holds three more people than the other car. How many people are in each car?**

   (A) 8 in one car and 5 in the other

   (B) 9 in one car and 4 in the other

   (C) 7 in one car and 6 in the other

   (D) 3 in one car and 10 in the other

Name _____   Date _____

Solving Word Problems

Directions: Read and work each problem. Find the answer, and mark your choice.

1. **Four friends started a muffin business. They charge customers $2.75 per muffin. They spend $0.48 per muffin on ingredients. If the friends sold 4 dozen muffins on Saturday and divided the profits evenly, how much money would each person earn?**

    (A) $26.04

    (B) $22.24

    (C) $27.24

    (D) $18.86

2. **Two numbers have a product of 96 and a quotient of 6. What are the two numbers?**

    (F) 36, 6

    (G) 24, 4

    (H) 32, 3

    (J) 28, 5

3. **Nora and Grace share a room that measures 14 feet by 16 feet. They can't agree on what color carpeting to get, so they plan to split the room in half evenly and carpet each side separately. What is the area each girl will need to carpet?**

    (A) 76 square feet

    (B) 224 square feet

    (C) 112 square feet

    (D) 56 square feet

4. **Which number sentence shows how you arrived at the result for question 3?**

    (F) $\frac{14}{2} \times \frac{16}{2}$

    (G) $\frac{(14 \times 16)}{2}$

    (H) 14×16

    (J) $\frac{14}{16} \times 2$

Directions: Use the information in the box to answer the questions that follow.

> Javier is 4 years older than Gina.   Gina is twice as old as Maggie.
> Javier is 4 times Elijah's age.   Elijah is 5 years old.

5. **How much older is Gina than Elijah?**

    (A) 3 years

    (B) 8 years

    (C) 7 years

    (D) 11 years

6. **Which number sentence correctly shows the relationship between Elijah's and Javier's ages?**

    (F) $J = 4E$

    (G) $J = 4/E$

    (H) $E = 4J$

    (J) $J + 4 = E$

Name _____ Date _____

Solving Word Problems

218

Directions: Read and work each problem. Find the answer, and mark your choice.

1. Mr. Burnham is going to build a fence around a square area on his property. The total length of the fence is 128 feet. Which equation shows the total area that will be enclosed by the fence?

   (A) $(128 \div 4) \times 2$

   (B) $(128 \div 4)^2$

   (C) $(128 \times 4) \div 2$

   (D) $128^2 \div 4$

2. Marshall earns $9.50 an hour working part-time at the Greener Gardens Nursery. Each week he works a total of 18 hours, and he is paid by check once every two weeks. If 12% of what he earns is taken out of each check to pay for taxes, how much is Marshall's paycheck?

   (F) $150.48

   (G) $342

   (H) $383.04

   (J) $300.96

3. Kirsten has a piece of cloth that is 4.5 feet long by 6 feet wide. She is going to use it to make napkins. Each napkin requires 324 square inches of fabric. How many napkins can she make with the cloth?

   (A) 8

   (B) 10

   (C) 12

   (D) 14

4. A glass holds 400 mL of water. How many glasses would it take to fill a container that can hold 7 L of liquid?

   (F) 28

   (G) $17\frac{1}{2}$

   (H) 57

   (J) $1\frac{3}{4}$

5. A moving company charges $0.30 per cubic foot to ship items using their trucks. If you need to move 45 boxes, and each box is 24 inches long, 18 inches wide, and 18 inches tall, how much will it cost?

   (A) $60.75

   (B) $67.50

   (C) $87.48

   (D) $8,748

6. A gift shop has received a shipment of 125 glass ornaments. Each ornament weighs 680 grams. The ornaments will be displayed on glass shelves that can each hold at most 38 kg of weight. How many shelves will be needed to display all the ornaments?

   (F) 5

   (G) 4

   (H) 3

   (J) 2

Chapter 10: Applications

Solving Word Problems

Directions: Read and work each problem. Find the answer, and mark your choice.

1. **Olly gave Nakima half of his grapes. Nakima ate half of the grapes and gave the rest to Nick. Nick kept 6 grapes and gave 12 to Ben. How many grapes did Olly have at the beginning?**

   (A) 36

   (B) 18

   (C) 72

   (D) 44

2. **Leo's dad is a dentist. He gave Leo a bag full of toothbrushes to bring in to his health class. There were 32 toothbrushes in the bag. 25% were green, 25% were blue, and 50% were red. Which of the following statements is not true?**

   (F) There were 16 red toothbrushes.

   (G) There were an equal number of green and blue toothbrushes.

   (H) There were more red toothbrushes than green and blue combined.

   (J) There were 8 green toothbrushes.

3. **Find the mystery 3-digit number. The sum of its first two digits is 3. The product of its second and third digits is 10. This number's only prime factor is 5. What is the number?**

   (A) 25

   (B) 125

   (C) 219

   (D) 128

4. **The number of people at the town talent show is 200 when rounded to the nearest hundred and 150 when rounded to the nearest ten. Which of these could be the number of people at the talent show?**

   (F) 199

   (G) 178

   (H) 159

   (J) 154

5. **Joe Peretti runs Joe's Lunch on Wheels. He sells lunches to construction workers, landscapers, and others who work outdoors. On average, he sells 54 turkey sandwiches per day. He sells $\frac{1}{3}$ as many egg salad sandwiches as turkey sandwiches. He sells twice as many meatball subs as egg salad sandwiches. How many meatball subs does Joe sell each day?**

   (A) 36

   (B) 18

   (C) 27

   (D) 32

6. **What is the total number of sandwiches Joe sells per day?**

   (F) 106

   (G) 54

   (H) 108

   (J) 98

Mean, Median, Mode, and Range

Directions: For each store, calculate the mean, median, mode, and range of prices for soccer cleats. All prices have been rounded to the nearest dollar.

1. Store 1 Prices

$45 $32
$45 $70 $45
$20 $48 $55
$50 $32

Mean: _____

Median: _____

Mode: _____

Range: _____

2. Store 2 Prices

$35 $40
$35 $25 $75
$50 $63 $80
$42 $35

Mean: _____

Median: _____

Mode: _____

Range: _____

Just a reminder . . .

Mean: average number

Median: middle number of ordered data

Mode: the value that occurs most often

Range: the difference between the largest and smallest values

3. Store 3 Prices

$85 $50
$45 $60 $45
$80 $85 $20
$85 $50 $100

Mean: _____

Median: _____

Mode: _____

Range: _____

4. Store 4 Prices

$55 $60
$88 $60 $32
$80 $48 $64
$80 $60

Mean: _____

Median: _____

Mode: _____

Range: _____

Mean, Median, Mode, and Range

Directions: Use each set of numbers to answer the questions that follow.

The following list shows the test scores for the students in Mr. Wong's history class:

98, 92, 94, 88, 82, 81, 96, 95, 88, 78, 88, 91, 91, 93, 89

1. What is the median test score?

(A) 88

(B) 91

(C) 93

(D) 92

2. What is the mode?

(F) 91

(G) 98

(H) 78

(J) 88

3. What is the range among the scores?

(A) 18

(B) 20

(C) 19

(D) 15

The following numbers show how many hot dogs each of the contestants ate at Nate's Great Hot Dog Challenge at the Bloom County Fair:

3, 8, 11, 7, 7, 7, 6, 9, 4, 2, 13

4. What is the mean number of hot dogs eaten?

(F) 7

(G) 8

(H) 9

(J) 11

5. 7 is the mode, median, and _____ of hot dogs eaten.

(A) range

(B) maximum

(C) mean

(D) None of the above

6. The judges realized that they had miscounted how many hot dogs one of the contestants ate. Rupert ate 11 hot dogs, not 7. Which statement is not true?

(F) The median has not changed.

(G) The mean is higher.

(H) The range has not changed.

(J) The total number of hot dogs eaten has not changed.

Mean, Median, Mode, and Range

Directions: Read and work each problem. Round your answer to the nearest whole number, and mark your choice.

Sunny Days per Month												
City	**Jan.**	**Feb.**	**Mar.**	**Apr.**	**May**	**Jun.**	**Jul.**	**Aug.**	**Sep.**	**Oct.**	**Nov.**	**Dec.**
Port City	14	12	10	15	21	23	18	17	24	18	16	21
Landsville	22	20	18	14	16	22	19	17	20	23	19	18
Martinton	24	19	23	17	24	23	20	21	26	24	19	22
Brasstown	24	20	17	17	20	19	24	22	23	21	20	26

1. For the year shown, what is the mean number of sunny days in a month for Port City?

(A) 16

(B) 17

(C) 18

(D) 19

2. What is the range of sunny days per month during the year for Martinton?

(F) 7

(G) 8

(H) 9

(J) 10

3. What is the mode of sunny days per month during the year for Brasstown?

(A) 17

(B) 20

(C) 17 and 24

(D) 26

4. Which town had the greatest median number of sunny days per month during the year?

(F) Port City

(G) Landsville

(H) Martinton

(J) Brasstown

5. Which town had the least mean number of sunny days per month?

(A) Port City

(B) Landsville

(C) Martinton

(D) Brasstown

6. Based on the number of sunny days for all four cities, which month was sunniest?

(F) January

(G) June

(H) September

(J) October

7. Which month had the greatest range of sunny days?

_____

8. Which month had the smallest range of sunny days?

_____

Organizing and Displaying Data

Directions: Read and work each problem. Find the answer, and mark your choice.

The soccer team members needed to buy their own shin guards, socks, shoes, and shorts. Two players volunteered to do some comparative shopping to find the store with the best deals. Use their charts to answer the questions that follow.

Sports Corner	
Socks . . . . .3 pairs for $9.30	
Shoes . . . . .2 pairs for $48.24	
Shin Guards . . . . . .4 pairs for $32.48	
Shorts . . . . .5 pairs for $60.30	

Sam's Soccer Supplies	
Socks . . . . .2 pairs for $6.84	
Shoes . . . . .3 pairs for $84.15	
Shin Guards . . . . .5 pairs for $35.70	
Shorts . . . . .4 pairs for $36.36	

1. How much does it cost for one pair of shin guards at the store with the best deal?

(A) $7.14

(B) $8.12

(C) $32.48

(D) $4.76

2. How much would it cost to buy one pair of shoes and socks at Sports Corner?

(F) $27.22

(G) $57.54

(H) $31.47

(J) $28.22

3. How much would it cost to buy one pair of shoes and socks at Sam's Soccer Supplies?

(A) $27.22

(B) $31.47

(C) $29.11

(D) $31.57

Mr. VanderSy's class earned $582 during the school year in order to purchase new books for the library. The graph below shows the percentage of money earned from each activity. Use it to answer the questions that follow.

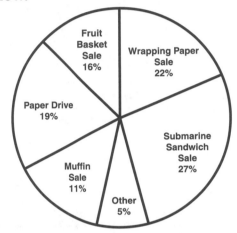

4. How much less was earned on the paper drive than from the wrapping paper sale?

(F) $17.46

(G) $23.46

(H) $18.46

(J) $16.46

5. Which fundraiser earned the most money?

(A) the fruit basket sale

(B) the wrapping paper sale

(C) the submarine sandwich sale

(D) the paper drive

6. How much money was earned from the muffin sale?

(F) $63.02

(G) $123.02

(H) $64.02

(J) $73.03

Organizing and Displaying Data

Directions: Study the results of Zoe's experiments with plants. Use the graphs to answer the questions that follow.

Plant A

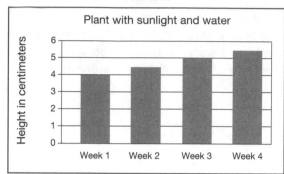

Plant with sunlight and water

Plant B

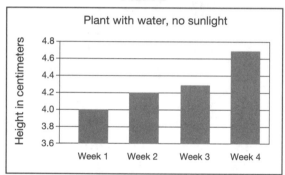

Plant with water, no sunlight

1. How much did plant A grow between weeks 1 and 4?

- (A) 2 cm
- (B) 1.5 cm
- (C) 1 cm
- (D) 0.4 cm

2. How much did plant B grow between weeks 1 and 4?

- (F) 0.8 cm
- (G) 0.6 cm
- (H) 0.7 cm
- (J) 0.4 cm

3. When was the slowest growth for plant B?

- (A) Weeks 2–3
- (B) Weeks 3–4
- (C) Weeks 1–2
- (D) Weeks 4

4. Why is the height measured in increments of 1 cm for plant A and 0.2 cm for plant B?

- (F) Plant A grew very slowly.
- (G) Plant A did not grow as much as plant B.
- (H) Plant B did not grow as much as plant A.
- (J) Zoe made an error in her graphs.

Make sure you understand what each graph is representing.

Organizing and Displaying Data

Directions: Use the graph below to answer the questions that follow.

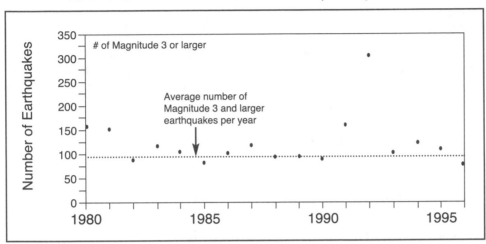

North Coast California: Number of Earthquakes per Year

1. **In which year did the greatest number of earthquakes occur?**

   (A) 1990

   (B) 1991

   (C) 1992

   (D) 1993

2. **In which year did the fewest number of earthquakes occur?**

   (F) 1981

   (G) 1986

   (H) 1991

   (J) 1996

3. **Based on the data, what is an average number of earthquakes per year on the north coast of California?**

   (A) about 250

   (B) about 150

   (C) about 100

   (D) about 50

4. **The y-axis is marked in increments of _____.**

   (F) 5

   (G) 10

   (H) 25

   (J) 100

5. **What is the difference between the number of earthquakes in 1990 and 1992?**

   (A) 100

   (B) 200

   (C) 75

   (D) 25

Organizing and Displaying Data

Directions: Make a stem and leaf plot for the following data.

Example

To use a stem and leaf plot, each value in the data is split into a "stem" and a "leaf." The "leaf" is most often the last digit of the number. The other digits to the left of the "leaf" are the "stem." For example, in the number 214, the "stem" would be 21 and the "leaf" would be 4. You can show this in a table, such as this:

Stem	Leaf
21	4

The legend for the table would be: Legend: 21 | 4 means 214. If you have multiple entries, the leaves for each stem go in the same row. For example, the data 214, 216, 223, 217, and 224 would be shown this way in a table:

Stem	Leaf
21	4, 6, 7
22	3, 4

Ms. Jenson's class completed a math test. The test scores out of 50 possible points were 49, 35, 37, 47, 43, 50, 44, 45, 48, 38, 41, 50, 45, and 50.

Math Test Scores (out of 50 points)	
Stem	**Leaf**

Legend: 3 | 5 means 35.

To find the median in a stem and leaf plot, count off half the total number of leaves. What is the median grade for the math test?

_____

Organizing and Displaying Data

Directions: Read and work each problem. Find the answer, and mark your choice.

The graph below shows the average number of rainy days per month in Sun City, Florida. Use the graph to answer the questions.

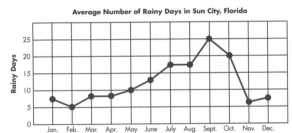

Average Number of Rainy Days in Sun City, Florida

Major Religions of Canada

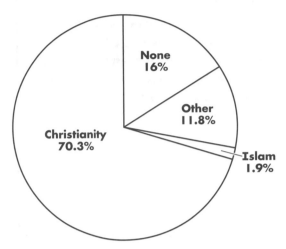

1. **Based on this graph, which two months should have been the best for tourists?**

   Ⓐ January and February

   Ⓑ February and November

   Ⓒ March and April

   Ⓓ April and December

2. **Which two-month period shows the greatest change in the number of rainy days?**

   Ⓕ May and June

   Ⓖ June and July

   Ⓗ October and November

   Ⓙ August and September

3. **How many inches of rain fell during the rainiest month?**

   Ⓐ 20 inches

   Ⓑ 25 inches

   Ⓒ about 18 inches

   Ⓓ None of these

4. **What percentage of people in Canada practice Islam?**

   Ⓕ 0%

   Ⓖ 1.9%

   Ⓗ 11.8%

   Ⓙ 16%

5. **What percentage of Canadians practice a religion that is not Christianity?**

   Ⓐ 13.7%

   Ⓑ 11.8%

   Ⓒ 1.9%

   Ⓓ 14%

Name _____   Date _____

Sample Test 10: Applications

Directions: Read and work each problem. Find the answer, and mark it.

Example

The enrollment at King Middle School has increased 20% from last year. The enrollment last year was 650. By how many students has the enrollment increased?

(A) 120

(B) 130

(C) 150

(D) 90

Answer: B

1. Your uncle bought 375 feet of wire fencing. He put up 325 feet today and saved the rest for tomorrow. Which equation shows how many feet of fencing he has left?

(A) $375 + \square = 325$

(B) $375 - 325 = \square$

(C) $\square = 375 + 325$

(D) $375 - \square = 325$

2. The sweaters on sale come in three styles: pullover, cardigan, and turtleneck. They come in three colors: black, white, and red. How many possible outcomes are there?

(F) 9

(G) 6

(H) 3

(J) 12

The chart below shows how the space in a store was divided among the different departments. Use the chart to answer the questions.

3. What fraction of the space in the store is the bakery?

(A) $\frac{1}{4}$

(B) $\frac{1}{8}$

(C) $\frac{1}{5}$

(D) $\frac{1}{10}$

4. What percentage of the space in the store is devoted to frozen foods?

(F) 30%

(G) 25%

(H) 40%

(J) 12.5%

5. If the total space in the store is 3,000 square feet, how many square feet of space is taken up by packaged foods?

(A) 400 square feet

(B) 550 square feet

(C) 600 square feet

(D) 60 square feet

GO

Sample Test 10: Applications

Directions: Read and work each problem. Find the answer, and mark it.

6. If you try to guess the month that someone was born, what is the probability that you will guess the correct month?

(F) $\frac{1}{12}$

(G) $\frac{1}{6}$

(H) $\frac{1}{24}$

(J) $\frac{1}{13}$

7. Tony was a novice jogger. The first week, he ran $\frac{1}{2}$ mile on his first try, $1\frac{1}{4}$ mile on his second try, and 2 miles on his third try. If Tony ran the same distances the next week, how far would he run in total for the two weeks?

(A) $3\frac{3}{4}$ miles

(B) $7\frac{1}{2}$ miles

(C) $6\frac{3}{4}$ miles

(D) $8\frac{1}{2}$ miles

8. 14 teachers and 246 students will travel to the state capital. One bus holds 38 people. How many buses are needed altogether?

(F) 6 buses

(G) 7 buses

(H) 5 buses

(J) 8 buses

The graph below shows the average basketball attendance for the season. Use the graph to answer the questions that follow.

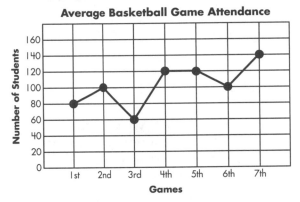

Average Basketball Game Attendance

9. What was the increase in attendance from the first to the seventh game?

(A) 50 students

(B) 60 students

(C) 140 students

(D) 70 students

10. Between which two games was there the smallest increase in attendance?

(F) 1st and 2nd games

(G) 6th and 7th games

(H) 5th and 6th games

(J) 2nd and 3rd games

11. How many students altogether attended games?

(A) 140 students

(B) 160 students

(C) 720 students

(D) 600 students

GO

Name _____   Date _____

Sample Test 10: Applications

Directions: Read and work each problem. Find the answer, and mark it.

12. The convenience store has a choice of chocolate, vanilla, and strawberry frozen yogurt in either a sugar cone or a waffle cone. How many choices are there?

(F) 9

(G) 6

(H) 3

(J) 5

13. In question 12, what is the probability that you will choose a chocolate frozen yogurt on a waffle cone?

(A) $\frac{1}{3}$

(B) $\frac{1}{5}$

(C) $\frac{1}{6}$

(D) $\frac{1}{9}$

14. About 16 million people live in Florida. About how many of them live in cities?

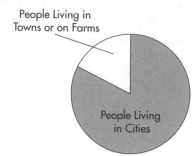

People Living in Towns or on Farms

People Living in Cities

(F) 13 million

(G) 8 million

(H) 5 million

(J) 3 million

Directions: Use the data to answer the questions that follow.

The test scores for a French class are 86, 94, 70, 81, 92, 74, 75, 89, 76, and 97.

15. What is the mean of the data?

(A) 27

(B) 83.4

(C) 83.5

(D) 89

16. What is the median of the data?

(F) 27

(G) 83.4

(H) 83.5

(J) 89

17. Create a stem and leaf plot using the data set.

Stem	Leaf

GO

Sample Test 10: Applications

Directions: Read and work each problem. Find the answer, and mark it.

18. **Mrs. Perez wants to find out what the average tomato yield is in her garden. Here are the weights, in pounds, of the tomatoes she picked for the last 5 years: 16, 18, 13, 22, 17. What is the mean?**

    (F) 16 pounds

    (G) 18.8 pounds

    (H) 17 pounds

    (J) 17.2 pounds

19. **Samuel's New Year's resolution is to write to his friends and relatives more often. He sends 1 postcard in January, 2 in February, 3 in March, 4 in April, and so on. By the end of the year, how many postcards has he mailed in all?**

    (A) 56

    (B) 78

    (C) 82

    (D) 98

20. **Samuel decided not to send any postcards in the month of December. Which number sentence shows how to find the new total of postcards he sent?**

    (F) $t + 12$

    (G) $t - 12$

    (H) $t \times 12$

    (J) $t \div 12$

21. **Two numbers have a product of 64 and a quotient of 4. What are the two numbers?**

    (A) 16 and 4

    (B) 16 and 8

    (C) 64 and 4

    (D) 32 and 2

22. **Keely is choosing a doll for her little sister's birthday. She can choose a doll with blue eyes, black eyes, or brown eyes. The doll can have brown hair, red hair, blond hair, or black hair. How many possible outcomes are there?**

    (F) 7

    (G) 8

    (H) 12

    (J) 14

23. **One letter is randomly chosen from the word *assessment*. What is the percentage of likelihood that *s* will be chosen?**

    (A) 10%

    (B) 4%

    (C) 40%

    (D) 60%

STOP

Practice Test 3: Math
Part 1: Concepts

Directions: Read each problem. Find the answer, and mark it.

1. Which figure has the same shaded area as figure A?

A

Ⓐ

Ⓑ

Ⓒ

Ⓓ

2. Which number is ten thousand more than 399,587?

Ⓕ 400,587

Ⓖ 409,587

Ⓗ 499,587

Ⓙ 490,587

3. What is another name for 60?

Ⓐ (4 × 6) × 6

Ⓑ 6 × (4 + 6)

Ⓒ (20 × 2) ÷ 2

Ⓓ 4 × (18 ÷ 3)

4. Which fraction is another name for $\frac{2}{5}$?

Ⓕ $\frac{16}{40}$

Ⓖ $\frac{4}{40}$

Ⓗ $\frac{4}{15}$

Ⓙ $\frac{12}{48}$

5. Point J is closest in value to

Ⓐ 6.2

Ⓑ 6.5

Ⓒ 6.125

Ⓓ 7.5

6. What number is missing from the pattern shown below?

| 8, 10, 14, 20, _____, 38, 50 |

Ⓕ 24

Ⓖ 26

Ⓗ 28

Ⓙ 25

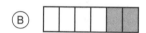

GO

Practice Test 3: Math
Part 1: Concepts

Directions: Read each problem. Find the answer, and mark it.

---

7. Which of these does not have the same value as the others?

(A) $\frac{24}{3}$

(B) $\sqrt{64}$

(C) 32×0.25

(D) 0.08

8. How many of the fractions in the box are greater than $\frac{3}{5}$?

$\frac{2}{5}$	$\frac{3}{4}$	$\frac{6}{7}$	$\frac{1}{2}$	$\frac{20}{25}$	$\frac{7}{10}$

(F) 1

(G) 3

(H) 4

(J) 2

9. Which of these statements is true about the number 378,654?

(A) It has a 3 in the thousands place and a 4 in the ones place.

(B) It has a 7 in the ten thousands place and a 6 in the tens place.

(C) It has a 3 in the hundred thousands place and a 5 in the tens place.

(D) It has an 8 in the ten thousands place and a 6 in the hundreds place.

10. What should replace the box in the number sentence below?
$(7 \times \Box) - 9 = 54$

(F) 8

(G) 7

(H) 5

(J) 9

11. Which statement is true about the number sentence $798 \div 10 = \Box$?

(A) $\Box$ is more than 80.

(B) $\Box$ is more than 90.

(C) $\Box$ is less than 80.

(D) $\Box$ is more than 700.

12. Which fraction is in its simplest form?

(F) $\frac{9}{12}$

(G) $\frac{12}{20}$

(H) $\frac{4}{5}$

(J) $\frac{2}{8}$

13. A barrel is 36 inches from top to bottom. The water in the barrel is $12\frac{1}{2}$ inches deep. How much space is there from the surface of the water to the top of the barrel?

(A) $s = 36 \div 12\frac{1}{2}$

(B) $s = 36 \times 12\frac{1}{2}$

(C) $s = 36 - 12\frac{1}{2}$

(D) $s = 36 + 12\frac{1}{2}$

14. Which of these is an improper fraction?

(F) $\frac{45}{90}$

(G) $\frac{37}{36}$

(H) $1\frac{2}{9}$

(J) $\frac{9}{10}$

15. $\sqrt{81}$

(A) 11

(B) 7

(C) 8

(D) 9

GO

Name _____ Date _____

Practice Test 3: Math
Part 1: Concepts

Directions: Read each problem. Find the answer, and mark it.

16. Which of these is another name for $\frac{13}{4}$?

　(F) 4

　(G) $3\frac{1}{3}$

　(H) $8\frac{1}{4}$

　(J) $3\frac{1}{4}$

17. Estimate the sum of 369 plus 547. Round both numbers to the nearest ten and solve. Then, round to the nearest hundred and solve. What are the estimated sums?

　(A) 920 and 900

　(B) 890 and 900

　(C) 910 and 900

　(D) 900 and 1,000

18. Misaki has 6 apples, Hailey has 5 oranges, and Kate has 4 bananas. What fraction of the fruit does Hailey have?

　(F) $\frac{1}{15}$

　(G) $\frac{1}{3}$

　(H) $\frac{1}{5}$

　(J) $\frac{3}{5}$

19. Which of these is a prime number?

　(A) 33

　(B) 11

　(C) 18

　(D) 32

20. Which of these is 0.494 rounded to the nearest tenth?

　(F) 0.4

　(G) 0.5

　(H) 0.410

　(J) 0.510

21. Which is the greatest whole number listed below that makes the number sentence below true?
$6 \times \square < 70$

　(A) 12

　(B) 10

　(C) 13

　(D) 11

22. What should replace the $\square$ in the number sentence below?
$8 \times 7 = (6 \times 6) + (4 \times \square)$

　(F) 4

　(G) 6

　(H) 5

　(J) 7

23. Which of these is the expanded numeral for 57,076?

　(A) 50,000 + 7,000 + 70 + 6

　(B) 5,000 + 70 + 6

　(C) 5,700 + 70 + 6

　(D) 50,000 + 700 + 6

24. What does the underlined numeral name? 4<u>5</u>6,786,774

　(F) millions

　(G) hundred millions

　(H) ten thousands

　(J) ten millions

25. Which of these numbers shows $\frac{29}{7}$ as a mixed fraction?

　(A) $4\frac{1}{7}$

　(B) $\frac{7}{29}$

　(C) $4\frac{2}{7}$

　(D) 0.34

Name _____ Date _____

Practice Test 3: Math
Part 1: Concept

Directions: Read each problem. Find the answer, and mark it.

26. Which of the tables follows the rule shown below?
Rule: Multiply the number in column A by 24 to get the number in column B.

(F)

A	B
2	36
3	42
5	54
7	66

(G)

A	B
2	16
3	22
5	34
7	46

(H)

A	B
2	12
3	16
5	15
7	17

(J)

A	B
2	48
3	72
5	120
7	168

27. Khalid has a bag with 13 marbles. His father puts some more marbles in the bag. He now has 28 marbles. Which equation shows how many marbles his father gave him?

(A) $28 \div 13 = \square$

(B) $13 + \square = 28$

(C) $28 \times 13 = \square$

(D) $13 - \square = 28$

28. What is the value of y if $y + 15 = 87$?

(F) 72

(G) 82

(H) 92

(J) 102

29. Riley spent $\frac{1}{3}$ hour washing the dishes and $1\frac{1}{4}$ hour vacuuming. Which equation shows how much time he spent doing chores?

(A) $\frac{1}{3} \times 1\frac{1}{4} = t$

(B) $1\frac{1}{4} \div \frac{1}{3} = t$

(C) $\frac{1}{3} + 1\frac{1}{4} = t$

(D) $1\frac{1}{4} - \frac{1}{3} = t$

30. What number comes next in the pattern?
120, 108, 96, 84, 72, _____

(F) 66

(G) 64

(H) 58

(J) 60

31. Evaluate $7a + 12b - 2c$, if $a = 11$, $b = 3$, and $c = 9$.

(A) 95

(B) 85

(C) 106

(D) 78

STOP

Practice Test 3: Math
Part 2: Computation

Directions: Read each problem. Find the answer, and mark it.

1. 6,788 + 3,528 + 6,743 =
- (A) 17,059
- (B) 16,059
- (C) 17,058
- (D) None of these

2. 7,500
  × 60
- (F) 45,000
- (G) 450,000
- (H) 420,500
- (J) None of these

3. 896 ÷ 33 =
- (A) 28 R2
- (B) 27 R5
- (C) 27
- (D) None of these

4. $\frac{5}{9} \times \frac{3}{8} =$
- (F) $\frac{4}{9}$
- (G) $\frac{5}{12}$
- (H) $\frac{5}{24}$
- (J) None of these

5. 92,654
  − 43,879
- (A) 4,877
- (B) 67,775
- (C) 48,775
- (D) None of these

6. 6)4,387
- (F) 731 R1
- (G) 731
- (H) 732 R2
- (J) None of these

7. 994 × 738 =
- (A) 732,572
- (B) 723,572
- (C) 833,572
- (D) None of these

8. 77.59
  − 5.8
- (F) 72.79
- (G) 71.79
- (H) 72.68
- (J) None of these

9. $\frac{8}{9} - \frac{3}{6} =$
- (A) $\frac{7}{8}$
- (B) $\frac{5}{6}$
- (C) $\frac{7}{18}$
- (D) None of these

10. 3.4 + 7.5 + 0.9 =
- (F) 12.6
- (G) 11.8
- (H) 14.2
- (J) None of these

Practice Test 3: Math
Part 2: Computation

Directions: Read each problem. Find the answer, and mark it.

11. $5\frac{3}{4}$
    $+1\frac{4}{7}$
    (A) $6\frac{8}{9}$
    (B) $7\frac{1}{4}$
    (C) $7\frac{9}{28}$
    (D) None of these

12. $(3 + 7) - (3 \times 7) \div 7 =$
    (F) 8
    (G) 7 R8
    (H) 7
    (J) None of these

13. $25.5 \div 3 =$
    (A) 7.6
    (B) 8.5
    (C) 7.5
    (D) None of these

14. 8,976
    $-$ 60
    (F) 53,856
    (G) 438,560
    (H) 538,560
    (J) None of these

15. $13\overline{)549.9}$
    (A) 41.3
    (B) 42.6
    (C) 51.41
    (D) None of these

16. $8\frac{1}{12}$
    $-6\frac{3}{4}$
    (F) $1\frac{1}{3}$
    (G) $2\frac{3}{4}$
    (H) $1\frac{1}{12}$
    (J) None of these

17. $45.6 + 33.9 =$
    (A) 78.5
    (B) 79.4
    (C) 79.5
    (D) None of these

18. $245 \times 8 =$
    (F) 2,453
    (G) 1,985
    (H) 1,960
    (J) None of these

19. $\frac{7}{9}$
    $+\frac{11}{18}$
    (A) $1\frac{7}{18}$
    (B) $1\frac{7}{18}$
    (C) $1\frac{7}{9}$
    (D) None of these

20. 45,603
    $-44,984$
    (F) 719
    (G) 818
    (H) 619
    (J) None of these

Name _____ Date _____

Practice Test 3: Math
Part 2: Computation

Directions: Read each problem. Find the answer, and mark it.

21. $(8 \times 9 - 5 \times 9) \div 4 =$

  (A) 6

  (B) 6 R3

  (C) 5 R9

  (D) None of these

22. $5\frac{3}{4}$
  $+ 7\frac{2}{3}$

  (F) $13\frac{5}{12}$

  (G) $12\frac{3}{4}$

  (H) $13\frac{1}{3}$

  (J) None of these

23. **Which of the following are prime factors of 30?**

  (A) 10×3

  (B) 15×2

  (C) 5×6

  (D) $3 \times 5 \times 2$

24. $568 \div 16 =$

  (F) 35 R8

  (G) 35

  (H) 35 R6

  (J) 36 R8

25. $5(\sqrt{36} - 2) + (48 \div 4) =$ _____

  (A) 36

  (B) 24

  (C) 32

  (D) None of these

26. **What are the prime factors of 125?**

  (F) 5^3

  (G) 5×25

  (H) $5 \times 5 \times 3$

  (J) $5^2 \times 25$

27. **If 699 – 24 = 675 then 675 + 24 =** _____

  (A) 24

  (B) 26

  (C) 675

  (D) 699

28. $3\frac{4}{7} - 1\frac{3}{4}$

  (F) $1\frac{23}{28}$

  (G) $1\frac{3}{8}$

  (H) $\frac{23}{28}$

  (J) None of these

29. $349.268 + 40.9 =$

  (A) 308.368

  (B) 390.168

  (C) 389.68

  (D) 390.16

30.   6.91
  $\times 1.4$

  (F) 8.31

  (G) 9.7

  (H) 9.64

  (J) None of these

STOP

Practice Test 3: Math
Part 3: Geometry

Directions: Find the correct answer to each problem. Mark the space for your choice.

1. What is the perimeter of this rectangle?

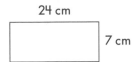

24 cm

7 cm

- (A) 62 cm
- (B) 31 cm
- (C) 168 cm
- (D) Not given

2. A room is 18^2 feet. What is the area of the room?

- (F) 36 square feet
- (G) 324 square feet
- (H) 72 square feet
- (J) 648 square feet

3. Which pair of shapes is congruent?

- (A)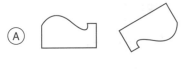
- (B)
- (C)
- (D)

4. What is the perimeter of the rectangle below?

24 in.

14 in.

- (F) 38 in.
- (G) 76 in.
- (H) 336 in.
- (J) 10 in.

5. What is the area of this circle?

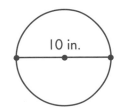

10 in.

- (A) 31.4 in.^{2}
- (B) 62.8 in.^{2}
- (C) 78.5 in.^{2}
- (D) 314 in.^{2}

6. Draw and name a polygon with four sides and four right angles. Opposite sides are parallel.

GO

Practice Test 3: Math
Part 3: Geometry

Directions: Find the correct answer to each problem. Mark the space for your choice.

7. Which of the following figures is a trapezoid?

(A)

(B)

(C)

(D)

8. Which of the following is not a prism?

(F)

(G)

(H)

(J)

9. Which of these are the coordinates of the triangle?

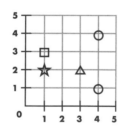

(A) (1, 2)

(B) (3, 2)

(C) (1, 3)

(D) (4, 4)

10. Which of the following figures does not have a line of symmetry?

(F)

(G)

(H)

(J)

11. A box is 7 inches wide, 10 inches long, and 5 inches high. Find the volume of the box.

(A) 350 cubic inches

(B) 22 cubic inches

(C) 700 cubic inches

(D) 70 cubic inches

12. What is the measurement of the missing angle?

(F) 20°

(G) 310°

(H) 110°

(J) 70°

45°

25°

STOP

Practice Test 3: Math
Part 4: Measurement

Directions: Find the correct answer to each problem. Mark the space for your choice.

1. Pizzazz Pizza Parlor gave the sixth-grade class a 25% discount on pizzas they purchased for a party. Each pizza originally cost $12.00. How much did the sixth graders pay per pizza?

(A) $3.00

(B) $9.00

(C) $8.00

(D) $6.00

2. 130 inches is

(F) exactly 10 feet.

(G) more than 3 yards.

(H) between 9 and 10 feet.

(J) less than 3 yards.

3. Rebekah lives in an apartment that is 6 stories tall. About how tall is the building?

(A) 60 feet

(B) 100 feet

(C) 600 feet

(D) 10 feet

4. Sonya earned $6.00 by baby-sitting. She added that money to some allowance she had saved and bought a new video game for $22.79. She had $2.88 left over. How much allowance had Sonya saved?

(F) $19.91

(G) $13.78

(H) $19.67

(J) $18.77

5. What fraction of one week is 12 hours?

(A) $\frac{1}{12}$

(B) $\frac{1}{14}$

(C) $\frac{1}{24}$

(D) $\frac{1}{8}$

6. School begins at 8:45 A.M. The sixth graders eat lunch 2 hours and 45 minutes later. Lunch lasts 30 minutes. Which clock shows the time the sixth graders return to class after eating lunch?

(F)

(G)

(H)

(J)

7. Which of these statements is true?

(A) 11 quarters are worth more than 19 dimes.

(B) 50 nickels are worth more than 25 dimes.

(C) 6 quarters are worth more than 16 dimes.

(D) 15 nickels are worth more than 9 dimes

GO

Practice Test 3: Math
Part 4: Measurement

Directions: Find the correct answer to each problem. Mark the space for your choice.

8. About how much does an orange weigh?

(F) 600 grams

(G) 6 ounces

(H) 60 ounces

(J) 6 pounds

9. 7,500 m = _____ km

(A) 7.5

(B) 0.75

(C) 75

(D) 750

10. Suki and her family are going on vacation. They leave the house at 7:30 A.M. They drive for 4 hours and 18 minutes. They stop for lunch, which takes 42 minutes, and then they drive the remaining 3 hours and 10 minutes of their trip. What time do they arrive?

(F) 2:36 P.M.

(G) 3:20 P.M.

(H) 3:40 P.M.

(J) 4:19 P.M.

11. The temperature on the backyard thermometer is 21°C. It drops 6 degrees as a storm rolls in. What is the temperature now in degrees Fahrenheit?

(A) 15°F

(B) 59°F

(C) 39°F

(D) 82°F

12. For a science experiment, Elena needs to fill 5 buckets with $\frac{1}{2}$ liter of water each. How many milliliters is this in total?

(F) 25 mL

(G) 2,500 mL

(H) 250 mL

(J) 25,000 mL

13. Justin sold $240 worth of fruit baskets for a school fundraiser. The next year, his totals were 16% higher. What were his sales totals the second year?

(A) $254.80

(B) $276.40

(C) $278.40

(D) $291.00

14. About how long would it take to drive 15 miles on the highway? (Assume there is no unusual traffic.)

(F) about 45 minutes

(G) about an hour

(H) about 5 minutes

(J) about 15 minutes

STOP

Practice Test 3: Math
Part 5: Applications

Directions: Find the correct answer to each problem. Mark the space for your choice.

1. Jupiter has 16 moons, Mars has $\frac{1}{8}$ the number of moons that Jupiter has. How many moons does Mars have?

   Ⓐ 8
   Ⓑ 2
   Ⓒ 4
   Ⓓ 6

2. Which equation shows the total attendance at the science fair if 67 girls and 59 boys attended?

   Ⓕ $67 - 59 = \square$
   Ⓖ $67 + 59 = \square$
   Ⓗ $67 \div 59 = \square$
   Ⓙ $67 \times 59 = \square$

3. Suppose you wrote the word *vacation* on a strip of paper and cut the paper into pieces with one letter per piece. What is the probability of picking the letter *a*?

   Ⓐ 1 out of 8
   Ⓑ 2 out of 8
   Ⓒ 4 out of 5
   Ⓓ 2 out of 7

4. A carpenter has 12 pieces of wood that are each 9 feet long. He has to cut 2 feet from each piece of wood because of water damage. Which equation shows how much good wood is left?

   Ⓕ $(9 + 2) \times 12 = \square$
   Ⓖ $12 - 2) \times 9 = \square$
   Ⓗ $(12 \times 9) - 2 = \square$
   Ⓙ $(9 - 2) \times 12 = \square$

Use the graph below to answer the questions that follow.

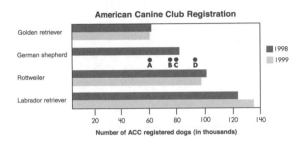

American Canine Club Registration

5. The number of registered German shepherds in 1999 was 62,006. Look at points A, B, C, and D on the graph. Which point indicates where a bar should be drawn to complete the graph?

   Ⓐ point A
   Ⓑ point B
   Ⓒ point C
   Ⓓ point D

6. The number of registered Labrador retrievers in 1998 was

   Ⓕ between 100,000 and 120,000.
   Ⓖ less than 100,000.
   Ⓗ between 120,000 and 140,000.
   Ⓙ more than 140,000.

GO

Practice Test 3: Math
Part 5: Applications

Directions: Read each problem. Find the answer, and mark your choice.

7. Find the mode for 85, 105, 135, 85, and 65.

(A) 70
(B) 85
(C) 86
(D) 95

8. Find the median for 85, 105, 135, 85, and 65.

(F) 70
(G) 85
(H) 86
(J) 95

9 Find the mean for 85, 105, 135, 85, 65, 80, and 84.

(A) 70
(B) 85
(C) 86
(D) 91.3

10. What is the range for 85, 105, 135, 85, 65, 80, and 84?

(F) 70
(G) 85
(H) 86
(J) 91.3

Directions: Tyler did an experiment with three planes to see how their flight would be affected by the angle of the wings. He recorded his results in a graph. Use the graph to answer the questions that follow.

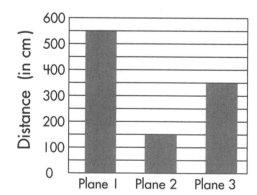

11. Which statement is not true?

(A) Plane 3 flew more than 2 times as far as plane 2.
(B) Plane 1 flew 4 times as far as plane 2.
(C) Plane 3 flew 350 cm.
(D) Plane 2 flew 200 cm less than plane 3.

12. What is the average distance Tyler's planes flew?

(F) 425 cm
(G) 300 cm
(H) 290 cm
(J) 350 cm

Practice Test 3: Math
Part 5: Applications

Directions: Read each problem. Find the answer, and mark your choice.

13. Nico's family is getting a new circular pool in the backyard. The radius is 8 feet. Which equation shows how to find the pool's area?

(A) $A = \pi 16^2$

(B) $A = \pi 8^2$

(C) $A = \frac{\pi}{8}$

(D) $A = \frac{\pi}{16^2}$

14. Mrs. Dunwald is a substitute ballet teacher. The following list shows the number of hours she worked each week for the last 7 weeks: 6, 18, 4, 9, 6, 22, 11. What is the range of hours she worked?

(F) 6 hours

(G) 8 hours

(H) 22 hours

(J) 18 hours

15. What is the difference between the median and the mode in question 14?

(A) 3 hours

(B) 2 hours

(C) 6 hours

(D) 8 hours

16. A group of students is in line in the cafeteria. What is the correct order, from first to last? Kate is between Carter and Jasmine. Carter is behind Li. Aiden is not next to Carter. Aiden is not last.

(F) Aiden, Li, Carter, Jasmine, Kate

(G) Jasmine, Kate, Carter, Li, Aiden

(H) Aiden, Li, Carter, Kate, Jasmine

(J) Li, Carter, Kate, Jasmine, Aiden

17. You know that your friend was born between 8:00 P.M. and 9:00 P.M. on August 16. What are the chances you will guess the exact time of her birth?

(A) $\frac{1}{30}$

(B) $\frac{1}{60}$

(C) $\frac{1}{24}$

(D) There is no chance.

18. Find the mystery 3-digit number. The sum of its first two digits is 5. The product of its second and third digits is 16. This number has a square root that is between 10 and 15. What is the number?

(F) 149

(G) 12

(H) 414

(J) 144

19. Carla's mom asks her to buy 2 gallons of 2% milk. There are no gallon-size containers of 2% milk left at the store. How many quarts of milk should Carla buy?

(A) 4 quarts

(B) 8 quarts

(C) 2 quarts

(D) 6 quarts

GO

Practice Test 3: Math
Part 5: Applications

Directions: Read each problem. Find the answer, and mark your choice.

20. There are 10 silver earrings and 10 gold earrings in a jewelry box. Luisa reaches in without looking. What is the probability that she will pick a gold earring?

(F) $\frac{1}{2}$

(G) $\frac{1}{3}$

(H) $\frac{1}{4}$

(J) $\frac{1}{5}$

21. A group of teachers are ordering sandwiches from the deli. They can choose ham, beef, turkey, or bologna on white bread, wheat bread, or rye bread. How many different meat and bread combinations are possible?

(A) 12

(B) 16

(C) 7

(D) 9

Directions: The sixth-grade class at Trenton Middle School collects items to donate to a local homeless shelter. The chart below shows an inventory of items collected. Use the chart to answer the questions.

Items	Last Year	This Year
Snack foods	21	32
Paper goods	28	42
Instant foods	22	38
Canned goods	42	63
Infant clothing	42	40

22. What is the average number of items collected last year?

(F) 31

(G) 43

(H) 30

(J) 55

23. What is the average number of items collected this year?

(A) 31

(B) 43

(C) 30

(D) 55

24. What was the difference in the mean number of items collected?

(F) 31

(G) 13

(H) 12

(J) 43

25. Which item showed the greatest increase from last year to this year?

(A) Snack foods

(B) Paper goods

(C) Instant foods

(D) Canned goods

page 9
1. C
2. G
3. C
4. H
5. A
6. J
7. C
8. G

page 10
1. A
2. H
3. D
4. H
5. A
6. F
7. B
8. J

page 11
1. A
2. F
3. B
4. G
5. D
6. G
7. D
8. G

page 12
1. C
2. G
3. D
4. F
5. A
6. G
7. D
8. H

page 13
1. C
2. G
3. C
4. G

page 14
1. buy
2. cents
3. due
4. it's
5. there
6. here
7. they're

8. read
9. where
10. too
11. right

page 15
1. B
2. F
3. C
4. J
5. C
6. H

page 16
1. D
2. G
3. B
4. F
5. C
6. H
7. D
8. G

page 17
1. B
2. G
3. C
4. J
5. B

page 18
1. A
2. F
3. C
4. H
5. D
6. F
7. D
8. J

page 19
1. C
2. F
3. B
4. H
5. A
6. H
7. B
8. H

page 20
9. B
10. H
11. C

12. J
13. D
14. G
15. B
16. F
17. D
18. H

page 21
19. C
20. G
21. C
22. J
23. C
24. G
25. A
26. G

page 22
27. B
28. H
29. C
30. F
31. D
32. G
33. A
34. H

page 23
1. D
2. G

page 24
1. C
2. F
3. B
4. H

page 25
1. B
2. H

page 27
1. B
2. G
3. D
4. H
5. D
6. F

page 28
1. B
2. H

page 29
1. B

2. G

page 30
1. D
2. G

page 31
Answers will vary.
Possible answers
shown.
Fact: He filled one
glass pitcher with tap
water and another with
bottled water.
Opinion: This one
tastes great!
Fact: Lefse is a soft
flatbread made from
potatoes, milk, and
flour.
Opinion: Lefse tastes
best when eaten with a
little jelly.
Fact: At 5:30, Ruby
opened her eyes.
Opinion: The sound
of that alarm was so
annoying!

page 32
1. C
2. G
3. C
4. J

page 33
1. C
2. H
3. C
4. H

page 34
1. myth
2. science fiction
3. realistic fiction
4. nonfiction

page 35
1. C
2. J
3. A
4. G
5. C

page 36
1. C
2. F
3. D
4. G
5. D
6. G
7. D
8. H

page 38
1. B
2. H
3. A
4. J
5. B
6. F

page 40
1. B
2. H
3. B
4. H
5. C
6. F

page 42
1. C
2. J
3. C
4. G
5. B
6. G

page 43
1. B
2. F

page 45
1. A
2. J
3. D
4. H
5. B
6. G

page 47
1. C
2. J
3. A
4. G
5. D
6. H
7. A

page 49
1. C
2. G
3. A
4. G
5. C
6. J

page 50
1. A
2. G

page 52
3. A
4. H
5. B
6. F
7. B
8. F

page 54
9. A
10. H
11. B
12. H
13. B
14. J
15. A
16. J

page 55
1. C
2. H
3. A
4. G
5. C
6. F
7. C
8. F

page 56
9. B
10. H
11. A
12. H
13. B
14. G
15. A
16. J

page 57
17. C
18. F
19. D

20. G
21. C
22. H
23. A
24. G

page 58
25. A
26. H
27. B
28. H
29. B
30. H
31. D
32. G

page 60
1. D
2. J
3. B
4. J
5. A
6. J

page 62
7. B
8. J
9. C
10. J
11. A
12. G

page 64
13. B
14. J
15. A
16. H
17. B
18. H

page 65
1. B
2. J
3. C
4. G
5. C
6. H

page 66
1. A
2. G
3. A
4. H
5. A

6. F
7. C
8. G
9. A
10. H

page 67
1. D
2. H
3. A
4. H
5. B
6. J

page 68
1. B
2. H
3. D
4. F
5. B
6. H
7. C
8. G

page 69
1. A
2. J
3. B
4. H
5. A
6. G

page 70
1. D
2. H
3. B
4. H

page 71
1. B
2. F
3. C
4. G
5. B
6. G

page 72
1. A
2. H
3. B
4. F
5. B
6. H
7. A

8. G
9. D
10. F

page 73
1. D
2. H
3. B
4. H
5. A
6. J
7. A
8. J
9. C
10. G
11. D
12. F

page 74
1. A
2. G
3. D
4. G
5. A
6. G
7. B
8. F

page 75
9. A
10. G
11. A
12. H
13. A
14. G
15. C
16. F

page 76
17. C
18. F
19. D
20. H
21. D
22. J
23. C
24. F

page 77
25. B
26. H
27. D
28. G
29. C

30. F
31. B
32. H

page 78
1. have
2. attract
3. are
4. have
5. have
6. climb
7. eat
8. are
9. is
10. has

page 79
are, is, fly, know, are, catch, tie, take, dive, keep, are, perch, have

page 80
1. are
2. are
3. like
4. is
5. are
6. are
7. has
8. sit
9. takes
10. smells
11. wait
12. are
13. are
14. kicks
15. read

page 81
1. B
2. H
3. A
4. H
5. D

page 82
1. A
2. G
3. C
4. J
5. A
6. G
7. A
8. J

9. A
10. J

page 83
1. B
2. H
3. D
4. F
5. C
6. J

page 84
1. B
2. G
3. C
4. G
5. B
6. H
7. B
8. H

page 85
1. D
2. G
3. D
4. H
5. C
6. G

page 86
1. B
2. G
3. C
4. F

page 87
1. B
2. H
3. C
4. H

page 88
1. compound
2. simple
3. compound
4. simple
5. simple
6. compound
7. compound
8. compound
9. simple
10. compound

page 89
1. C

2. G

page 90
1. A
2. H
3. B

page 91
1. A
2. H
3. D
4. G
5. B

page 92
1. B
2. F
3. B
4. H

page 93
1. A
2. J
3. C
4. J

page 94
1. A
2. G
3. D
4. H
5. D

page 95
1. C
2. G
3. D
4. G
5. B
6. H
7. D

page 96
1. B
2. H
3. D
4. H
5. A
6. Answers will vary. Possible answer: Since it is a technology book, she should use the more recent copy, which will

contain current
information.

page 97
1. A
2. H
3. B
4. G
5. C

page 98
1. C
2. F
3. B
4. F
5. A

page 99
6. G
7. C
8. G
9. A
10. H
11. C

page 100
12. G
13. D
14. H

page 101
15. C
16. H
17. C
18. H
19. B
20. H
21. A
22. J

page 102
23. B
24. G
25. D
26. G

page 103
1. A
2. J
3. B
4. F

page 104
1. 2
2. 3
3. 1
4. 3
5. 2
6. 2
7. 3
8. 1

page 105
1. A
2. J
3. C
4. F

page 106
Answers will vary
but should all include
figurative language.

page 107
Answers will vary. In
the first paragraph,
students should identify
three organizations. In
the second paragraph,
students should give
reasons why they
would be interested in
volunteering for those
organizations. In the
concluding paragraph,
students should explain
what contributions
they would make to
these organizations as
volunteers.

page 108
Answers will vary.
Students should identify
the problem and
explain why they think
it is a serious problem.
Students should also
explain what they think
world leaders could
do to help solve the
problem.

page 109
Answers will vary.
Students' writing should

be logically organized,
and they should include
specific examples and
details.

page 110
1. C
2. H
3. D
4. G
5. A
6. J
7. B
8. H

page 111
9. B
10. F
11. B
12. H
13. The Proclamation
of 1763 forbade
British subjects
to settle beyond
the Appalachian
Mountains.
14. During the
Revolutionary
War, fighting
occurred from
Quebec in the
north to Florida in
the south.
15. The Americans
were angry about
paying the taxes
required by the
Stamp Act of
1765.

page 112
16. J
17. C
18. J
19. C
20. F
21. D
22. J

page 113
23. C
24. J
25. A

26. G

page 114
27. A
28. F
29. B
30. G
31. C
32. H
33. D
34. G
35. D
36. F

page 115
37. B
38. H
39. A
40. F
41. B
42. H
43. D
44. F
45. A

page 116
1. C
2. J
3. D
4. J
5. C
6. G
7. A

page 117
8. H
9. C
10. J
11. B
12. G
13. D

page 118
14. G
15. A
16. G
17. D
18. F
19. D
20. H

page 119
21. C
22. H
23. B

page 120
24. J
25. B
26. H
27. B

page 121
28. G
29. A
30. H
31. C
32. F

page 122
Answers will vary. Students' responses should include a clear purpose for writing and a topic developed with supporting details.

page 123
1. A
2. H
3. D
4. F
5. C

page 124
1. B
2. G
3. C
4. F
5. C
6. J
7. B
8. G

page 125
1. D
2. H
3. D
4. G
5. B
6. H
7. D

page 126
1. B
2. H

3. A
4.

1	2	3	4	5	6	7	8	9	10
11	12	13	14	15	16	17	18	19	20
21	22	(23)	24	25	26	27	(28)	29	30
31	32	33	34	35	36	37	38	39	40
41	42	43	44	45	46	47	48	49	50
51	52	53	54	55	56	57	58	59	60
61	62	63	64	65	66	67	68	69	70
71	72	73	74	75	76	77	78	79	80
81	82	(83)	84	85	86	87	(88)	89	90
91	92	93	94	95	96	97	98	99	100

5. Z

page 127
1. B
2. H
3. A
4. G
5. D

page 128
1. C
2. G
3. B
4. J
5. D
6. G
7. A
8. F

page 129
1. C
2. G
3. C
4. G
5. C

page 130
1. 0, 3, 6, 9, 12, 15
2. 3, 9, 15, 21, 27, 33
3. $x + 4$
4. $4x$
5. $x - 2$
6.

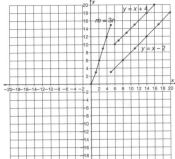

page 131
1. C
2. G
3. D
4. G
5. A
6. G
7. C
8. J

page 132
1. B
2. H
3. C
4. F
5. A

page 133
1. B
2. G
3. A
4. H
5. A
6. J
7. B
8. G

page 134
1. 0.8
2. 0.38
3. 1.67
4. 0.78
5. 0.42
6. 2.8
7. 0.43
8. $\frac{6}{10}$ or $\frac{3}{5}$
9. $\frac{42}{100}$ or $\frac{21}{50}$
10. $\frac{25}{1,000}$ or $\frac{1}{40}$
11. $\frac{85}{100}$ or $\frac{17}{20}$
12. $\frac{192}{100}$ or $1\frac{23}{25}$
13. $\frac{56}{100}$ or $\frac{14}{25}$
14. $3\frac{125}{1,000}$ or $3\frac{1}{8}$

page 135
1. D
2. G
3. D
4. H
5. D
6. G
7. A
8. G

page 136
1. 87%
2. 45%
3. 2%
4. 34.2%
5. 0.39
6. 0.07
7. 0.018
8. 1.32
9. 0.0005
10. C
11. G
12. D

page 137
1. C
2. J
3. B
4. H
5. B

page 138
1. B
2. H
3. B
4. G
5. B
6. J

page 139
1. D
2. H
3. A
4. G
5. D
6. F

page 140
1. C
2. G
3. B
4. G
5. B

page 141
1. B
2. H
3. A
4. J
5. C
6. F
7. A
8. J

page 142
1. B
2. G
3. B
4. H
5. A

page 143
1. A
2. H
3. B
4. H
5. B
6. J
7. C
8. J

page 144
1. C
2. J
3. A
4. H
5. C
6. J

page 145
1. A
2. F
3. B
4. J
5. A
6. H

page 146
1. C
2. G
3. A
4. H
5. D
6. G
7. C

page 147
8. F

9. B
10. H
11. A
12. H
13. C
14. G
15. C

page 148
16. J
17. D
18. F
19. B
20. F

page 149
21. B
22. F
23. C
24. F
25. B
26. G
27. C

page 150
1. C
2. F
3. B
4. J
5. A
6. G
7. C
8. J

page 151
1. A
2. G
3. C
4. H
5. A
6. J
7. B
8. G

page 152
1. B
2. F
3. D
4. H
5. A
6. F
7. C
8. J

page 153
Students should show
their work.
1. 91
2. 34
3. 17
4. −14
5. −10
6. 16
7. 76
8. 0

page 154
1. C
2. F
3. C
4. G
5. A
6. J

page 155
1. D
2. F
3. C
4. J
5. A
6. F
7. Answers will
   vary.
8. Answers will
   vary.

page 156
1. $2 \times 2 \times 5 \times 5$
2. $2 \times 3 \times 5 \times 7$
3. $2 \times 2 \times 11$
4. $2 \times 3 \times 5 \times 5 \times 7$

page 157
1. A
2. J
3. C
4. F
5. B
6. J
7. A
8. G

page 158
1. B
2. F
3. B
4. H

5. C
6. J
7. D

page 159
1. B
2. F
3. A
4. J
5. C
6. F
7. B
8. F
9. B
10. H

page 160
1. C
2. J
3. D
4. J
5. B
6. G
7. C
8. G

page 161
1. A
2. G
3. D
4. F
5. C
6. F
7. B
8. F
9. A
10. G

page 162
1. C
2. F
3. A
4. J
5. B
6. F
7. C

page 163
1. B
2. G
3. C
4. G
5. A
6. H

7. A
8. J
9. C
10. H

page 164
1. D
2. H
3. D
4. H
5. D
6. F
7. B

page 165
1. C
2. H
3. A
4. G
5. D
6. H
7. D
8. F
9. A
10. G

page 166
1. C
2. G
3. C
4. J
5. C
6. G
7. A

page 167
1. B
2. H
3. B
4. F
5. C
6. J
7. A
8. G
9. A

page 168
1. B
2. F
3. B
4. G
5. C
6. F
7. D

8. G

page 169
9. B
10. F
11. B
12. H
13. B
14. G
15. A
16. H
17. B
18. J

page 170
19. C
20. J
21. C
22. H
23. C
24. F
25. D
26. F
27. C

page 171
28. G
29. B
30. H
31. A
32. J
33. A
34. G
35. D

page 172
1. B
2. G
3. D
4. F
5. C
6. J

page 173
1. right 60°
2. obtuse 110°
3. obtuse 20°
4. acute 50°
5. right 50°
6. acute 71°

page 174
1. 127°
2. 75°

3. 55°
4. 105°
5. 90°
6. 115°

page 175
1. A
2. 8 left, 2 down
3. reflection across the y-axis
4. reflection across the x-axis

page 176
1. yes
2. yes
3. yes
4. yes
5. no
6. yes

page 177
1.
2. none
3.
4. none
5.
6.

page 178
1. B
2. F
3. C
4. H
5. rectangle; Students should draw a rectangle.
6. scalene triangle; Students should draw a scalene triangle.

page 179
1. rectangle; 90°
2. parallelogram; 128°
3. square; 90°
4. trapezoid; 54°
5. trapezoid; 120°
6. parallelogram; 120°

page 180
1. pyramid
2. prism
3. pyramid
4. prism
5. neither
6. prism

page 181
1, 6, 6, 0
0, 12, 8, 0
8, 5, 0, 0
Possible answers:
1. pyramid
2. cylinder
3. cube
4. rectangular prism

page 182
1. $C = 25.12$ in.
   $A = 50.24$ in.^{2}
2. $C = 314$ mm
   $A = 7,850$ mm^2
3. $C = 9.42$ in.
   $A = 7.065$ in.^{2}
4. $C = 62.8$ ft.
   $A = 314$ ft.^{2}
5. $C = 5.024$ cm
   $A = 2.0096$ cm^2
6. $C = 3.14$ mm
   $A = 0.785$ mm^2

page 183
1. D
2. G
3. B
4. F
5. B
6. G
7. D

page 184
1. C
2. H

3. D
4. F
5. A

page 185
1. B
2. H
3. B
4. H
5. A

page 186
1. C
2. G
3. D
4. F

page 187
1. 180 in.^{3}
2. 216 m^3
3. 198 mm^3
4. 20 in.^{3}
5. 528 cm^3
6. 2,178 in.^{3}
7. 96 m^3
8. 192 cm^3

page 188
1. $F = (2, 6)$
   $L = (5, 6)$
   $A = (5, 4)$
   $G = (5, 2)$
2. $B = (-2, 2)$
   $O = (1, 2)$
   $X = (1, -1)$
   $D = (-2, -1)$
3. $S = (2, -3)$
   $H = (2, -5)$
   $A = (-2, -5)$
   $P = (-2, -6)$
   $E = (-5, -6)$

page 189
1. C
2. G
3. C
4. H
5. D
6. F

page 190
1. B
2. J
3. B

4. F
5. A
6. G

page 191
7. A
8. H
9. C
10. J
11. prism
12. pyramid

page 192
13. $C = 125.6$ mm
    $A = 1,256$ mm^2
14. $C = 47.1$ in.
    $A = 176.625$ in.^{2}
15. $C = 13.188$ m
    $A = 13.8474$ m^2
16. reflection across
    the y-axis
17. B
18. H
19. C

page 193
20. F
21. C
22. H
23. A
24. G
25. D

page 194
1. B
2. G
3. A
4. J
5. A

page 195
1. B
2. J
3. A
4. H
5. B
6. H
7. A
8. G

page 196
1. D
2. J
3. C

4. H
5. A
6. G
7. B
8. F

page 197
1. B
2. G
3. D
4. G
5. B
6. G
7. D
8. J

page 198
1. C
2. F
3. D
4. H
5. B
6. J

page 199
1. B
2. H
3. A
4. G
5. B
6. H
7. A
8. H
9. A

page 200
1. A
2. G
3. C
4. G
5. C
6. G

page 201
1. C
2. F
3. A
4. H
5. D

page 202
1. C
2. G
3. A

4. J
5. C
6. J

page 203
1. A
2. G
3. B
4. H
5. A
6. G

page 204
1. C
2. F
3. D
4. G

page 205
1. C
2. F
3. A
4. J

page 206
1. draw line to
   grams
2. draw line to
   milliliters
3. draw line to feet
   (or meters)
4. draw line to
   meters (or feet)
5. draw line to
   pounds
6. draw line to
   gallons
7. draw line to tons
8. draw line to liters
9. draw line to
   millimeters
10. draw line to miles

page 207
1. B
2. J
3. A
4. J
5. A
6. G
7. C
8. J

page 208
1. B
2. H
3. B
4. F
5. B
6. J

page 209
7. A
8. H
9. A
10. H
11. B
12. F
13. D

page 210
14. H
15. A
16. G
17. D
18. F
19. C
20. G

page 211
Sample answers are shown below. Students' methods of displaying the outcomes may vary.

1.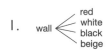

2.

3.

page 212
1. B
2. J
3. Students' answers will vary but should generally state that increasing the sample size (i.e., picking cards 100 times rather than 2 times) should cause Jose's prediction of the empirical probability to more closely resemble the theoretical probability of $\frac{12}{52}$.

page 213
1. C
2. F
3. A
4. J
5. A
6. J

page 214
1. B
2. G
3. A
4. J

page 215
1. A
2. F
3. B
4. F

5. B
6. F
7. B

page 216
1. C
2. F
3. A
4. F
5. A

page 217
1. C
2. G
3. C
4. G
5. D
6. F

page 218
1. B
2. J
3. C
4. G
5. A
6. H

page 219
1. C
2. H
3. B
4. J
5. A
6. H

page 220
1. Mean: 44.2
   Median: 45
   Mode: 45
   Range: 50
2. Mean: 48
   Median: 41
   Mode: 35
   Range: 55
3. Mean: 64.1
   Median: 60
   Mode: 85
   Range: 80
4. Mean: 62.7
   Median: 60
   Mode: 60
   Range: 56

page 221
1. B
2. J
3. B
4. F
5. C
6. J

page 222
1. B
2. H
3. B
4. H
5. A
6. H
7. March
8. April

page 223
1. A
2. F
3. B
4. F
5. C
6. H

page 224
1. B
2. H
3. A
4. H

page 225
1. C
2. J
3. C
4. H
5. B

page 226

Stem	Leaf
3	5, 7, 8
4	1, 3, 4, 5, 5, 7, 8, 9
5	0, 0, 0

The median grade for the math test was 45.

page 227
1. B
2. H
3. D
4. G
5. A

page 228
1. B
2. F
3. B
4. G
5. C

page 229
6. F
7. B
8. J
9. B
10. F
11. C

page 230
12. G
13. C
14. F
15. B
16. H
17.

Stem	Leaf
7	0, 4, 5, 6
8	1, 6, 9
9	2, 4, 7

page 231
18. J
19. B
20. G
21. A
22. H
23. C

page 232
1. A
2. G
3. B
4. F
5. C
6. H

page 233
7. D
8. H
9. C
10. J
11. C
12. H
13. C
14. G
15. D

page 234
16. J
17. A
18. G
19. B
20. G
21. D
22. H
23. A
24. J
25. A

page 235
26. J
27. B
28. F
29. C
30. J
31. A

page 236
1. A
2. G
3. B
4. H
5. C
6. F
7. D
8. G
9. C
10. G

page 237
11. C
12. J
13. B
14. H
15. D
16. F
17. C
18. H
19. A
20. H

page 238
21. B
22. F
23. D
24. F
25. C
26. F
27. D
28. F

29. B
30. J

page 239
1. A
2. G
3. A
4. G
5. C
6. Answers will vary. Possible answer: a rectangle

page 240
7. C
8. F
9. B
10. J
11. A
12. H

page 241
1. B
2. G
3. A
4. H
5. B
6. H
7. A

page 242
8. G
9. A
10. H
11. B
12. G
13. C
14. J

page 243
1. B
2. G
3. B
4. J
5. A
6. H

page 244
7. B
8. G
9. D
10. F
11. B
12. J

page 245
13. B
14. J
15. A
16. H
17. B
18. J
19. B

page 246
20. F
21. A
22. F
23. B
24. H
25. D